Dear Sir or Madam

Dear
Sir or Madam

by Mark Rees

A journey from
female to male

Mallard

First published 1996 by Cassell (now Continuum)

This edition (revised and expanded) published 2009 by

Mallard
21 Culverden Avenue
Tunbridge Wells
Kent
TN4 9RE

A CIP catalogue record for this book is available from the British Library

ISBN 978-0-9562734-0-6

Printed and bound in the UK by CPI Antony Rowe (Eastbourne)
48-50 Birch Close, Eastbourne, East Sussex BN23 6PE

Distributed by Gardners Books, 1 Whittle Drive, Eastbourne, East Sussex, BN23 6QH
www.gardners.com

Dedicated to all who have
helped me on my journey,
especially my mother,
ALICE (BILLIE) REES
1907 – 1988

To Sam,

with very best

wishes,

Mark

Contents

Preface to the Second Edition

THERE is something very frustrating about getting a book published but then to find that after a relatively short time many important and relevant developments have subsequently taken place that would certainly have merited inclusion.

Such was the fate of *Dear Sir or Madam,* which was first published in 1996. By 2003 it was out of print but Cassell had no plans to republish, in spite of continuing interest. With the added impetus of significant legislative developments in the next couple of years I decided that it would be an appropriate time to revise and expand the original text.

What become a self-imposed venture was made possible by the encouragement and practical help of four talented friends, for which I am immensely grateful. They were Frances Day, who undertook the mammoth task of typing the original text onto disk; Anne Simpson, who used her professional expertise to proof-read and edit where necessary, and graphic designers Gillian Shaw and Ian King whose skill in redesigning the cover and fitting graphics into the text was invaluable. The inclusion of pictures was an innovation because the first edition had no photographs except on the cover. Given the topic of the book, some people had remarked that pictures would have been welcome. At least I was now in the position to include what I saw fit.

I have, with their permission, retained the original Foreword by Professor Gooren and Preface by Lord Carlile, formerly Alex Carlile MP QC. In spite of the legal developments that have taken place since these pieces were written, I believe that they are still relevant and am grateful to both men for their support.

Although 'transsexual' is a term which I have used throughout this book it is one I abhor. It has been used purely for convenience, not conviction. To begin with, it is not a noun, but an adjective. To describe a person as a transsexual may be easy (and I do it myself) but it should be 'transsexual *person*'. The *'trans'* prefix implies that one moves *across* from one sex to another. That is impossible. Some experts, especially the late Dr C N

Armstrong, have suggested that the condition is a form of intersex. That being so, we cannot even pretend to have 'changed sex'. It is instead a movement towards that which most closely approximates to our gender identity, but no one 'changes sex'.

Secondly, to call it 'sexual' suggests that it is a form of sexuality. We are lumped together with homosexual people. It should be now be clear that this is not the case. Transsexual people exhibit the same variety of sexual orientation as the rest of the population. The area of the brain that determines gender identity is separate from that which determines sexual orientation. This would explain why gays and lesbians don't want to change sex, unless they are also transsexual, as some are. If a new term could be coined for the condition, which would not engender prurient media interest nor lead people to think it a 'sexuality', it would do us all a great service.

But what term? 'Inter-sexual' might leave us all being called 'It'. (A neutral gender pronoun in our language would be helpful to everyone.) I would be equally unhappy with the term 'Gender Dysphoric'. My problem wasn't with my gender identity, it was with the gender role into which I was forced until the age of twenty-eight. I have no gender role dysphoria now. Someone told me that in France the condition is known as the Benjamin Syndrome, after the earliest specialist in this field of medicine. That would seem a kinder term than the transsexual one. Whatever we are called, what is most important is that we are seen primarily as people. In most of our roles our transsexual status is totally irrelevant.

Mark Rees
2009

Foreword to the First Edition

TRANSSEXUALISM is an error in the sexual differentiation process, the development of becoming a man or a woman…the person involved bears no personal responsibility for his or her condition. It is not a matter of choice.

Most legal systems pertaining to the determination of sex pay absolute reverence to one criterion – that of the external genitalia – whereas there are several criteria or characteristics of sex, such as the genetic, the gonadal, that of the internal genitalia, and that of the sexual differentiation of the brain. The latter, the sexual differentiation of the brain, is rather new information. I cannot say we have a complete picture, but the scientific information can no longer be ignored and it goes without saying that it has relevance for the subject of transsexualism.

It has always been assumed that the sexual differentiation (of a foetus) was completed with the formation of the external genitalia, but it is NOT. Since the beginning of the 20th century we have known that the brain also undergoes a sexual differentiation. It is firmly established scientifically that in lower mammals it takes place relatively late in development – in most species just before birth.

We know that the human brain also undergoes a degree of sexual differentiation. Three areas of the brain have now been documented to be sex-dimorphic. The surprising thing really is that sex difference only becomes manifest three to four years after birth. This is amazing information. Long after you have been born, and your sex has been determined by the criterion of the external genitalia, your brain has still a long way to go to become sexually differentiated. These scientific findings may shed light on the problem of transsexualism where we find a contradiction between the genital sex on the one hand and the gender identity on the other. Very recent evidence found that a structure in the brain that is different in size between men and women had an unambiguously female size in the brains of five male-to-female transsexuals on whom post-mortem investigations could be done.

In transsexuals there is a contradiction between the genetic, gonadal and genital sex on the one hand and the brain sex on the other. For all these people who had the misfortune to incur a sex error of the body in their development, solutions have to be found. It would be absolute medical ignorance, medical incompetence, even abuse, NOT to rehabilitate a person with a sex error of the body.

Professor L J Gooren
Free University Hospital
Amsterdam
The Netherlands

Preface to the First Edition

SHORTLY after I became a Member of the Westminster Parliament in 1983 I discovered a group of people who, despite all the developments in rights legislation since 1945, had been left disregarded and without sympathy. These people were transsexuals. Their plight was brought tellingly to my attention for the first time by a letter from Mark Rees. When I received it I was as ignorant as most about such people. I had read of April Ashley, who had made the headlines when I was a law student in London years earlier, and of some other sensationalised cases; but I had no idea of the causes of transsexualism, the dilemmas faced by those affected, nor for that matter of the extraordinary deficit in legal and individual rights which they faced.

The clarity and urgency of Mark Rees's letter made me write back to him. Since then I have kept in close contact with him, have assisted the group Press for Change which he started with others, and have researched the issue facing transsexuals. I have tried to interest other politicians in their plight with mixed success. I have urged government ministers to change the law to bring it closer to that of some of the more enlightened countries, thus far with no success. With the assistance of a remarkable London solicitor, Terrence Walton, I have ready in my office a private member's bill which I hope one day to present to Parliament with a realistic hope of success. Why, bearing in mind the panoply of political issues of a more populist and widespread kind, do I feel so strongly about this one?

The simple answer is that, as a liberal lawyer with Utilitarian tendencies, I think that I can spot injustice when I see it and I see it in relation to transsexuals. If a person passes the harsh tests set by medical science before gender reassignment therapy can be completed, and functions with total success in the acquired gender, why should they have to suffer the indignity and mental agony of being forced in law to be the opposite of who they really are? Mark Rees is a good example. There is no doubt that Mark is a man in looks, voice and behaviour. However, the law demands that for ever he should be a woman by legal status. He can have no substitute for his original birth certificate, cannot marry save in the wholly artificial role of a woman (with the absurd consequences that two transsexuals could marry each other, but the groom would have to pretend to be the bride and vice versa), and has no employment protection specifically related to his sexuality.

I don't think that society feels any sense of hostility towards transsexuals, though curiosity sometimes merges into prurience if some journalists are to be regarded as a reflection of their readers. It is just that the scale of the problem is poorly appreciated, and for politicians there aren't many votes in transsexualism. This sensible, sensitive and serious book should be required reading for anybody with even a slight interest in the subject. It has the power to reform their views of the importance and urgency of the issues.

What Mark Rees achieves better than anyone before is to describe the process – inexorable, physiological and psychological – which led to his inevitable gender reassignment. Teenage years are confusing enough for the everyday boy and girl as they learn and unlearn relationships. Mark tells with chilling clarity of how the dawning of the inevitable changed not only his perceived sexuality but also everything in his life. The sad story of the breakdown of relations with his sister has elements of Greek tragedy. The transition from tomboy to real man makes good reading, but it goes very much further in drawing us within his frightening process of self-discovery. His relationships with women are described with a frankness which leaves us in no doubt that the scars of a society which discouraged that self-discovery are deep and lasting. His struggle for jobs, despite his sharp brain and capacity for hard and sustained work, are a testament against prejudice.

This is a good book, but it is much more besides. It is a brave and honest plea for justice, an attack on prejudice, and a story of suffering and success. It should leave the reader with a significantly improved understanding of transsexualism, and a sense of anger at the slowness of the progress to improve the lives of transsexual people.

Alex Carlile   House of Commons, London, August 1995

Acknowledgements for the First Edition

THE gestation period of this book has been a long one. Without encouragement I would have aborted it years ago. I am therefore grateful to those people who persuaded me to carry on, especially my good friend, writer Wendy Cooper, who also generously gave of her time and advice.

Posthumous thanks are due to the late Mr John Todd of Darton, Longman and Todd, who made me realise that a publisher could be interested in my story.

Sheila Watson, of Watson-Little, worked tirelessly for years to find a publisher before we decided to put aside the manuscript until times were better. It is fitting that my present successful contact with Cassell came about through Sheila's suggestion. I am very thankful for her past efforts and continuing personal interest.

To my present agent and personal friend, Jane Collins of Collins & Collins, I owe thanks. She encouraged and advised when prospects seemed hopeless. Gratitude is also due to Tim Pain, my first editor, who helped me prepare the vital first chapters and synopsis for submission to Cassell.

There are others, too numerous to mention, who have said 'Keep trying'. I hope they will now realise that their efforts have been rewarded.

This book has been added to as the years have passed, with the result that it became the literary equivalent of an archaeological site. My patient and exceptionally good-humoured editor, Rebecca de Saintonge, cut through layers and helped me dig out, clean, sort and arrange the worthwhile 'artefacts' into a presentable display.

It was an onerous task to decipher my appalling typing and Rebecca's annotations. Gill Powell overcame these problems and expertly typed the manuscript. She certainly deserves my thanks.

Lastly, I must express my appreciation of Steve Cook of Cassell. Without his efforts you would not be reading this now.

Mark Rees   Rusthall, Tunbridge Wells, 1995

Glossary

Gender identity
'The sense of belonging to one sex or the other.'
Professor L Gooren

'The inner conviction that we are male or female, whether or not that conviction reflects our physical appearance or the gender role society imposes on us.'
Professor Milton Diamond. (He calls gender identity 'sexual identity'.)

'The private experience of gender role and gender role is the public manifestation of gender identity.'
Professor John Money

Gender role
'We communicate this sense of belonging to the one sex and not to the other to the outside world in our gender role.'
Professor L. Gooren

'Society's idea of how boys and girls or men and women should behave.'
Professor Milton Diamond

'Gender role is everything a person says and does to indicate to others or to the self the degree that one is either male, female or androgynous. It includes but is not restricted to sexual and erotic arousal and response.'
Professor John Money

'Gender is not physical at all...it is essentialness of oneself, the psyche...male or female are sex, masculine and feminine are gender.'
Jan Morris *(Conundrum)*

Intersex
'The criteria of sex are: 1. Chromosomal sex, 2. Gonadal sex, 3. Apparent sex, 4. Psychological sex. Usually, all four criteria are of the same sex, and intersex is when one or more of the criteria are of different sex.'
C N Armstrong, MD, FRCP, DPH

Sexual orientation
'May be heterosexual, homosexual or bisexual. Independent of gender role or identity.'
Professor Milton Diamond

Transsexual
One in whom gender identity and gender role are at variance. Sexual orientation may be heterosexual, homosexual, bisexual or asexual. The gender role reassignment is permanent. Prior to treatment the individual is said to be 'gender dysphoric', i.e. profoundly ill at ease with one's gender role.

Transvestite
Usually a heterosexual male who occasionally changes gender roles but rarely permanently. The transvestite lives two roles, the transsexual person only one.

FTM: A female to male transsexual person.

MTF: A male to female transsexual person.

Chapter one

Cod Liver Oil and Syrup of Figs

THE elderly lady might not have been a brilliant painter but she was good enough to impress a twelve-year-old. I chatted to her when on holiday with my family on the Isle of Wight, enthralled as she painted her seascapes. One day, quite suddenly, she asked me if I were a boy or girl. It was quite a reasonable enquiry, my hair was short and I was wearing a tee-shirt and shorts, but so too was my younger sister and as far as I knew, no one had asked her a similar question.

'I'm a girl.' The words almost stuck in my throat, but why? Yet my discomfort then was nothing compared to what awaited me as I entered my adolescence. That summer day in 1955 marked the beginning of my troubled teenage years. The stranger's innocent, if not tactful, query was to be the forerunner of almost two decades of similar questions, which were often couched in less friendly tones.

The fact that I was there at all was something of a miracle. Twelve years earlier, in December 1942, I had been born at Tunbridge Wells Maternity Home, one of two-month premature fraternal twins. My mother told me that we were each put into a drawer as we were very underweight and weak. I had always wondered about that, but a midwife friend confirmed that it was unlikely that incubators were available at that time and it would have been the practice to wrap the tiny baby up with cotton wool and place in a drawer to help keep it warm. My father said that we looked like skinned rabbits. When he registered our births, my sex was recorded as 'girl'. That entry was to have a major effect upon my life.

Dad may well have recorded my twin sister's death at the same time because she died when only five days old. The cause given on Carol's death certificate was 'Pre-maturity'. My mother never saw her and was not united with me until I left the incubator after ten days. Carol was buried in a tiny unmarked grave in the 'Children's

Corner' of Rusthall's New Churchyard. Although having no conscious memory of her I am still, decades later, very aware of this loss. My mother told me of her death but spoke of it in a very matter-of-fact way. It is only comparatively recently that I have realised that she must have suffered grief but in those days emotions were kept well controlled.

The Second World War was into its third year when I was born. My recollections of that period are few although I do have vague memories of being fed pink blancmange by Mum and simultaneously hearing the thump of the anti-aircraft guns on Rusthall Common. Another memory is of visiting the local ARP post with our next-door neighbour, 'Aunt' Rose, who was a Warden. Apparently I had a Mickey Mouse gas mask and my own siren suit, so was well equipped. Our area was relatively unscathed by enemy action but my mother told me that some bits of ceiling fell in my room when a retreating Nazi bomber discharged its cargo outside the village.

Anticipating an air raid

My parents had met in happier times. Mum and her best friend, Edna, had gone on a P&O cruise in 1933. I think it cost them £16 each. Her friend had rather liked one of the crew of the *Mongolia,* but my mother was somewhat indifferent. Nonetheless, five years later, Mum married him when they were in their early thirties.

Both Mum and Dad had been born in the first few months of 1907.

Having come into the world within the sound of Bow bells, my mother was, according to local tradition, a Cockney. She only occasionally used rhyming slang, and, I suspect, did so with her tongue in her cheek. Her father, William Bailey, was an engineer at W J Bush, the essence distillers and her mother, Alice, nee Mason, was a dressmaker. It seemed that they had a reasonably comfortable situation since both my mother and her elder brother (also William) were sent to fee-paying schools.

My parents, probably at the time of their engagement

Dad's background was very different. His family lived in rural Berkshire although he had been born in Middelburg, South Africa, the son of William Rees, an Army NCO from Carmarthen and Emma, nee Rynhoud, an Afrikaaner schoolmistress. (Seven out of the ten Rynhoud children became teachers.) Grandpa Rees was a Wesleyan Methodist and the upbringing of his four children was quite strict. I think it was quite a shock for the family when confronted with Dad's 'city girl', my mother, in her tailored business suit. My father was quite reserved but Mum came from a much more extrovert family. She was therefore the more outgoing of my parents although both were basically unassuming.

Much of my mother's early adult life was spent at the tennis club, taking part in amateur dramatics and playing the piano, at which she was exceptionally gifted. She had the talent to have become a professional musician but her father sent her to Pitman's College to train for secretarial work. He thought it offered more security than music. Perhaps he was right but nonetheless my mother was always in great demand as a pianist, most of it unpaid. In her retirement she seemed to be constantly travelling around the locality playing for various groups and events and certainly gave countless people great pleasure. She was very amused and flattered to be engaged to play professionally at the local Trinity Arts Centre in Tunbridge Wells at the age of seventy-nine. My father did not play any instrument but would spend hours happily listening to my mother play. Both my parents enjoyed dancing of which they did a great deal in their younger days.

Whole family photograph, including the cat

After their marriage in 1938 they lived with my mother's parents in Hackney. My father, who was a professional merchant seaman, was away for much of the time, so until my birth in 1942, my mother lived the life of an unmarried working woman. She was a secretary in a City firm but the company was evacuated to Kent in September 1940 as the Battle of Britain raged overhead.

Mum told me that her first reaction on arriving in Rusthall was, 'What a God-forsaken hole!' She must have grown to like it because she spent the rest of her life in Rusthall, a village about a mile and a half to the west of Tunbridge Wells. Its name probably originated from the proliferation of iron springs in the locality, as did the name of Tunbridge Wells.

Mum rented a house in Rusthall, where she was joined by her

recently widowed mother, 'Nan' Bailey. Dad of course was at sea all this time, probably with the convoys and no one knew where he was, how long he would be away or even if he would survive. (It was due to my mother winning the toss of a coin that he did not re-enlist on the *SS Rawlpindi* for what turned out to be its fatal final trip.) Nonetheless, amongst his effects I found five campaign stars. It was typical of his modesty that they were still unwrapped and in their box.

People liked my parents. They were conscientious, generous and kind and shared a great sense of humour. My childhood was happy but disciplined. Good manners were regarded as of the utmost importance and for that lesson I have always been grateful to them.

In February 1946, when I was three, my sister Jane was born. My parents had hoped for a boy, but apparently overcame their disappointment when she arrived. Unlike me, the 'skinned rabbit', she was a 'bonny baby' but I was not too keen on this pink squawking creature and suggested to my mother that she return it to the baby shop. Gradually I appreciated having a sister. I do not recall much of our early life together except that she used to share her biscuits with me and I used to make up stories for her, illustrated with cut-outs held over the bedside lamp which made shadows on the ceiling.

My memories of my 1940s infancy are many: Norman the baker who called with hot loaves covered with a cloth in his basket; Mr Burch the grocer, and his brisk wife, both in immaculate starched white overalls, amongst the square biscuit tins; Mr. Sewell the fishmonger, with his horse and cart, and my diminutive but formidable Nan telling him what to do with the fish if it did not meet her exacting standards. There was *Chick's Own,* Enid Blyton's *Sunny Stories* and, from school, *Milly Molly Mandy* for reading practice and *Children's Hour* with 'Uncle Mac' on the BBC Home Service. My mother cooked with dried eggs which I thought were delicious, we were dosed with 'Parish's Food' which was not, 'Syrup of Figs' which I liked and cod liver oil which was horrid.

Amongst my favourite toys was a rabbit called Peter, who had excellent sartorial taste. He wore yellow trousers and bow tie, a waistcoat and tweed jacket. I wanted to have clothes like Peter and was also keen on Rupert Bear's outfit. (Although my present attire does have echoes of Peter's dress, I have never quite succumbed to Rupert's yellow check trousers.) Another much-loved toy was a big red wooden lorry into which I would load toy bricks. Jane and I were given the choice of a doll each. My sister chose a baby doll, but I chose the then very modern teenager doll with developed breasts. I certainly did not want to wear copies of her clothes but was happy to dress and undress her. Our parents were very tolerant of our toys and did not restrict us to girls' playthings. I suspect Dad had mixed motives in buying us a toy clockwork train set because he spent considerable time with us making sure it worked. We both played with dolls in their pram, toy soldiers, puppets, trains, cowboy outfits, (Jane and I both sported toy pistols) bricks and cars. Dad also made us bows and arrows. As time went on my toys became more obviously masculine. I saved my pocket money to buy a small Meccano set. In my late childhood and teens I spent much time painstakingly assembling and painting plastic kits of ships and cars. I longed to drive a red MG Midget, an as yet unfulfilled ambition. By this time my sister was occupying herself with trying to look grown-up and feminine.

My well-dressed Peter Rabbit came with me into hospital, when, at the age of five, I had my tonsils and adenoids removed. It was a frightening experience. I howled when visiting time ended and my mother had to leave me, which was probably as hard for her too. It is good that a more humane approach is practised nowadays and parents can spend much more time with their children.

This was altogether a traumatic period. My beloved Nan Bailey was also ill. Jane and I were sent away to stay with a good friend of my mother's and when we got back Nan was no longer there. Mum told us that Nan had gone to heaven. I kept looking up into the sky hoping to see her. Death was one taboo at that time and sex was the other.

In my childish innocence I blamed myself for Nan's illness. She had died of lung cancer. (Although not a smoker, Grandad and Uncle were. Grandad had died of a smoking related illness in 1940 and Uncle Bill was to die of lung cancer some years later.) During Nan's illness I had suffered from whooping cough and badly infected tonsils and could hear her also coughing as I lay in my bed. For years I was convinced that she had caught her cough from me.

It was a terrible time for my mother, having to cope alone with my robust two-year old sister while nursing both her dying mother and me. In addition my parent's marriage was going through a difficult time, which, thank goodness, later resolved itself.

My next trauma was starting school. After my long illness I was thin and pale, 'like wax' my mother said, and totally unprepared for the lively children who were my peers. The sudden transition from the safety of home to this alien place was frightening. I hated school. The bigger children teased me and I was too timid to answer back. Instead I yelled to go home, which could not have helped the teacher.

Fortunately my time at Rusthall Infants' School was short. I can just recall the desks with tip-up seats, the cold outside toilets, our little slates and chalk and the magnificent rocking horse that the school possessed and now stands, restored to its former splendour, in the Tunbridge Wells Museum. (The old school building eventually became the local library.) Because of my poor health I was moved to a nearby school for delicate children, the Open Air School, and remained there for three years. My mother went for a week to help the headmistress sort out her clerical work and remained there for twenty-seven years.

I settled at this school and began to play with the other pupils. Leaving the girls with their dolls and skipping I pleaded with the boys to be allowed to join in their games. I much preferred being with them. It was however rather humiliating to be given the role of ranch housekeeper whilst the cowboys went out after the Indians but I kept quiet lest they excluded me altogether.

During this period I had my first and last affair with a male. Robin kissed me behind the cloakroom door. We were six. It had been a very daring thing to do. Later the person who really attracted me was Josephine, the little girl who lived in the big house at the end of our garden. She was a pretty feminine child with dark eyes and brown curly hair. I made her a brooch out of clay and painted 'J' on it but do not recall ever giving it to her. For some reason my mother did not approve. We were not encouraged to become very friendly with anyone in case they did not want to be friends with us. 'One should not impose oneself on people' was her maxim, although she was always friendly when approached by others. This attitude was, I suspect, due to her own lack of self-confidence, perhaps an inferiority complex, but her reservations did not stop me from chatting to Josephine over the fence.

With my seafaring father absent for long periods it was inevitable that my mother became the major figure in my life, yet, although loving her dearly, I identified much more with my father, in spite of him being a virtual stranger. He was my role model and I was pleased when Mum said I was like my father, either in his patience or stubbornness, depending on her mood. I do not know what engendered my admiration for my father; perhaps it was just because he was a man, because good as he was, my mother was certainly his equal.

With Nan dead and Dad away our neighbours were very important. They had been very supportive to my mother during difficult times. As was then the custom, children often called neighbours 'uncle' or 'aunt'. This seemed a happy compromise between the rather formal 'Mr' or 'Mrs' and the subsequent very informal first name form of address. Our Welsh neighbours became my surrogate extended family. 'Aunt' Rose and her husband, 'Uncle' Brin, lived next door together with 'Auntie Barnes', Rose's elderly widowed mother, and 'Uncle Albert', their lodger. My real uncles and aunts were geographically distant individuals whom we saw comparatively rarely. This was unusual in a village community where many people had relatives, in if not the next house, then probably in the next road. If local people shared the same surname it was very likely that they were related. Our neighbours, also without local relatives, likewise regarded us as part of their extended family. Rose always referred to me as her Godchild, which technically was untrue, but she had a much greater affection for me than did my real Godmother who was an atheist and disliked me. (Mum was usually quite a good judge of character but not in this instance!) It was Rose, a keen singer, who encouraged me in my own choral activities that were to be such a delight to me later when little else gave joy.

When Brin and Albert cycled home from work together, Jane and I would run to meet them at the end of our road. They would dismount, lift us onto their saddles and push us on their bikes the short distance home. Uncle Brin looked after their garden and more than once I was lifted back home over the wall with the gift of a freshly picked tomato clutched in my hand. Albert did the odd jobs and had a workshop, which was heaven to me. I spent hours 'helping' him there, watching as wood shavings flew onto the shed floor and pieces of wood took shape as a cupboard or something equally useful. I enjoy the smell of freshly cut wood still. Albert was always patient with me and helped to fill the void left by my father.

At the age of seven I joined the Brownies and made friends with Lynda Woodman. A sturdy, practical, straightforward and sometimes dominant girl, she was most unlike Josephine. Perhaps these attributes, which could be regarded as masculine (although she was never 'butch') enabled me to see her as a chum. We played together a great deal, usually with string puppets and a toy farm, but I have no memory of us ever playing with dolls. Later we graduated into the Girl Guides where I was the only one to sport a sheath knife on my belt, which would probably now put me before the juvenile court for carrying an offensive weapon, but then it was just regarded as a useful tool.

Mum sent me for piano lessons when I was seven but I was lazy at practising so she decided not to waste any more money on that venture. Given her own musical talent it must have disappointed her and it is certainly something that I have forever regretted. It would seem that when given such opportunities one is often too immature to realise their worth, but when mature enough to appreciate them one is past carrying them out. I was obviously not, however, without ambition because on the front of my first music book I drew a picture of a concert pianist acknowledging rapturous applause and labelled it, 'Me'. The figure drawn was a man in white tie and tails.

Although my mother was not at that time a churchgoer, Jane and I were sent to Sunday school in the dreary brick 'Mission Church' that had been built in the late nineteenth century for 'the working people of the village.' A few adults attended, probably to help keep order, and Miss Black, who always wore a turban, played the ancient harmonium as we sang 'Jesus bids us shine'. The sickly Victorian picture of a white Gentle Jesus surrounded by well-scrubbed and well-mannered children from all parts of the Empire is still there today but the harmonium has been retired and replaced by a 'Music Group'. Miss G was in charge of the 'Children's Church'. She rode a sturdy black bicycle, had her hair pulled back into a bun, wore a belted tweed coat, grey ankle socks and Clark's sensible sandals and always (probably wisely) took her bicycle pump into church.

My child's mind was puzzled by the ankle socks. Adult female clothing was a mystery to me. I believed that all women were compelled to wear stockings and all the other dreadful things I had seen on my mother and aunt: girdles, suspenders, stockings, bras and – even worse – corsets. I thought it bad enough having to wear navy school knickers, so felt very sorry for women. Female attire was obviously designed by a misogynist. It never occurred to me that most women did not mind such garments or that I would one day be expected to wear similar. Until nearing puberty it did not occur to me that I would develop into a woman; it was something so inconceivable that no thought was given to it.

'Dressing-up' was one of my favourite activities because it gave me the opportunity to wear male clothes. I wanted to be a boy even then but as many of my peers were also 'tomboys' it was not considered unusual. It was something we would 'grow out of'. One of the advantages of being a Brownie was that the pack held fancy dress parties when I could dress as I wanted. My mother sometimes disagreed and once made me go as a (very disgruntled) flower-girl.

Later on I had a dream of forming an all-girl cavalry whose sole function would be to parade in gold-encrusted uniforms. Far from seeing myself as different I took it for granted that all girls wanted to be boys and would share my masculine interests.

At the age of eight I was moved to the village girls' primary school. My sister started attending the infants' school at the same time which I decided ruined her – she was no longer my baby sister. From now on my education was to be totally gender segregated, so in addition to living in an exclusively female home (except when Dad was on leave) my schooling was also spent entirely in female company. I do not remember being too upset by this because my chum, Lynda, was also at the same school. Although not very good at skipping or the ball games the girls played, I seemed to enjoy myself. We sometimes played 'families'. One advantage of being in a single-sex school was that I could take on male roles, so usually played 'father' in these family games.

On the perimeter of the school field were old air-raid shelters. During the summer we built camps behind them and in winter slid gleefully down their frozen earth roofs. School dinners were taken in the Rusthall Working Men's Club at the other end of the village and we walked in a crocodile along the High Street every lunchtime. I still have awful memories of soggy puddings and watery swede.

I enjoyed history, especially copying decorated letters from medieval manuscripts. (It is interesting that subsequently I developed a great interest in pre-Reformation monasticism and its legacy, which included the illuminated manuscripts created in the monasteries.) Another lesson I particularly enjoyed was weaving. Miss Woods had looms in her classroom and it was something quite special to be allowed to use one. I was very proud to have woven a scarf.

We listened to the BBC Schools Programmes and it was during one of these (*Music and Movement* I think) that the programme came to an abrupt halt and the death of King George V1 was announced. From what I recall the broadcaster asked us to go into mourning after which I solemnly wore a purple scarf with my navy school raincoat. At school the following year, 1953, we were given Coronation mugs and the combined village schools held a pageant. I recall my sister being dressed up as a peeress in a dyed red curtain with strips of cotton wool 'ermine' sewn on it by Mum. My role was far less stately; I think our class did marching routines, which was a mercy for me because whilst I would have been happy as a peer, the part of countess would not have pleased me at all. Shortly before the Coronation the school hired coaches and we drove to London to see the decorations. We watched the actual Coronation on a neighbour's television set with its tiny black and white screen, then later in colour at the cinema.

My mother, sister and I, off to meet my father

It was exciting for me to have a seafaring father. I fear that by this time I might have become a little snob because Dad had become an officer and had his own steward, which I shamelessly related to my schoolmates. Whenever his ship docked, Mum, Jane and I went to meet him and often stayed on board overnight. I enjoyed sleeping in a cabin with bunks, eating in the First Class Dining Saloon and having morning tea brought to us by Manuel, Dad's smiling and gentle Goanese steward. He was very kind to us. What I could not understand was why the Goanese were referred to as 'boys' because to my innocent eyes they looked like men. This recollection is not a happy one, but I cannot blame my parents and their generation; they were conditioned by their culture and time as we all are.

When Dad was on leave, which was seldom more than a week or so, we would all go to see his family at Sandhurst in Berkshire. Jane and I had fun in Grandpa's hen-coop because it was part of an old aircraft cockpit into which we used to climb, ignoring the hens and flying away on imaginary sorties. Retired schoolteacher Grandma Rees was a warm person and clearly retained her regard for children and used to do her best to keep us amused. Of necessity she had to be thrifty so little was wasted and her cupboards were full of produce which had been made into chutney, preserves – and wine in spite of her strict Methodist husband. The smell of apples still evokes for me Grandma Rees' house.

School was more than tolerable (except for arithmetic and needlework) but out of school was fun, despite our lack of car, television, computer and electronic games. I was the proud owner of a rounders bat, which gave me a certain amount of popularity. Sometimes I took it to school but more often played with friends on Rusthall Common.

Lynda had a bike, which I did not, but generously tried to teach me to ride on hers. I was very cross because my young sister managed to learn first, but it is interesting to note that neither Lynda nor Jane continued to ride in adulthood whilst I still do so. (Grandpa Rees rode well into his eighties and I hope to do the same.)

Lynda was not my only out-of-school companion. I became friends with John Guest, a boy of about my own age who lived in the same road, and was allowed to join him on operating his electric train set, an item that I shamelessly envied. Like the MG Midget, I never got one. We and our younger sisters built secret camps on Rusthall Common, walked the dogs that belonged to Nurse Page at number 22, and went for cycle rides with other village boys along the local lanes.

At the age of ten I was happily ignorant of any problem of gender identity and still assumed that all girls wanted to be boys, but if I were unaware of my own situation, other people already had inklings, as I was to discover later. Years after my gender reassignment my mother admitted that she had taken me as a small child to the family doctor because she was concerned about the size of my clitoris and thought I was changing sex. The doctor assured her that there was no cause for anxiety. In 1980, in the absence of any close family in addition to my mother, 'Aunt' Rose made a supporting Statutory Declaration for my Appeal to the European Commission for Human Rights. My mother had stated in her Declaration that she had had a job to get me to wear girl's clothes, even when very young. Rose said that from very early days I had exhibited masculine behaviour and even when wearing frocks had not looked like a girl and had always walked with a masculine gait. My subsequent change of role had been no surprise to Rose or any other close neighbours.

Their awareness was, however, of little help in those days. Had I been born thirty years later it is possible that diagnosis and treatment could have been obtained at an early age because St George's Hospital at Tooting in London later opened a clinic for children and adolescents suffering from gender identity problems (gender dysphoria). If my role change had taken place earlier than it did then much needless suffering could have been avoided, both for my family and me.

My childhood innocence was ended by two awful events. The first was the eleven-plus examination. Everything was geared to gaining a place at the grammar school. It seemed as if a child's whole life depended upon it, which in a way it did, because it was rare for anyone who failed the exam to go on to university and a profession. Of course my parents were anxious for me to pass, but my earlier illness had meant lost schooling so they engaged a private tutor to coach me. I was also promised a bicycle if successful. I failed. It was my first real experience of failure and it was a terrible blow which has haunted me ever since. I was, in my mind at least, marked as inferior and had let down my parents.

The second, shattering experience was for me the onset of puberty, with all its physical implications. My childhood, which had been relatively carefree, was nearing its end.

Chapter two

School days

MY best friend, Lynda, had been successful. She went to the grammar school. I was sent to the Church of England secondary modern (lower) school. Inevitably we grew apart, although not by choice, and I relied more on my neighbour, John, for company, but my involuntary estrangement from Lynda was only to be temporary.

I resented being a failure, being parted from the intimacy of the church village school and friends and sent to a school that I hated. It was punishment indeed. Such were my memories that I was delighted to see the old tile-hung building subsequently demolished. On reflection in my mature years I realise that this was the destruction of a historic old building in one of the oldest parts of Tunbridge Wells, which, in later 'heritage conscious' times, might not have been permitted.

The regime at Murray House, as it was called, was strict and humourless. My few memories are of old desks, needlework and cautionary tales of what happened to naughty girls. Although it was a church school I recall little of warmth there. After such an experience it was incredible that I remained in the church for so long.

My best subjects were (ironically) 'Christian Faith', history and English. Arithmetic (which was taught in a very uninspiring way) and needlework were my most despised subjects. I also hated domestic science when we were introduced to it the following year, gazing wistfully at the boys from the adjacent school going into their metal work and woodwork classes whilst we were being told how to iron clothes and make a blancmange with cornflour. I did quite well in cookery, however, probably because I could eat the results. Even at the age of eleven I aggressively resented the fact that we had to study 'feminine' arts, and throughout my school career hated this gender stereotyping. Years later, after having changed roles, I cooked for myself and mended my own socks, to my mother's surprise, but then I was free to choose.

My form mistress, an ageing spinster, was a very religious person who would doubtless have been horrified to know that the only subject which I remember with any clarity, was not then on the curriculum. It was sex education, which was taught by the more erudite pupils in seminars held by the outside toilets, usually to the accompaniment of sniggers. Little wonder we perceived sexual activity as shameful, a topic for dirty jokes. I do not, however, remember being much affected by these 'lessons'. Like all kids, I probably considered it daring to learn 'dirty things', but that also included the lavatorial. Although wanting to be a boy, at that stage I was sexually indifferent. It is possible that my peers were more aware of their sexuality than I was. My development came later. Years after leaving school I met the 'ageing' form mistress at church and realised she was neither so old nor as formidable as I had thought.

I did not make any long-lasting friendships at that school, but do remember one girl for a very unusual reason. She had large and masculine hands, which she probably hated, but I was very envious of them.

After a year it was a relief to be transferred to the senior school, Bennett Memorial, which was a much more pleasant environment, although also very formal. We had to call the mistresses 'Madam'.

We had a very kind Christian Faith teacher, a Miss Stenning, and I continued to gain high marks for both that subject and English. Miss Stenning took some of us to Canterbury Cathedral. I was totally enthralled by the beauty of the building and the music. Unfortunately I dropped a bottle of orange squash, which broke, in the south-west porch which lessened some of the delight of the visit, but nonetheless it was a wonderful experience. I still remember the hymn sung at Evensong, 'Dear Lord and Father of mankind, forgive our foolish ways' which seemed appropriate after my mishap in the porch. Had I known that twenty years later I would be back in Canterbury as a male undergraduate, server and cathedral guide, I would have thought it a miracle. In a way it was. My own personal belief was then still probably very much a child's one, although I had long passed the stage of looking up into the sky for my dead Nan. The God I then believed in was a benign being, a cross between my kindly next-door neighbours and my favourite relative (apart from my parents) Great-Aunt Jessie – the person to run to when things were a bit fraught at home. He may also have been a bit of a Magician-God, who could miraculously sort out problems, and a Santa Claus who, if I were good and did my best, would reward me. 'God', however conceived, was something we took for granted in my church schools and Sunday 'Children's Church'. My projection of God at that age was undoubtedly a positive one and certainly I did not see myself as sinful and in need of redemption by a bloody sacrifice, nor did I ever do so.

My sense of failure was lessened by success in the thirteen-plus scholarship, although even the subsequent acquisition of a degree never fully repaired the damage caused by the eleven-plus. My mother, in her old age, admitted that her own feelings of academic inferiority stemmed from her scholarship failure over sixty years earlier, in spite of her father paying for her to attend the grammar school. These feelings were not lessened by the fact that she was an exceptionally gifted pianist. My father's situation was the reverse. He passed his scholarship but was unable to attend the grammar school because Grandma could not afford the uniform. Maybe it was their own low self-esteem and fear of failure that caused them to discourage me from 'aiming too high'.

Initially, Jane gave Mum and Dad greater joy than I did. She passed her eleven-plus and went on to grammar school. What I did not realise until many years later was that she really was their 'blue-eyed girl' (although in reality mine were the blue eyes!). Both 'Aunt' Rose and Great-Aunt Jessie, who used to stay with us from time to time, became quite upset because they believed that my sister received preferential treatment. Mum admitted this eventually, in her old age, when the 'blue-eyed girl' had broken her heart. I cannot recall being aware of this difference in treatment, probably because I lived in another world for much of the time, either playing with friends or buried in books. I do not blame my parents. One child was beautiful, healthy, lively and academically set to fulfil their hopes, the other, born a 'skinned rabbit', dreamy, initially very sickly and miserable-looking, a tomboy who baulked at the dresses her mother wanted her to wear and preferred to stay in dungarees. Who wouldn't have preferred my sister?

If the scholarship success was one of my joys of 1955, the arrival of a dog into the family was another. Jane and I pestered Mum to buy a flea-infested, cross-bred black spaniel from a local pet shop. We called her Judy. We removed the fleas but kept their host, who was a very good-natured and friendly animal. My sister was soon to find boys of more interest than a dog, so I became Judy's regular walker. She was alongside me, a loyal friend, throughout my lonely puberty and young adulthood.

My new school, Tonbridge County Technical School, known colloquially as the 'Tech', promised to be much less stifling than the church school and I looked forward to starting there in the September of 1955. The equivalent boys' school was situated in Tunbridge Wells, not Tonbridge, a fact which caused some awkward moments after my role-change when asked for the address of my former school. Local people would know that the Tonbridge school was for girls. Usually I tried to give a vague location but it did cause me some anxiety.

Tonbridge County Technical School

I was very happy at the Tech in spite of its outside loos which froze in winter and the music room with its leaking roof. It was comparatively small, friendly and very democratic. Prefects were unknown and pupils shared in the discipline, being elected to the School Council to make the few rules which did exist. It was a system that worked very well. Much of the credit for such a radical approach was due to the Headmistress, Marjorie Coward, who made it her business to know every pupil individually. I never knew her lose her temper, although she did admit once that she had to raise her voice 'in an unseemly manner'! She was always gently but firmly in control and wasn't above using kindly humour, 'If you roll your sleeves up, dear, I'll think you want to do the washing up', I overheard her tell one pupil who'd infringed the dress code.

We kept in touch after I left school and in spite of the difference in our ages she became one of my most loved friends, helping me through many a sticky patch with her humour, wisdom and compassion. She was also a deeply spiritual person but never imposed her beliefs on others. Marjorie Coward was loved by all with whom she came into contact and her death in 1984 left a void which has never been filled.

Life at school could have been very happy for me, had it not been for puberty. My schoolfriends seemed to reach it before I did. They began to take an interest in boys and wanted to attract them, slavishly following fashions (it was the age of the 'waspie' belt and 'beehive' lacquered hair), wearing make-up and pushing their growing breasts into stiff new bras. However gauche their efforts it was a sign that my contemporaries were very much aware of the approaching womanhood. I wanted none of it and desperately hoped that I'd escape this terrible thing.

By now I regarded myself as male, cursed with a female body, a feeling which grew more intense as my peers became more feminine. In spite of pleading with the Almighty that I'd find myself developing into a man, I too began to develop breasts, although, little comfort, they were small. If anyone were tactless enough to remark that my figure was developing I'd deny it and desperately try to conceal the offending parts, which were to me a deformity I abhorred. As far as I was concerned this new body prevented me from living what was to me a normal life, i.e. that of a male.

I became aggressively concerned to make no concession whatsoever to my anatomical sex and made every effort to hide it. Even in the hottest weather I scorned dresses and sweltered in the more masculine but officially acceptable alternative winter uniform of skirt, shirt and tie, often wearing a blazer too. In winter, instead of wearing a figure-hugging jersey, I wore my blazer indoors. The thick navy skirt had the advantage of concealing my lack of petticoat, required by both modesty and fashion in the 1950s. My sartorial eccentricity was tolerated with good humour. As a member of the school choir I was obliged to wear a frock for the annual summer concert. This meant a battle between my love of singing and hatred of wearing feminine attire. I didn't want to miss singing 'Sumer is icumen in' after weeks of practice. A compromise had to be reached. I wore my winter uniform to school, changed just before the concert and immediately afterwards resumed my shirt and tie. After one concert some of my school friends hid my winter uniform. Utterly furious and miserable I was forced to remain in the frock until the end of school. I am certain that to the culprits it was just a bit of fun. They did not realise the anguish it caused me. It was to be forty years before I sang the medieval round, 'Sumer is icumen in' again, but was expected to wear a dinner jacket on that much happier occasion.

Although I hated wearing women's clothes, it worried me greatly lest I were seen as 'horsey' or 'butch'. Certainly I did not identify with mannish women and was repulsed by the thought of being classed as one. I did not want to be seen as a woman, either feminine or 'butch'. Yet – and this seemed paradoxical to some, especially my mother – I enjoyed seeing others looking feminine and attractive. If however, my gender, my true self, were male, then this is self-explanatory.

What of my mother? Years later she said that she'd not realised how bad my situation was. I cannot help wondering if this were an example of denial. She just couldn't face what was becoming increasingly obvious. I'd grown out of my tomboy stage but was becoming more masculine, in spite of my puberty. She was clearly perplexed and worried. Her concern often manifested itself as anger. I wasn't 'normal', I was awkward and, as my ambiguous appearance began to provoke comments, her response was that I invited such remarks. Mum couldn't understand why I was so unfeminine, hating women's clothes, 'walking like a man' and wanting a man's job. It seemed as if she and my father regarded my behaviour as being deliberate, that I was trying to be awkward. One day she blurted out that she had once asked the doctor if I were changing sex. I wondered at the time if that were an attempt to frighten me into femininity. If so, it was doomed to failure.

Doubtless Dad would have been aware of all the upheaval, but his periods of shore leave were short and infrequent. I never really knew what he felt, but it saddened me terribly that my parents had to put up with me as I was, that I wasn't a successful young man, or a successful anything, of whom they could be proud. I was not able to convince them that it was not 'cussedness' that drove me, but something which to me was natural behaviour. Certainly I never set out to 'walk like a man'. My mother often accused me of stubbornness – in many areas of my life – and mentioned to Miss Coward that I was so.

'Not stubborn, Mrs Rees, but determined.'

I was going to need much determination.

Chapter three

The Hated Bra

LIFE at home was becoming a series of battles, nearly every argument stemming from my perceived 'cussedness'. One of the great battles was of The Bra. I angrily spurned the bra which my mother bought me when I was fourteen. To have worn it would be not only accepting my femininity, but accentuating it. I could do neither. Mum was understandably concerned by my reaction and even more so when she discovered that I had, in rage and revulsion, screwed up and hidden the offending item. After entreaties and arguments with her repeating that I wasn't normal, my poor mother withdrew from the war zone, confused and hurt, whilst in the privacy of my room I pummelled my hated breasts with fury. I was made even more angry when seeing my male peers from neighbouring schools becoming more manly, and was so frustrated and envious that I changed my homeward route to avoid seeing them.

One of the most traumatic happenings was the start of periods. Desperately I had prayed to be spared, but at fourteen, later than all my classmates, menstruation began. I was horrified and disgusted and tried to ignore the whole messy business, pretending that it wasn't happening, but it was useless. My mother had to be told.

'You're a woman now,' she said almost proudly. To her it must have been an immense relief, confirming that I was normal, but few words have brought me so much pain.

Outlets for my pent-up feelings were found in day-dreams and story writing. I scribbled adventures of a girl who had miraculously changed sex into a physically normal young man. He grew a beard and thereafter I became quite obsessed by the desire to have one myself. At every opportunity I drew bearded men. Whiskered faces covered my school rough books and every scrap of paper. (Interestingly, although quite good at art I was never able to draw feminine-looking women.) A beard was a very visible sign of masculinity, which was why I wanted one. Having heard that shaving stimulated growth I twice shaved the 'fluff' from my face, but to no avail. Unsatisfied with trying to imagine how I'd look as male, I made cut-outs of male attire which were then superimposed on my school photograph. Sometimes, when alone in the house, I'd get my father's old uniform jacket from the spare-room and having padded myself out a little, put it on. I was certain that I would make a much better-looking man than woman.

In common with my schoolfriends, I went through the 'crush' stage, but unlike them did not go on to finding boys attractive. Instead the objects of attraction were young women but I never envisaged having a relationship with a woman as a woman; such an idea was abhorrent. My body was, to me, so repulsive that I didn't want to see it myself, let along allow anyone else to do so. I realised that what others took for granted – sexual relationships – would be barred from me. Life thus promised to be one of isolation.

My chief out-of-school memories are of lone walks with our dog, Judy, my most uncritical companion. A dog gives love to the person, not to the shell, the outward appearance. Life for me and all other transsexual people would have been much more tolerable had more human beings possessed this ability. I had a few friends, but on the whole didn't have much in common with many of the girls, especially when they talked about boys – and pop music! At the same time, being apparently female, I could not have the kind of friendship which I would have liked with boys – that of a chum. So my dog was companion and confidante.

With Judy in our garden

Paradoxically, I was popular at school – a fact of which I have only recently been made aware by old friends. They accepted my unfeminine behaviour and I was seen very much as one of the group, although one girl called me homosexual, which made me very angry. At that point I'm not sure that I understood the term fully, although she may have done, being more worldly than I was. One friend, Madeline, with whom I am still in close contact, recently suggested that the girls recognised the male in me and found that attractive. One classmate said at the time that I would have looked better with a beer and a pipe than as a girl! Madeline's theory would explain why, although different, I was accepted instead of being rejected by 'the herd'.

One thing which she did remember was that, very uncommonly for an adolescent, I went my own way and ignored the current fashions. She said how she'd desperately tried to get a raincoat 'just like the others' spurning the one her mother had got her, whilst I'd pestered my father to get me one like his. I was the only pupil with a trenchcoat. Unlike the others, not only did I wear a blazer for most of the time, but one with leather-bound cuffs, which Madeline had never seen on a girl before. The girls wanted heeled shoes without being too concerned with the depth of shine, whilst I strode around in flat-heeled highly polished lace-up shoes. It was the fact that they all tried to be like each other, whilst I went my own way, which Madeline noted as the big difference between us.

She remembered me as 'the class clown', especially in the hated 'modern dance' lessons. Being the comic was my way of having some control, of allowing people to laugh with me rather than at me because of my awkwardness. I set the agenda. My efforts at drawing cartoons also gained me a reputation for skill and wit, and gave me some status which boosted my low self-esteem. Looking back it seems that my most productive times for such drawings were often during the periods of greatest stress.

One of the reasons for hating modern dance was that we were obliged to wear scanty black games slips which I loathed because they did not conceal my hated figure. I abhorred changing in front of my colleagues. We also wore these slips for games. I was hopeless at games, but at least the lessons gave me an opportunity to work out some aggression, although my efforts to 'liven them up' were seldom appreciated.

However, school gave me only temporary relief. My problem, whatever it was, would not go away. It dogged my whole life. The outside world was less kind than my school chums, 'When are you going to change sex, Brenda?' a boy shouted at me across the local high street one day. (I met him over thirty years later. He was a very affable middle-aged man. I hoped I was too.)

Mistakes and remarks like this were increasing and I could not expect much sympathy from my mother because 'you invite such remarks'. Besides, my sister was causing my parents great worry by her excessive interest in boys and by her generally bad behaviour. I didn't want to add to my mother's burdens. Although years later, when I changed roles, Jane was very supportive, at that point I would not have sought her confidence.

I was able to speak to a few close friends. They may not have understood, though they were sympathetic; but what could they do? Professional advice was needed but I was afraid that my doctor would dismiss my 'silliness' or say that nothing could be done. What I expected I don't know, because it was very improbable that a 'sex-change' was feasible. Although only fifteen I knew that was the only treatment which would help. Subsequent events proved me correct.

I was quite religious by that time, perhaps because of my increasing unhappiness. Surely God would understand me? Oddly enough, I have no recollection of blaming him for making me as I was, although I became very despairing when my pleas for help were apparently ignored. I believed God could perform miracles, so he could surely change my sex. I prayed daily for this. When nothing happened I made a bargain that if he worked this miracle I would be confirmed. This one-sided agreement lasted until I decided that maybe God wanted an act of faith, so presented myself for Confirmation anyway.

Such was my devotion that I was quite prepared to withdraw had I been forced to wear the white dress and veil which was then customary for girl candidates in the Church of England. This problem was overcome by wearing my choir robes but I could not escape the dreaded veil which was removed as soon as decently possible. Yet even subjecting myself to this humiliation had left him unmoved. Life became worse, not better. My cries for help were apparently ignored by a God whom I had visualised as a cosmic conjuror who would miraculously get me out of my hell. Nonetheless, having seen the name of the Diocesan Moral Welfare Officer on the church noticeboard, I decided to contact her. I organised my visits to coincide with school choir practice to give myself an excuse for my late arrival home.

The Moral Welfare Officer (MWO) was an elderly and bespectacled lady, with grey hair pushed into a bun under a very nondescript hat which appeared to be a permanent fixture. She was used to 'young gels in trouble' but that sort of trouble wasn't likely to be mine. Her advice was to go to church and say my prayers, which was of little help. God was now off my visiting list. So was the Moral Welfare Officer, especially as my mother was becoming very suspicious of the extraordinarily late choir practices. I had awful visions of my mother chastising the innocent music mistress. Mum and I had also had rows about the letters I'd received from the MWO. She became very cross when I would not divulge the name of the sender. It had been a fruitless effort. I had to tolerate the situation as best I could.

Some of the many rows I had with Mum stemmed from my apparent stubbornness about a career. In those days before the Equal Opportunities Act women were barred from many jobs. Given that I idolised my father it was natural that I wanted to follow him into the Merchant Navy and in particular into his company, P & O, but none of the jobs open to women on the liners interested me in the slightest. I didn't want to be a stewardess, nurse, Woman Assistant Purser or children's hostess, especially as there seemed little advancement. Dad (and I have since wondered if he were teasing me) told me of a Scandinavian ship crewed entirely by women. I wrote to the embassy concerned only to receive a polite but negative reply.

Other ideas included teaching, the services, the police, law and medicine. Teaching was a family profession on Dad's side and a possibility, but I could not have coped with it on a personal level. The number of insults, jokes and mistakes engendered by my ambiguous appearance were making me extremely self-conscious. Children were, and remain, the worst offenders, so I wanted to avoid them as much as possible. Nursing evoked only lukewarm interest; besides I would not enter what was a predominantly female profession. My parents scorned my thoughts of a career in law or medicine, telling me to accept my limitations. Interest in the police was soon quashed by Dad who remarked that policewomen had to be attractive and good mixers. I inferred that he saw me as neither, nor did I consider myself as such. He said I'd end up as a bus conductress.

The armed services seemed quite attractive; after all the uniforms were fairly masculine, but the thought of sharing quarters frightened me. In those pre-Women's Lib days anyone not wearing a bra or petticoat would have been thought very peculiar, although I did wear stockings and a suspender belt, which I detested. I knew I was different but did not want to be told I was.

Having had organ lessons for a couple of years I asked about becoming an organ-builder. The dour Youth Employment Officer made enquiries but elicited the same response from all the firms – they would accept only boys as apprentices.

I decided to make my own way. I had had enough of school and everything associated with it. (This was probably typical adolescent behaviour, so I was normal in one respect). It was time for freedom! In a flurry of independence, I left at the end of the summer term and got myself a job on a local farm, but Miss Coward's obvious regret that I'd decided not to take my GCEs made me question my decision. After a chat with the local vicar, Canon Mantle, I decided that perhaps mucking out the cowshed indefinitely was not my path to freedom. I returned to school for the next academic year, really rather relieved, especially when I learned that one of my former classmates had taken the farm job and it had nearly killed her. I wanted a future.

Whilst delighted to be back within the womb of the Tech I knew that it wouldn't be long before I was thrust into a seemingly uncaring and critical world where I had to find a job and cope with a problem of which no one seemed to have any knowledge. On the one hand my own sense of failure and inferiority convinced me that I'd never have a decent career, on the other I knew that, denied a normal life, a worthwhile occupation for me was of immense importance. I sat the exams in total despair, not really caring whether or not I'd pass, convinced that success would be no guarantee of a good job because my problems would thwart all efforts. Whatever I did or wherever I went they would haunt me and no one would understand. As it turned out I passed all the exams I sat.

It was customary for fifth formers to see Miss Coward at the end of term to discuss a timetable for the Sixth Form. The school offered only Art at A-level, so university entrance (which I'd longed for but hadn't dared to mention) was out of the question. I felt hopeless.

'My mother thinks it a waste of time my staying on at school another year because I don't know what to do,' I remarked miserably.

'Frankly, so do I,' she said.

That was it. I was to leave school four days later.

Chapter four

He, She or It?

'SHE wants a job made for her,' said my mother crossly.

It was the day after my interview with Miss Coward. My mother and I were back with the gloomy Youth Employment Officer. Mum's anger covered her anxiety. It was understandable but I wished she'd not come. I sat silently in blank despair, feeling powerless as events raced on. My concern wasn't only over employment but also the thought of being thrust into a world which had so far seemed hostile and jeering. How could I cope after leaving the haven of school? I was conscious of the YEO's monotonous voice suggesting various mundane jobs. Surely I could do better than that? Did she think I was stupid?

My parents certainly didn't think me capable of getting a degree, although years later I discovered that Miss Coward did. I loved English and had spent much of my childhood reading and writing – 'scribbling', as someone described it, not unkindly. In my day-dreams I was beginning to think that it would be good to gain a BA, but didn't dare mention it. My parents would just have told me to be realistic.

In the misery of my last three days at school I realised that it was futile to hope for anything more than a very ordinary job. Now I had to ask myself not what I wanted, but what was possible, even if it were to become the bus conductress or Woolworth's assistant that Dad had predicted. Earlier, friends had suggested I become a professional cartoonist. I was lukewarm about it, but our very kindly art mistress encouraged me to contact the Principal of the Tunbridge Wells School of Art. After term ended the Youth Employment Officer suggested I undergo assessment by an occupational psychologist. In my hypersensitive state I inferred she thought me mentally unbalanced. After all, my parents had said I should be attending the nearby school for girls with learning difficulties. Ignoring my protestations, Mum had an appointment made for me to see the psychologist. To me the art school seemed a lesser evil so I immediately applied for a place and was accepted. The psychologist's appointment was cancelled.

In the meantime my GCE results had arrived. I was very pleased to have passed all five subjects, English language, literature, history, religious studies and art. But what difference would all that make now? Miss Coward wrote on the result slip. 'This puts a different complexion on things', but I paid little heed to it. She had assumed I would now return to school but I hadn't realised it, to my great loss. Instead I went unwillingly to the art school.

It was housed in an old building adjoining the public library in the centre of Tunbridge Wells. Later it became the Adult Education Centre where I spent many happy hours but my spirits were decidedly low as I began that first term. My gloom was lifted, however, by the discovery that Lynda Woodman was also a new student. She and her friends welcomed me warmly and were to give me much support in the coming months.

Each new student was issued with a drawing board and allocated a locker by the genial caretaker. Although I was (very reluctantly) wearing a new skirt, he attempted to give me a key to a locker in the boys' cloakroom. 'I'm a girl,' I said crossly, wishing it hadn't been necessary to say it. He stared incredulously at me. 'You're not, are you?' Other students were listening with interest. I felt very embarrassed. 'How many boys wear skirts and nylons?' I replied. 'If you like I'll go home and fetch my birth certificate.' Clearly perplexed, the caretaker handed over a key to a locker in the girls' cloakroom.

From the beginning I missed the security and warmth of the Tech. It had been a place where I'd felt accepted, could grow and be a person. This was not so in the art school. From the outset I felt an object of derision.

The caretaker had unwittingly given some of the students ammunition to fire at me. The snipers were mostly male and all virtual strangers. They seldom missed an opportunity to make snide references to my ambiguous appearance. One day in class a boy sneered, 'We don't know what sex you are, mate'. Hardly a meal passed without some reference to 'the queer'. Although Lynda and her friends told the offenders to shut up, I stopped eating in the school and took sandwiches to eat out.

I began to despise my tormentors, who were in a minority. Most of the students were friendly and the staff likewise but I couldn't feel as close to them as to the teachers at the Tech. Nor did I feel able to ask them for help.

Socially it was a bad beginning, but vocationally I also felt in the wrong place. I lacked the dedication that was necessary, although I enjoyed pottery and metalwork, perhaps because both gave me the opportunity to bang out my frustrations. The pottery teacher, Mrs Trend, was one of the few people who made life in that alien place bearable. I began to think that any number of psychological tests would have been better than the mental torture I was now suffering.

Life was little better out of school. Either people mistook me for a boy or others, usually teenagers, intentionally abused me. It was a continual reminder of my ambiguity. Girls wore jeans and had short hair as I did but were not singled out for such treatment. It wasn't that I tried to look odd, or to 'walk like a boy', so what was it that caused such derision? I began to dread leaving the house and tried hard to avoid passing people at close quarters. When taking the dog out I'd slip along side-paths rather than face approaching walkers.

Nor was I safe from torment even in my own home. I still remember vividly the time one of my parents' friends said to my mother – in front of me – 'He, she or it?' Another day when I thought of leaving art school and answering an advert for a girl assistant in a West End music shop, my father remarked, ' I wouldn't bother. Customers like to know the sex of the person behind the counter.' 'Can't you take a joke?' said my mother after I had expressed my distress at such a comment, 'Besides, you invite such remarks.'

Why did my usually caring parents behave like this? I'm certain that they wouldn't have done had there been more information available at that time. All they saw was an adolescent who was being more difficult than most teenagers, for reasons they could not understand. Did they fear that I was sexually abnormal or deviant? If so, that was something to hush up. Perhaps they felt guilty, believing that my behaviour was the result of their inadequate parenting skills. Undoubtedly they must have experienced bitter disappointment.

They clearly did not see a person who was suffering, not from 'cussedness' or 'imagination', but from a medically recognised and treatable condition. The world's first Professor of Transsexuality, Louis Gooren, was later to describe it as 'a lethal disease' because so many victims attempt suicide.

Most people of their generation only heard of such things through salacious articles in the gutter press which confused, probably wilfully, a potentially tragic problem of gender identity, with a bizarre form of sexual deviance. We were labelled as freaks and perverts. No wonder my parents couldn't cope with it. Although their apparent lack of sympathy hurt, how could I blame them?

Dad died before my role-change. I don't know how he would have reacted, but in her later years my mother became my greatest ally. She grieved that she'd not been able to understand earlier. Her support more than compensated for previous misunderstandings. When she learned of the verbal abuse that I was suffering (and still suffer) I had to restrain her from hunting out the culprits; she would probably have ripped them apart with her tongue if not her hands.

How much better the lives of transsexual people and their families could have been had there been reliable information available, information which would have, to a certain degree at least, countered and dispelled the notion that the condition was something shameful. It was a condition that needed treatment. So, too, did society.

During the art school lunch breaks I scoured the shelves of the next-door public library, desperate to find out if my condition, which seemed to be a case of having the wrong body for my mind, was recognised. Was I unique? It was the experience of feeling totally alone which made it so hard to bear. How could I ever get help if my problem didn't exist officially? I couldn't find any information except about homosexuality, but it seemed that homosexuals didn't want to 'change sex'. Yet what else could I call myself? In fact there had been a couple of female-to-male role reassignments in 1944 (Michael Dillon and Robert Allen) but I didn't discover this until twenty years after my own role change.

Having exhausted the little material I could find, I began to read about medicine in general, especially its history, which was fascinating. I became more and more certain that this was my vocation. It was a way of helping people, of satisfying my enquiring mind and, because it was onerous, would fill what otherwise promised to be a lonely life. Not least, it might give me some status in the community. Would the local kids abuse the doctor? Perhaps they would in 2000 but probably not in 1960.

My unhappiness at home, at art school and out in the street where every passer-by was a potential tormentor, and the isolation all this engendered, drove me deeper into depression. Even memories of the Tech began to be tainted with doubts. Had Miss Coward used my career uncertainty to rid the school of a pupil she suspected of being homosexual? I didn't then have the courage to ask her.

The renewal of my friendship with Lynda was my salvation. Here was someone to whom I could talk. She soon realised that I found women attractive but I didn't tell her for some time that my desire was as a man. Lynda's steadfast support was to help me through one of the most difficult periods of my life. We agreed that 'expert help' was needed but were a bit uncertain what 'expert' should mean. I wrote to the 'agony aunt' of *Woman* magazine, Evelyn Home (Peggy Makins) and, to avoid my mother becoming suspicious over any reply, Lynda agreed to provide a postal address. Predictably, Miss Home recommended I see a doctor, perhaps a lady one privately if I could not face my own GP. She didn't think a 'sex-change' would be possible. If that were the case, I wondered, why bother to see a doctor? However, I always hoped that one day a doctor would say, 'Yes, I can help you to become a man'. It was going to be a very long wait.

Chapter five

Glimmer of Hope

FOR the time being I found solace in choral singing. Already a member of the local church choir I joined Tunbridge Wells Choral Society. So accustomed had I become to snide comments that the courteous welcome given to me by the members seemed unbelievable. They could not have realised how much their friendliness was appreciated. This and the music (my first work was Handel's *Messiah)* made the Monday night rehearsals the happiest time of the week. The only snag was that the ladies had to wear long black skirts for concerts. This was even worse than having to wear an ordinary skirt. I coped with it by pretending that it was a cassock.

However, my weekly escape into music didn't end the pain. With my permission, Lynda discussed my problem with our friendliest tutor. Mrs Trend was firm with me. 'You can't go on like this; something is bound to give unless you see a doctor.' She was right, but how could I ask my mother for the doctor's fee? My chance came unexpectedly. During an argument my mother angrily exclaimed that the neighbours were talking about me, wondering if I were male or female. She scrubbed furiously at the dishes in the sink. 'If anything happened to you we'd have to move, we couldn't stand the shame.' (I assumed that 'anything happening' meant a sex-change not sudden death.)

'If you don't change your ways I'll take you to see a doctor.'

'But I want to see a doctor, Mum.'

She was surprised. Her anger subsided and she gave me the necessary money for a private consultation with Dr Florence Gelber, a much loved and respected local GP. One large hurdle had been overcome. The next was to get myself to the surgery. Even Dr Gelber's reputation did not allay my anxiety as the time of the appointment drew near. Lynda decided to accompany me.

'I can't go,' I protested as we walked to the doctor's.
'She'll laugh and tell me not to be silly.'

'Nonsense, she won't' said Lynda, as she virtually dragged me along the road.

'She's bound to. Everyone does. She'll tell me to go home, pull myself together and put on make-up and feminine clothes.' But my friend did not loosen her grip.

Dr Gelber was a very attractive woman probably in her early forties. She was tall with elegantly-styled greying hair and warm brown eyes. Her mellow and cultured voice conveyed reassurance and concern but nonetheless I inwardly shook as she smiled. 'Well, what's the trouble?'

I felt myself flush, and staring miserably at the wall of her small surgery tried to summon up courage.

'I...I...find it difficult to tell anyone about this.' The doctor was now tactfully examining her fountain pen. Embarrassment and shame tied my tongue, but I'd come prepared. 'If you are willing, I'd like you to read this letter I wrote to someone but never had the courage to post.'

Dr Gelber read a few lines. 'How unfortunate,' she said. Relief swept over me. She was sympathetic. The doctor asked me how intensely and for how long I'd felt the way I did and what kind of singing voice did I have. I told her 'alto' and added that singing was the only thing I liked about being a girl – which was a stupid comment because men sing too.

Inevitably she wanted to give me a physical examination. In spite of her reassurance I hated the experience, not only of being seen naked (even by a doctor) but also the act of undressing. This was because by 1960s standards my 'abnormality' would be revealed. I was wearing neither bra nor petticoat and sporting a man's watch. (If I rolled up my sleeves in public the watch was always surreptitiously removed and concealed in a pocket, a ritual so ingrained that I did it at the doctor's.)

The examination was mentally rather than physically uncomfortable. Dr Gelber placed a comforting hand on me and spoke gently, an action which considerably lessened my tension. I was apparently normal, although she thought my feet were large (size $7\frac{1}{2}$) for a girl of my stature (5' $4\frac{1}{2}$"). She explained that both sexes had male and female characteristics, men had nipples and women a rudimentary penis, the clitoris. Both sexes possessed male and female hormones but in different proportions. A slight imbalance could cause quite drastic results, both physically and mentally. It was to be eighteen years before I would meet another doctor who spoke in those terms. Obviously Dr Gelber did not regard me as deluded.

'I can't give you an internal examination now, but before we go any further with the physical side of things we'd better see what things are like mentally. Have you any objection to seeing a psychiatrist?'

I had, but because the doctor had gained my trust I agreed. She assured me that I could be helped, adding that it rather depended on what I wanted to be, which I found rather an enigmatic statement. If 'sex-changes' were apparently impossible, what choice could I have?

The doctor then wrote a long letter to a psychiatrist whilst I waited, wondering if this were to be the beginning of the end of my problem. Dr Gelber smiled kindly as I left her. 'Don't despair, you mustn't give up hope you know. You have nothing of which to be ashamed.'

Had she realised what she'd done for me? For the first time I felt that someone really understood and was able to offer hope and encouragement. I was able to hold up my head and treat the jeers with contempt instead of letting them destroy me. A glance at the doctor's handwriting on the envelope containing the letter to the psychiatrist was a constant reminder of her understanding and reassurance.

The following week, again accompanied by Lynda, I went to the Baltic Road Clinic in Tonbridge to see the psychiatrist. It was not a happy experience. We sat for ages in an empty and cheerless waiting room. It was small and cell-like, with hard wooden chairs, drab brown linoleum and old magazines. As the minutes ticked away so did my courage. I was very thankful for Lynda's company.

Dr George Bram was a pleasant-looking man in early middle-age, his deep voice betraying his Polish origins. He smoked as he read Dr Gelber's letter and stared hard at me as he inhaled. The silence was broken only by the dripping of a tap over his washbasin. I felt myself breaking into a cold sweat. Eventually he spoke.

'Tell me, do you ever desire sexual intercourse with a woman?' I felt sick. The tap continued its dripping.

'You understand what I mean?'

'Yes.'

'Well?'

'Yes.' I felt ashamed.

'Hmm.'

Dr Bram continued to stare, before putting some more, less embarrassing questions, and finally asking if I'd be willing to attend his hospital for a day of psychological tests. I didn't expect to gain anything from these but the thought of a day away from the art school prompted me to agree.

Mabledon Hospital was at Dartford, Kent, which meant a circuitous train journey. Lynda was willing to come but I didn't want her to sacrifice her studies. I was profoundly grateful to her for the help she'd already given me. For a girl of seventeen, she'd shown immense maturity.

When stating my destination I hoped the bus driver wouldn't think me a patient. My ignorance was appalling. As I walked up the long drive there were some patients gardening. Were they ever supervised or locked up, I wondered? Just how mad were they? Was I also considered mad?

In spite of obvious efforts to brighten up the drab rows of grey tin huts the hospital resembled a First World War army camp. I entered the 'Enquiries' hut with sinking spirits.

To my surprise I enjoyed the psychological tests, especially writing stories about pictures. For the word association test an elderly Polish sister read a list of words as quickly as she could in a (to her) foreign language. I had to respond with the first word which came to mind. Interspersed with the ordinary words were 'naughty' ones, such as 'man' and 'woman'. The test was gathering momentum.

'Cup.'

'Saucer.'

'Constipation.'

'All-Bran.'

Sister lowered the list and looked hard at me.

'All-Bran? Vot is dat? Vy do you say "All-Bran"?'

Lunch was taken in the patients' dining room. It soon dispelled my ignorance. Most people seemed more normal than those outside. All were voluntary patients and many Polish. I believe that some of them were displaced persons and Mabledon was their only home.

Mum came with me when I returned to Dr Bram's clinic a fortnight later. She saw him first, then I was called into his office. Something was brewing.

The doctor asked me if I'd be willing to enter his hospital as an in-patient. I was stunned. He told me to think about it and telephone when a decision had been reached. Apparently the tests had revealed that I had an inferiority complex and was very depressed. I could have told them that without undergoing any tests.

I don't know what the doctor hoped to achieve. All I wanted was harmony of mind and body and knew they'd not alter my mind, but my immediate thought was that hospital admission would release me from the present intolerable situation. It seemed worth risking the perceived stigma of being a 'psychiatric case' in order to gain some respite from all the jeers and mistakes. I could hope for little more, but my 'escape' was to cost me dearly.

Chapter six

The Psychiatric Hospital

Mabledon Hospital

SUMMER holidays were in the air, but not for me.

It was the 20th June, 1960. Mum drove me to Mabledon Hospital. We had a tearful parting. She must have been very unhappy and perplexed as she went home alone. I wept again after she had left and hated myself for doing so because it was what I saw as feminine behaviour.

I was under the care of a very attractive Turkish woman psychiatrist, Dr Urgup. She insisted on addressing me as 'Darling' which I thought very odd. No one had ever done so before. Although liking her, I hated our interviews. I didn't believe her when she said she knew nothing of my case. So I struggled through my life history, inhibited by the fact that she wrote down almost everything I said. Sometimes I lapsed into awkward silences which were made worse by her intense gaze, which I decided was a psychiatrist's ploy. It was irritating and distressing. How, I wondered, did she intend to help me? All I wanted was to 'change sex', but everyone said it was impossible.

If she intended to make me feminine she was wasting her time, so what the hell was I doing there? Yet apart from these twice-weekly sessions, life at the hospital was more tolerable than at art school. The other patients and staff treated me with great kindness, probably because at seventeen I was the youngest patient.

I got along well with my two or three room-mates although shared quarters posed problems (for me) because of my hatred of being seen undressing. Each morning I hurried to the toilet with a prepared bundle of clothes and dressed hastily in the cubicle. At night I went to bed before my colleagues came to the room, having first prepared the bundle for the next morning. It was more difficult to overcome the communal bathroom, with its one bath surrounded by washbasins. When no one was around I'd manage a very speedy strip-wash but bathed only when at home each weekend. I was as circumspect in women's company as I would have been with men.

I chose pottery and clay modelling for my occupational therapy. My only companion in the pottery room was Ken, a friendly man, who was probably in his late twenties or thirties. Both he and his wife were day-patients. Ken shared his morning flask of coffee with me and we often slipped out for a walk, which appeared not to cause his wife the least concern. Had they both sensed my ambiguity?

The occupational therapist was a very attractive woman. One day she asked me why I didn't wear dresses and make-up. Ken sprang to my defence,

'She's all right. I think that when she was young she played football with the boys.'

He rolled himself a thin cigarette and the matter was closed. Ken was however wrong about the football. The village boys wouldn't have wanted a soppy girl playing with them. Besides, being at an all-female school I knew very few boys.

My modelling was good enough to win prizes in the Hospitals' Group Show. It was also a mental and physical outlet, my frustrations being thumped out on the wet clay, which received its hardest punishment after I'd seen Dr Urgup. Waste clay was put into a bucket then periodically emptied onto a plaster slab to dry before being kneaded for re-use. Drying was speeded if we spread the clay and made air holes in it with our fingers.

When Dr Urgup visited the pottery room one day she was intrigued by this operation. She asked why I was making the holes? Her face bore a slightly worried, 'There-is-a-deep-significance-here' look. I explained the reason and she seemed relieved. Certainly I wasn't going to give her the satisfaction of knowing that I did enjoy pushing my fingers into the wet clay!

As summer slid into autumn so Dr Urgup worked her way through my life history and began to put forward a series of proposals to explain my abhorrence of my apparent sex:

a) Was it because I felt unable to compete with my younger sister so didn't even want to try? She tried to reassure me of my femininity, even telling me that I was pretty, which was about the worst thing she could have said. Had Jane been the elder and the first to attain womanhood her theory might have been more tenable, but I was the elder and therefore my younger sister should have been the one to be 'nervous of trying'.

b) My problem was part of growing up. I knew that adolescents often passed through a homosexual 'crush' stage and had witnessed such amongst my peers but to my knowledge none of them had felt as I did. None of them had any problems with gender identity, nor did they want to have sex with women as if they were men.

c) I was boyish because of being unconvinced of my physical sex. How I could remain unconvinced with periods baffled me. I was no less convinced (albeit angrily) of my apparent sex than my peers. Her offer to arrange for me to see a gynaecologist was declined. I didn't want a humiliating examination to confirm something that was already causing me intense mental anguish. Couldn't she realise that no amount of 'reassurance' was going to make me feminine?

My fellow-patients were more helpful than the zealous doctor. I felt able to confide in one of my ward-mates as she sat up in bed at night putting her hair in curlers. Mrs A, a middle-aged lady, confessed that although certainly no lesbian herself she'd found a masculine woman attractive. Neither of us was then able to articulate what I have since realised, that it is gender identity that makes a man or woman, not genitals. Generally they are congruent but in transsexual people they are at odds.

Another patient lent me a copy of the *News of the World* and thus enabled me to discover that I wasn't unique. In that issue, Georgina Turtle, formerly George, had written her life story. With changed gender pronouns, it could have described how I felt. It was wonderful to learn that I was not unique but the article was of little help otherwise. It did not name the condition and I was going to have to wait ten years before learning what it was and how a sufferer could be helped. The episode ended with Miss Turtle writing 'I decided to consult a psychiatrist'.

I hoped she'd found them more helpful than I had. As far as I was concerned my fellow patients understood me better than the doctors. Perhaps the psychiatrists should have read the *News of the World.*

I discussed my future career with Dr Urgup. I was convinced that medicine was for me although the chances of reaching that goal seemed as unlikely as did changing my gender. Dr Urgup told me that I needed to be helped first. She was, I believed, only partly right. With a purpose and a challenge then I'd be less introspective. I didn't want to be wrapped up in my own problems. With a normal life apparently denied to me I needed someone to say that I had potential and a future. All the doctor was able to tell me was that I was a woman. Perhaps she saw me as a deluded patient and her purpose was to release me into my true self, a feminine self. I saw her as someone determined to make me deny myself. There could thus be no meeting.

Apart from the infuriating encounters with the psychiatrist, the hospital was something of a haven, a refuge from the world with all its sniggers and questions. I was less at ease outside its walls. When attending a church near the hospital I thought the choirboys were laughing at me. This may or may not have been so, but it does illustrate my state of mind at the time. I felt safe only at Mabledon.

This security was not to last. Soon both staff and patients began to remark about both my appearance and mannerisms, wondering if I were male or female. Nowhere was safe and memories of the Art School hell were revived. Lifelong conflict, frustration and loneliness were surely all that awaited me, but I was too much of a coward to attempt suicide. Death terrified me more than hell on earth. Much anguish was caused because my condition was perceived by others as a psychological problem and therefore 'just in the mind', or 'imagination', and consequently, I assumed, my 'fault'. It was also seen as a sexual problem, so wasn't 'quite nice'. My feeling of guilt was thus exacerbated by one of shame too.

What would remove these feelings would be the discovery of a physical abnormality that would explain the situation so I would no longer have to accept responsibility for it. Dr Gelber had hinted that there might have been at least a hormonal cause. I decided to accept Dr Urgup's offer of an appointment with a gynaecologist. During a visit home following persuasion from my mother and sister, I saw my own GP, Dr Hicks, who was extremely kind and understanding. He didn't think it wise to rely on psychiatry alone; nor did he think a gynaecologist would be as helpful as an endocrinologist, so, following discussion with Dr Urgup, I asked Dr Hicks if a consultation could be arranged.

Meanwhile Dr Urgup advised that I leave the Art School. It was with considerable relief that I had my name removed from the register. That, at least, was something positive.

On the 4th October 1960 I made my way apprehensively to St Bartholomew's Hospital in London, accompanied by both my parents. I would have preferred to have gone alone although Mum, who had been sympathetic since discovering how deep-rooted my problem was and what distress it caused, was naturally concerned. My father, always taciturn, did not reveal much of his feelings.

The specialist was a little bespectacled man with a curt manner. As soon as he spoke I felt defeated and hopeless. His room was equally cheerless, sparsely furnished and with a stone floor. The only comfort was given by the nurse in attendance, a plump and smiling woman with a sympathetic manner.

'Did you play with dolls?' asked the doctor.

'I did.'

Perhaps I should have added that my doll was a well-endowed teenage one and that together with my feminine younger sister I played with toy trains, lead soldiers, toy guns, bows and arrows and also owned a Meccano set, but such was his attitude that I felt further information was not welcome.

'Sex diagnosis,' he growled at the nurse. I sensed her compassion.

When I was prostrate on the hard couch, which boasted only a coarse brown blanket, the doctor gave my abdomen a few rough prods. Menstruation prevented a more extensive examination. The prodding completed, the doctor pronounced me a 'normal female' and then sent me to the laboratory for a buccal smear and blood test to confirm that I was also chromosomally female.

My parents were asked to see the endocrinologist whilst I sat miserably in the green tiled waiting hall. They were relieved that there were no apparent abnormalities. I was not. My mother told me that the doctor had advised them to get me 'out of hospital and into a job', adding that as there were many 'horsey' women around, it was nothing to cause concern.

Once outside the hospital despair and rage overwhelmed me and I wept. My mother tactfully said little but Dad assumed an air of 'I told you so'. For years he had maintained that my problem was total imagination, I was just being 'cussed'. Now the doctor had apparently confirmed his view. Was it possible that my imagination could play such cruel tricks? Was I deluded? If so, why had so many people thought me male or at the very least, ambiguous?

My dejection was further increased by the fact that, by the time I returned to Mabledon Hospital, supper was over. Cross and hungry, I went to bed early and wrote in my diary. 'God forbid that I should ever become a "horsey" woman. I can stand it no longer, the taunts and insults of ignorant people, the dreadful feeling of awkwardness, the suppression of emotions and the feeling of inadequacy and failure'. These words could not convey fully my feelings as the most unhappy day of my life ended.

In spite of the endocrinologist's advice to leave the hospital I remained a patient at Mabledon for some weeks more and continued with the seemingly fruitless visits to Dr Urgup. Quite suddenly, during one interview, she suggested that I contact my former headmistress, Miss Coward, to ask if it were possible for me to return to school. This was beyond my wildest hopes. I told her it was impossible as it had been over a year since I'd left school. Nonetheless I could not forget the idea. Eventually I plucked up courage and wrote to Miss Coward, who in her prompt and sympathetic reply suggested a meeting. Miss Coward soon put me at ease. Over lunch I told her of the present situation and very tentatively put forward Dr Urgup's suggestion. To my surprise she responded as if the matter were already settled and we began to discuss my timetable as a member of the Upper Sixth. This made me wonder if Dr Urgup had contacted her. I never asked, but was grateful to them both.

Although very keen to leave Mabledon and return to school, doubts began to creep into my mind. Was it right that I should return to school? Wasn't I just taking refuge from the world? My parents were negative, believing that at my age I should have been earning a living. I believed, irrespective of the need for refuge, that it was better to delay wage-earning and acquire some qualifications which would enable me to enter a profession. I did not want to be a bus conductor. The other question was, would I cope with being in a community of young women? I had previously found one of my former classmates, whom I would meet again, attractive. She was a very demonstrative girl, which while not bothering the others, disturbed me. I was afraid of my growing desires.

In spite of these fears I decided the risk was worthwhile in order to study. By now I was absolutely determined to become a doctor. Unfortunately the Tech did not offer academic A-level courses but some further O-levels would be welcome. Before leaving Mabledon I bade farewell to Dr Urgup. She seemed genuinely interested in my future plans, but I didn't need her final advice to have more confidence in myself and be more feminine. 'Enjoy being a woman, darling!' She purred. But at least she'd got me back to school.

On the 1st November 1960 I rejoined my old school-friends at the Tech. The events of the past year seemed like a nightmare and it were as if I'd only been away for a few days until I discovered how much work there was to catch up on.

To the few who knew of what I regarded as "my problem", I tried to give the impression that it no longer bothered me, but on the first day back recorded in my diary how much I hated being a girl. This important day was marred by the start of a period, so instead of feeling bright and enthusiastic as anticipated, I sat miserably on the home-going bus with a headache, wondering if it were possible to get home without being sick.

Whilst I was delighted to be back, the fourteen months of comparative mental inactivity meant that returning to serious study was hard work. My schoolfriends helped out as much as they could, lending me notes and even writing them out for me, which I appreciated greatly. Soon I settled into the routine and was happier than I'd been for a long time, but was not out of danger. Sometimes in our Upper VI study, we gave vent to our youthful high spirits and indulged in horseplay. On one of these occasions one of the girls jokingly ran her fingers through my hair and embraced me. To my horror, I was sexually aroused. In retrospect I realise that this took the form of a clitoral erection, although at that time I wouldn't have known what an erection was. 'Wrestling' with the same girl another day I was taken aback when she suddenly broke loose,

'Stop it!' she cried, laughing. 'You're worse than a man!'

It would have been so much easier to be asexual, but I wasn't. My sexuality was a burden. As I abhorred the idea of a sexual relationship with a woman unless I was a man, it seemed there would never be an outlet for my desires. I was often troubled with arousal and erotic hopes and dreams. In my dreams I was forever pursuing a desirable woman but never quite reaching her. I'm not quite sure what my sex was in these dreams, presumably male because as a female I would not have chased anyone.

During the last weeks of term I pondered my future. Without A-levels I wouldn't get into medical school. At first I thought of studying at night and working during the day, but I couldn't seem to find the right job. I even considered joining the services, since they boasted opportunities for further education, but an interview with the Women's Royal Army Corps put me off. The officer referred to me as 'a bit of a tomboy', so I thought 'Oh hell I won't bother!' Certainly I could cope with the work, but my fear of being thought 'odd' deterred me. I decided to put aside all thoughts of a service career – for the time being at least.

Life at home was still difficult. My parents seemed to think that because the endocrinologist had found no abnormality that was the end of the matter and I would start to behave as a normal teenage girl. Little sympathy was forthcoming from my mother if I told her of the latest remark or insult regarding my ambiguous appearance. Instead she'd chastise me for my unfeminine walk. It seemed as if they were still convinced that my behaviour was contrived to annoy them.

Apart from singing with the local choral society there were no social activities in my-out-of-school life. I avoided them because of my hatred of dressing up, feeling awkward and being thought 'butch'.

Miss Coward, ever solicitous, was sympathetic regarding my various concerns and contacted Dr Bram on my behalf. The tap still dripped in Dr Bram's room, but it did not bother me this time. I was relieved that he had no plans to re-admit me to Mabledon. His advice was to join one of the services. Would I have the courage to do so?

Upper VI, (Miss Coward centre, me extreme right)

July 1961 finally came upon me. It was time to leave the Tech, this time for good, and as far as I was concerned, for bad. The feeling of loss was worsened by my apprehension about my future. I hated being asked about my career plans. I had none.

There was no thought of a holiday that summer, just the prospect of unemployment. I was fortunate to obtain a post at the local hospital, which I regarded as a temporary measure until something better was possible. Although basically menial, my work as a ward orderly had its rewards. It gave much patient contact. The patients, mostly elderly ladies, seemed to like me and I had my pockets stuffed with gifts of sweets and unwanted oranges. It was another place, apart from school and choral society, where I felt a person, not an object of derision. That meant much to me.

Although happy in a hospital environment, I had no desire to remain as a washer of bedpans and cleaner of toilets. Still I wanted to be a doctor, but in spite of passing another GCE there was still a long way to go before I could apply to medical school. After three months I decided it was time to leave to look for something more challenging. There just had to be something better. Could I find it?

Chapter seven

Rejection

MAYBE I could turn professional? Instead of singing only on Monday nights perhaps I could do it every day? I wrote to the BBC Chorus but they wanted fully-trained singers. That I wasn't. Various other ideas were pursued but none bore fruit. I began to despair. Perhaps I should reconsider the services?

I went with some other potential Officer Cadet candidates to the WRAC Officer Training Unit at Haslemere. It was a stimulating and enjoyable day, but to my dismay there was a clear emphasis on retaining femininity. This may have encouraged my colleagues but it had the opposite effect on me.

The charming and beautifully groomed Liaison Officer who accompanied us – described as 'a poppet' by the cadets – was an ideal role model for any young woman. It was not one I could follow. I'd be known as 'Butch Brenda' by the privates, if not by the officers too. The services could surely not be for me.

Dejected, I returned to the 'Situations Vacant' columns and the dreary Labour Exchange. I resigned myself to the demoralizing plop of 'We regret...' letters falling on the doormat. To me, the epitome of hopelessness was the dole queue, shuffling silently forward to 'sign on'. I wanted never to see it again – a vain hope. With no job, no hope, little money and having constant rows with my parents because of my perceived 'cussedness', Christmas 1961 was not a happy one for me.

In the New Year I took a job as a clerk in an insurance office. I hated it. The thought of addressing thousands of envelopes for the rest of my life filled me with utter misery, so despite my misgivings I filled in the Army application form. A decision had been made. I felt happier for it and began to look forward to a new life.

My application for a commission was rejected, but no reason was given. After an equally unsuccessful attempt to get into the ranks, I asked Dr Gelber to write to the Army. She did so and confirmed my suspicion that the medical rejections were due to my five months in Mabledon. It was the greatest blow since my eleven plus failures. Was I, in addition to being denied a normal life, also to be barred from a worthwhile career? Could I do no better than wash bedpans or address envelopes?

I felt a total failure and utterly hopeless. My subsequent many visits to Dr Gelber with various aches and pains, which were obviously psychosomatic, gave hope of getting away from the detested job and finding a sympathetic ear. This was my first, but not last, experience of the psychological damage that can be caused, not by unemployment but inappropriate employment.

Our local curate, Denys Crouch, became my mentor and I also returned to Dr Bram. He sent me to a colleague for a second opinion. Psychotherapy was recommended but I thought it would be futile. What I wanted was a decent career, not life in a consulting room. After much deliberation I decided to try the WRAF. They invited me to a three-day Selection Board at RAF Biggin Hill on 6th March 1963.

One anxiety was allayed when I found that the candidates were allotted single rooms, but soon after arrival I was summoned for a medical examination. That was odd because they weren't scheduled until the next day. I was told that because of my medical history (i.e. Mabledon) it was necessary for me to see an RAF consultant neurologist in London the following day. (They never explained why I had to see a neurologist rather than the usual psychiatrist.)

In the examination room the nurse told me to strip to my bra and pants. I didn't wear a bra and went hot with embarrassment. This was just what I'd feared. Few questions were asked. Dr Bram had written to say that I had previously suffered from depression. I told the examining doctor that I was now fine.

As I dressed, the nurse, a very attractive girl with blonde hair and blue eyes, asked if I'd like to tell her why I'd been in Mabledon. She said that I wasn't obliged to, but she was under oath and would not reveal any confidences. Her manner was sympathetic and I found myself telling her of my transsexuality (although I could not give it a name at the time). She didn't appear shocked, which is what I'd come to expect, but said I'd been brave to tell her. With a warm smile she patted my shoulder and told me not to worry. It was a tremendous relief to find in this rather awesome and impersonal place at least one person who seemed to understand. On reflection I wondered why she was so interested. Had the doctor asked her to question me?

Herded together in gowns for x-rays, I had great difficulty in concealing my lack of bra from my fellow candidates but in spite of these problems felt happy at the prospect of service life. It promised a worthwhile career and congenial company.

During a break I slipped into the simple but tranquil station chapel. Alone there I thanked God for leading me to Biggin Hill and implored Him to guide the Selection Board to accept me. (Perhaps my God had now become an Air Commodore.) Afterwards I rang Miss Coward and told her how happy I was to be with the RAF.

Next day I was at the RAF Medical Centre in London. The neurologist was a thin, pale and balding man with a strong Irish accent. He fidgeted constantly with a string of beads, perhaps a rosary, in his overall pocket.

'Why did you see the psychiatrist?' he asked.

'Because I hated art school.'

'Why?'

'Because I didn't get on too well with some of the students.'

'Why?'

'They were very rude and called out personal remarks every day.'

'Give me an example.' His voice sounded cold and bored. Foolishly I repeated the first comment which came into my head from those unhappy days. 'We don't know what sex you are mate!'

His face was expressionless as he looked at me.

'Hmm. Well, I think you will find the RAF too much of a strain.' The consultation was over.

On my arrival back at Biggin Hill I was summoned by the President of the Medical Board. He wrote something on a piece of paper, 'Take this downstairs.' Stunned, I took it and read 'Reason for Rejection: Temperamental Instability'.

I was furious. What they had done was more likely to make me unstable than the challenge of service life. Later I realised that they were probably concerned lest I were lesbian and therefore clearly a great threat to the stability both of the RAF and the nation. In a way, life would have been simpler had I been lesbian. They didn't know what I was, although probably would not have admitted it. Nor did I know.

I met some of my fellow candidates downstairs.

'Well, how did you get on?' asked one of the girls, kindly. To my shame, I burst into tears – how I despised this female chemistry which reduced me to such displays of emotion. The others listened to my account of the day's events and then took me to the mess for a coffee. It was not an entirely negative twenty-four hours. I was beginning to learn that whilst much of the world seemed hostile and uncomprehending there was compassion.

There was yet another summons, this time to see a RAF and a WRAF senior officer. What a sight I must have looked to those smart and efficient beings, a plain tweed-clad ambiguous creature with still-reddened eyes. Their purpose was to present me with the official rejection slip. Why couldn't they have posted it?

'Any questions?' asked the RAF officer. I had recovered some of my composure.

'Yes. Why does the RAF doctor say that service life will be too much of a strain when my own psychiatrist recommends it?'

'I don't expect your doctor knows what service life demands.'

'I believe he was an Army psychiatrist.' The officers looked at each other.

'Well, if you are not satisfied, ask him to write to the Medical Board. We can't do anything. It's up to the doctors.'

I went straight to a telephone and rang Dr Bram. He was angry,

'My dear girl, I know what I am talking about – I was the Director of a Military Psychiatric Unit!' He assured me that he'd write to the Board. In a way it was a slur on his professional judgement so his fury may not have been entirely on my behalf. I returned to the RAF officer and told him of Dr Bram's reaction. He seemed more sympathetic.

'Then you must get your doctor to write. For goodness' sake don't let it rest if you are not satisfied.'

'I won't,' I said and meant it.

I returned to the Chapel, wept and hated myself even more. Nor was I desperately keen on God. He'd really let me down this time.

The RAF did not escape without a fight. Over the next few months letters went back and forth between Dr Bram, the RAF and myself. Not until my case reached the Air Ministry did I concede defeat, but not very graciously. It had, however, been a good preparation for the battle which was to come many years later. I was not in awe of officialdom then, nor am I now.

Mum and Dad were very sympathetic. They knew I'd tried, but that didn't stop me from feeling that I'd let them down. Would they ever have reason to be proud of me? My sister wasn't giving them much joy, either. She'd left the local grammar school with few academic qualifications, was seventeen and pregnant. My parents surely deserved better children.

Denys Crouch wasn't surprised at my rejection. He said that the services weren't very keen on 'that kind of thing'. I could have assured them that in my female role I'd be no threat but knew they wouldn't understand. The services like to categorise people. My condition did not fit into any known compartment, at least not in 1963. One day it would, but not for some years.

Chapter eight

Unexpected Encouragement

ONE boon that had come out of my time at the hated insurance office was that I became friends with a fellow clerk, Christine, and her ordinand fiancé, John Huggett. Both concerned themselves very much with my problem and to my amazement suggested that I make enquiries about having my sex changed. It was what I wanted above all else, but I knew there would be obstacles. The doctors said it wasn't possible and besides, what about my family? What if I wanted to marry? Could I marry if I became a man?

Chris replied that if they really loved me they would want me to be happy. That was true, but would everyone see it that way? As for marriage Chris assured me that had John had a similar problem she would still want to be with him because she loved him. (None of us then knew that marriage in a new gender role would be unlawful.) Their support for me was so wholehearted that she hoped I would be able to attend their wedding as a man.

John wrote to support Christine's suggestion and said that they would do anything they could to help me and went on, 'From the little I know of you, in many ways you seem already like one of us men! It would seem that the only way in which you are different is your form... I'd say you'd make a very good man and be happy as such. That is why, humanly speaking, I think the only answer to your problem is to have the necessary hormones injected into you so that you change sex.'

Chris and John had recognised, perhaps unconsciously, that whilst my body was apparently female, my gender identity was male. They gave me courage to return to Dr Gelber. Perhaps she'd still say my wish could not be fulfilled, but on the other hand there might have been developments that made it possible. I felt hopeful, elated at the thought of being released from my prison and beginning to live as myself. Physical pain and other difficulties would be a small price to pay for this rebirth.

How soon my hopes were dashed. There was genuine regret in Dr Gelber's voice as she told me that nothing could be done in the way of surgery because it was all still in the experimental stage. (She may have meant the construction of a penis that is still experimental.) I was physically normal so a 'sex-change' was out of the question.

From a report she'd read, psychotherapy was useless in such cases, a point of view further confirmed in the succeeding thirty years. Dr Gelber said that I was unfortunate in having more maleness in me than female, but I would just have to accept it.

She assured me that although depressed I was not a depressive. There was good reason for my depression; it was exogenous. She was very sorry about the RAF because I badly needed a worthwhile career. Her very positive reaction to my later 'sex-change' convinced me that had she known of a possibility for me to undergo treatment earlier she would have encouraged and helped me. So there was no solution. It was ironic that almost immediately afterwards I attended a friend's wedding. Whilst happy for her I felt bitter, knowing that I'd never be able to marry. John and Christine were sorry to hear of my lack of progress and their support was greatly valued.

A strange consequence was that I met John's family, kind people but very Evangelical, and was distressed to hear them and their friends condemn Roman and Anglo-Catholics. My beloved Great-Aunt Jessie was an Anglo-Catholic so I resolved to find out more in order to defend her. One Sunday I attended Mass at St Barnabas' Church, Tunbridge Wells, the only Anglo-Catholic church in the district. It hadn't been my intention to do more than inspect it, but I was attracted by the music, the ritual, and not least by the genuinely warm welcome given to me by the vicar, Rowland Taylor. As a result of my joining this congregation the course of my life was to be completely changed.

The despised job in the insurance office soon came to an end. My employers decided that, judging from the number of service and other interviews I'd had, it was not my intention to stay with the firm. In spite of the prospect of further unemployment I was absolutely delighted to take my month's pay and leave.

My parents were more understanding than anticipated, although the subject of employment and problems encountered because of my 'queerness' continued to spark off rows. I had to accept this. My only regret about leaving the job was that I didn't see Christine daily, but she and John kept in contact. I was profoundly grateful for their generous and thoughtful friendship. Eventually we lost touch, but it was no surprise to discover years later that John had become a priest and that they both became well-known in evangelical church circles for their healing ministry.

I was now determined to get into either the police or one of the services and decided to adopt a strategy of acting out the feminine role, even to the extent of wearing the loathsome bra, in order to achieve my end. I wasn't sure how to cope with it, but thought it would be possible by detachment. The real me would remain under the shell. This strategy would not, however, include marriage; it was adopted solely to get a decent job.

There were many interviews, medical examinations, much form-filling and heart-searching as I was tempted to ignore the question, 'Have you ever been medically rejected by any other branch of the services?' The medical examination for the Metropolitan Police was the worst. I felt like an exhibit as, stripped to the waist, I was observed by two women police officers while the doctor told me that I was medically unfit. He'd conducted no physical examination whatsoever so I concluded that the decision had been reached as soon as they'd read 'Mabledon'. I felt humiliated. At an interview for another police force, the butch-looking woman officer asked why I didn't wear make-up! I decided this was a clear case of motes and beams!

Rejected by several police forces, the WRAC (commission and other ranks) likewise the WRAF, I wondered if I would ever be allowed to achieve anything or would I be one of life's failures? But there remained the Navy, or rather the Women's Royal Naval Service.

Previously I'd had little interest in the WRNS because they did not go to sea, besides that service seemed the most feminine. Nevertheless I decided to apply. What had I got to lose? Donning the hated bra and petticoat for my 'role-play' I set off for the medical and interviews which were held, not in dreary barracks, but aboard Captain Scott's old ship, the HMS *Discovery*, which was then moored by the Thames Embankment in London. Interviews apart, the venue made it an interesting experience.

As expected, the naval doctor, an avuncular figure in civilian dress, was dubious about my psychiatric history but promised to write to Dr Gelber before reaching a decision. It was the first time I'd been allowed to proceed to selection tests and an interview. Usually I'd been dismissed once my medical history had been revealed. The WRNS officer put me completely at ease, which was quite an achievement during those trying days. She was red-haired and I took quite a fancy to her. The Navy had treated me as a person. For the first time ever, I left an interview with hope.

HMS Discovery

It was justified. I was accepted and immediately wrote to thank Dr Gelber for her part. It was also a shock. Rejections had become so much part of my life that it took some readjustment to realise that someone had said 'yes' to me.

I took a temporary job as a driver for Vines, a grocer's shop in

Southborough, until my enlistment a few months later. It was fun to tour the countryside in the little van, meeting many people from all walks of life. Most were women at home and several seemed delighted to have a visitor, even if it were only me delivering groceries, but whether in the urban streets of Southborough or the outlying country lanes, my sex was frequently confused by customers.

With the future apparently determined, I began a correspondence course in O-level biology. I hoped that in four years' time, my WRNS engagement completed, I might have gained the necessary qualifications to go on to medical school. Failing that, a permanent career in the WRNS, perhaps as an officer, was a possibility.

Whilst much happier than before, I was still bothered by my sexual drive, especially as I'd been attracted very strongly to one of the young contraltos in the Choral Society. It was very frustrating. I never told her of my feelings. What was the point? I didn't want to ruin a friendship. It was, however, one of the strongest attractions I'd so far experienced.

Our curate, Denys Crouch, warned me that life might be difficult within a female community, but I hoped that the newness of WRNS' life would occupy my thoughts fully. Not all the Wrens would be attractive, surely? I did, however, resent having to sublimate this part of myself. Denys, alas, whilst very kind, never accepted that I wasn't really homosexual, even years after my role change. It was a view that the Navy was to share, to my cost.

Chapter nine

The WRNS

THE Union flag hadn't seen daylight since the Coronation, ten years earlier, but some neighbours waved it from their window as I left Rusthall for my life in the WRNS. A couple of my former school friends, Madeline and Jean, who were now student nurses, met me in London and insisted on travelling with me to Reading – although they hastily retreated before the arrival of the naval lorry which met the recruits at the station! I appreciated their company on this special journey.

We were driven to HMS Dauntless, at Burghfield, where our basic training was to take place. Here I met the first anomaly of service life – 'HMS' Dauntless wasn't of course a ship, but a collection of typical military huts, linked by black insulated pipes, functional but not beautiful. Only two men were on site, the stoker who looked after the boilers, and the chaplain who cared for our souls. Probably the former was more appreciated. Unusually for such an establishment, our rooms (called cabins) were only two-berth and had hot and cold water in each. This, plus the constant heating (it was the end of October) made me think that service life had much to commend it.

Initially we were permitted only a minimum of luggage. I unpacked my suitcase, which included, as always, paper, pen and dictionary, and found a small packet. I thought my mother had put in some sandwiches, not that they'd been needed, but when I unwrapped it found a very stale jam roly-poly. The pudding had not been one of Mum's greatest successes. She had dished it up during the preceding week on several occasions, to the accompaniment of rude comments from me and Aunt Jessie, who had been staying with us. It had become a family joke. Now the joke was on me. The neighbour's flag, Madeline and Jean's company and the pudding had given me pleasure. Perhaps I wasn't as unlovable as I'd come to believe.

Dauntless was our home for the first month of service life while we underwent 'Basic Training', which the recruits called 'Hard Labour'. For the first fortnight we wore shapeless blue wrap-over overalls, white socks and plimsolls. Only after signing away four years of our lives were we issued with the coveted uniform. When not cleaning for the multitude of inspections, or marching around the camp to the worn strains of 'Hearts of Oak' over the tinny Tannoy (which I enjoyed), we had lectures on every aspect of service life, from polishing our shoes (the spit was not officially sanctioned) to Queen's Regulations. There were further medical examinations and interviews with WRNS officers, none of whom charmed me as much as the one I'd met on Discovery, but they were affable enough. To us the most important person was our young Divisional Petty Officer. It took some time to get used to women barking orders but away from the parade ground and in 'mufti' PO seemed a very likeable and feminine person. She quite took my fancy. Frustrating as that was, at least it took my mind off the contralto in the Choral Society, whom I'd sadly left behind.

On the whole I enjoyed myself. The comradeship was welcome, so I tolerated the floor scrubbing and being shouted at by Petty Officers pretending to be fearsome. What I hated was PE because it involved a kind of 'Health and Beauty' activity – lessons on make-up, hygiene (which seemed an affront to any civilised person) and lectures on the birds and bees. I felt quite sorry for the elderly lady doctor assigned to this task. She used bits of felt anatomy to stick on the cloth board to illustrate her point and brought the house down when she announced with slight dismay, 'Oh dear. I've dropped my ovaries.'

Although trousers would have been better than a skirt, I was proud to go home for a couple of hours' leave in my new uniform. I think it gave my mother a little thrill. Although very irksome to me it had been a good idea to adopt the 'role-play' because it was making life easier than it had been.

In a uniform, as I had discovered at school, I was someone, without necessarily being me. It gave status and also anonymity. My 'oddness' was masked. At that time too, members of the public obviously had a respect and affection for the WRNS. Strangers chatted and it was good to be greeted by other servicemen and women when away from base. The uniform meant a great deal because it was a sign that I'd been accepted, something which until recently had seemed almost impossible. I had overcome the stigma of Mabledon. From now on I was going to go up. The career of Wren Rees BM 120540 had begun.

Visiting my father on his ship

As a potential motor transport driver I was sent on to HMS Seahawk, the Royal Naval Air Station at Culdrose in Cornwall, for driving instruction. (The fact that I already had a full licence was deemed irrelevant!) Anyhow, I enjoyed my free trips around Cornwall and was sorry when the course ended. I was pleased to be drafted to the air station and looked forward to enjoying the mild climate of the Lizard Peninsula for some months to come, but nothing is quite what it seems. I didn't find an airfield too exciting when it meant driving round it most of the day. The glossy recruiting brochure didn't show us cleaning our vehicles in the frosty weather, the water freezing as we worked; neither did it show the crowded smoky crewroom where we sat, often playing cards as we waited for another exciting errand from the control tower to a hangar on the far side of the airfield, but this didn't detract from the fellowship, which I was enjoying immensely.

My twenty-first birthday fell soon after my arrival at Culdrose. Mum sent me a delicious cake, which was vastly superior to the jam roly-poly. Dad sent a cable from his ship and my sister, now married to her first husband, sent me a superb book about music. Otherwise the occasion passed almost unnoticed. My only celebration was a drink in a nearby pub with a couple of Wrens. My parents were willing to give me a party when I went home but said that I probably wouldn't want one because I hated social gatherings and dressing up. It was the dressing up I hated. I had a party twenty years later.

Life was ticking along. My officer recommended me for advancement to Able rate, stating that I was 'hard-working, conscientious and an asset to the unit'. Despite the intellectual limitations of the work (i.e. it bored me!) I enjoyed the rest of service life, involving myself in chapel, fencing, drama club and the madrigal group. It was a joy to walk to the nearby coast at Looe Bar and look at the sea. Often it was a deep, almost turquoise blue, and in rough weather it was an awesome sight with huge deafening waves crashing onto the shore.

I was managing to cope with living in the mess with thirteen women, all of whom were friendly. Most of the women I liked eventually became officers. There were some Wrens at the station who were regarded as lesbian, although officially they did not exist. In retrospect I am certain that one or two of them were transsexual. Service life had attracted me, so why not them? Some, including NCOs and officers, fell foul of the authorities and were discharged, which was tragic because they worked as well as anyone else and were as decent as their fellow Wrens, sometimes more so. I identified slightly with the mannish Wrens, but not with those who were homosexual.

As a Motor Transport (MT) Wren the greatest progress I could achieve was a lorry-driving course and advancement to Leading Wren. I wanted neither. A commission was more attractive, but at that time candidates did not apply, they were selected. Only graduates could apply for Direct Entry commissions. I began to attend the Commission and Warrant Classes, hoping that I might be selected, but soon became disillusioned. The other women were no brighter than me, but had confidence and social polish. I didn't, at least not as a woman. It would be possible to cope with being an officer but not with being a 'lady'. I wanted to abandon the classes and just plod on, making the most of service life, and endeavouring to become eligible for entry to medical school by the end of my engagement. Already I was working for an O-level biology examination in my spare time. In this decision I felt I'd reached a kind of equilibrium. Then the blow fell.

One Saturday morning in July 1964 Second Officer Hadley beckoned me into her room as I was passing the administration block. She invited me to sit down,

'Tell me, Wren Rees, why are you so mannish?'

I was struck dumb. Was I having a nightmare? I looked at my shabby jeans,

'I'm sorry, Ma'am, but I'm wearing these old things because we are cleaning the mess'.

That didn't satisfy her. I knew she'd caught me out. There was no point in pretending any more. She was unexpectedly sympathetic and I found myself pouring out my life history, but she would not agree to my giving up the commission classes.

'You will continue to attend,' she said. 'It is up to us to decide your suitability.'

Why had she sentenced me to certain rejection, I wondered? Why not let me withdraw quietly?

My world had crashed. My 'role-play' had been a failure. The memories of the last few years returned to haunt me. This time God, if there were one, had really let me down. It would have been better not to have joined up. I felt desolate. To whom could I talk? I wanted to leave Culdrose, but that wasn't possible unless I deserted. I wrote to Denys Crouch who replied immediately and said that I had to face my problem and not run away from it. Certainly I should not miss the chance of a commission. He thought that the Second Officer was concerned because of the chance of my becoming involved with another woman which would cause a scandal were I an officer. Denys assured me that people did care for me; indeed he would willingly write to the chaplain, or the officer concerned, to express his conviction that I was self-disciplined enough to withstand this kind of temptation. It wasn't necessary – my only temptation was to despair.

He was right about not running away from problems but I disagreed with his assertion that I should become an officer. On my next weekend leave I met him and explained that it was my lack of femininity that posed more problems than my supposed homosexuality. He agreed that perhaps a commission was not the answer, and suggested I speak again to Second Officer Hadley. I very reluctantly returned to Culdrose but before I could see Second Officer I was summoned by the Officer-in-Charge, First Officer Dorothy Talma.

She had heard that I was unsettled, but said there was more chance of my being an officer than a doctor. I was reassured by her obvious concern, but my heart was no longer in the WRNS. Shortly afterwards I was involved in a very minor road accident. Although I was totally exonerated from blame it nonetheless added to my now depressed state.

There was one very positive event during this otherwise black period. I met the Anglican sisters of the Community of the Epiphany at Truro. This was my first contact with the religious but certainly not the last. There was nothing strait-laced or remote about them and I was struck by their love, happiness and good humour. Since then I've never been without friends in habits, irrespective of my own beliefs or lack of them, and have been very grateful for their support.

In the summer of 1964 I went to Germany to stay with a family in Düsseldorf. It was my first trip abroad. As part of my female act (which, in spite of Second Officer, I felt it was necessary to continue), I bought a pair of court shoes for my holiday. I hated the wretched things, as they made me feel so awkward.

'My God!' remarked a forthright WRNS friend, when she saw me in them, 'You look like a bloke in drag!' That finished the short career of the shoes – to my relief. I enjoyed my holiday, in spite of the shoes, but dreaded returning to Culdrose. What awaited me was even worse than I could have imagined.

Some weeks before summer leave I had been on weekend driving duty with just one other Wren. One of the male civilian drivers had been what I considered 'a bit of a nuisance'. While I was reading in the crewroom he'd come up behind me and touched my breasts – not that there was much to touch. I just pushed him away and continued reading. To me it was no more than the irritation of a passing fly, but my colleague, whom the man had also touched, reported the matter. It says something about my perception of myself that I paid so little heed to the incident while she took such a drastic step.

Notice of a formal inquiry greeted my return after leave. I was annoyed with the Wren for reporting it because the inquiry was a highly embarrassing experience. I was furious when the man's union representative suggested that we'd behaved in a way likely to encourage him! How I hated my female role as I stood before the station commander in my Number One (best) suit, answering very personal questions. To be fair, I could sense that our superiors were very sympathetic. Afterwards the Commander told us to forget the whole affair. The driver was moved to a part of the Air Station far away from Wrens. I didn't think much of his taste. As far as I was concerned, it was another nail in the coffin of my WRNS career.

Chapter ten

Fatal Attraction

A COUPLE of new Wrens arrived in the Motor Transport Section. Emma and Meg were clearly officer material and I became friends with them. We had some good times together and their company brightened both work and recreation. Little did I know that one of them was to contribute to my premature discharge.

I was sent on a fortnight's loan draft to HMS *Excellent*, the Royal Naval Gunnery School in Portsmouth. It was a very welcome change from the smoky crewroom at Culdrose with its blaring radio and tedious trips around the airfield day and night. Although I was away for only a short time it was good to have a letter from Emma. I missed her. We seemed to have a rapport that I'd not experienced with anyone else before. She appeared to know my thoughts almost before I did. My time away made me realise that my feeling for her was stronger than anything I'd ever felt for anyone else. I found her both mentally and physically attractive. Was this being 'in love'?

It was a joyful yet painful realisation. We could be close mentally but not physically. My extreme horror of a physical relationship was not because of the fear of service disapproval – others had risked it – but because of my abhorrence of my own body, being seen as a woman and unable to have a normal heterosexual relationship with a female. Had I been male there is no doubt that I would have wanted to 'have my way' with her, restricted only by my own moral code. Yet still, because of the lack of information, I regarded myself as some kind of 'deviant' lesbian. I couldn't find another label.

A few years later I attended a lesbian club. That finally convinced me that whatever others might have thought, I was certainly no lesbian. The women there didn't want to be men; they were happy in their gender role. What amazed me was the fact that two feminine women found each other attractive, but as I later realised, the root of the word 'homosexual' is the Greek 'homos' meaning not 'man' but 'same'. Never had I, nor ever would I, find a person like myself, i.e. the same gender (as opposed to genetic sex) attractive. What has since become clear is that gender identity and sexuality are separate and determined by different areas of the brain. Usually they are congruent but not always. This has explained to me something that was initially a great enigma, transsexual people who change roles only to become homosexual. One female-to-male friend had a phalloplasty (construction of a phallus) in order to please his man-friend.

Doreen Cordell, a social worker for the Albany Trust, who counselled me when I was about to change roles, declared that I had always been 'psychologically heterosexual'. She was right. Some years later Dr Gelber sent me a copy of the *Canadian Medical Post*, a medical newspaper, which contained a report on the difference between lesbians and female-to-male transsexual individuals. This supported all I have said – that they do not see themselves as lesbians and, before treatment, hate their partners seeing their bodies. The report stated that the partners of female-to-males are normal heterosexual women, not lesbians, and see their lovers as men, in spite of the lack of a penis. The partners were feminine, many had had earlier relationships with genetic males and often experienced orgasm with their female-to-male partners for the first time. The report stated that these relationships were stable and long lasting and that transsexual people made good parents of any children their partners had. My own observations confirm this, but none of this information was available to me during those traumatic weeks and months when I first realised I was 'in love' with Emma.

I continued to consider myself a 'deviant' lesbian and had to accept that my affection for Emma would have to remain unvoiced and that I would probably see her marry someone else.

Emma was no fool. She had observed that I took no interest in men – very unusual for a Wren. Perhaps unwisely, she began to question me. Her searching brown eyes made me feel as if she knew already so I told her how I hated my female body, of my time in Mabledon and so-called 'homosexual' tendencies. I was careful not to mention my feelings for her. Emma admitted that she was not entirely surprised; I'd had a hard time and she was genuinely sorry.

I had meanwhile been revising and was due to sit my GCE biology examination in London followed by a weekend at home.

Emma kindly drove me to Redruth station to catch the sleeper to Paddington.

'There's something you haven't told me, isn't there?' she said. I felt myself redden.

'What makes you think that?'

'I can tell.' My inside felt as if it were shaking. She was looking intensely at me.

'I can't tell you,' I replied, as calmly as possible.

'Very well, I shall be left to assume all kinds of things now.' As the train drew out of the station, Emma grasped my hand, 'You do trust me, don't you?'

'Yes, I do.'

As the train steamed through the night, I lay awake in the sleeping compartment, my mind in a turmoil. Did Emma know how I felt about her? Why had she so persistently questioned me? Should I tell her? To what end? Nothing could come of it except perhaps an end to our friendship. What should I do? I realised that for those couples who were concerned to remain celibate until after marriage there are strains, but for me the strain would be perpetual.

Once home, I hurried to see Denys Crouch. This was certainly something to avoid telling my mother. He'd feared such a happening but felt my intention to tell Emma was a wise one, although he believed she already knew. I did too. I wrote to Emma. It gave me a chance to think carefully about the wording and it gave her the opportunity to learn about it without my being there. I emphasised that she need fear no physical advances from me and I would never behave in a way to cause her hurt or scandal. If she wished, I would seek an immediate draft to another station.

When I returned to Cornwall, Emma met me at Redruth. She admitted that she'd been shocked by my letter but had had an inkling. I repeated my willingness to ask for a draft but she firmly said no. In the following weeks, every time she appeared depressed, I'd repeat my offer to ask for a draft and each time she said no, it wasn't necessary. Initially, she was remote, but slowly she seemed to return to her old self and I gave up asking her if she wanted me to move.

Although matters seemed calm, superficially at least, I considered it expedient to confide in Ken, the Chaplain (I had spoken to him earlier following my encounter with Second Officer Hadley). I also wrote to Dr Gelber. She suggested that I seek psychiatric help and also, in spite of what Emma said, ask for a transfer. I did neither. As I saw it, the problem was physical, not mental. I didn't want psychotherapy for being in love. As for seeking a draft, Emma and I were friends, so why should we part?

I should have taken Dr Gelber's advice about a draft. One evening, quite unexpectedly, Emma and Meg came to my mess and said they wanted me to go out with them. Emma's manner was such that I felt distinctly uneasy but nonetheless joined them. Even my unease did not prepare me for what followed.

Meg drove us to a quiet cove and stopped her car. Emma turned on me and declared that she couldn't bear having me around any longer. I was repulsive to her and she hated me. If I didn't get a crash draft or leave the WRNS she'd report me to First Officer. Her eyes were full of what I perceived then as hatred. Was this the girl I'd seen gently comforting a distressed colleague, who'd been so kind to me personally and been such good company, who'd asked me to trust her? Was this the woman I'd loved? Meg tried to smooth things. She'd known the purpose of the conference but had not expected such vehemence.

Perhaps I could have coped with such behaviour immediately after my disclosure but for a couple of months I'd been lulled into a false state of wellbeing. Why had she let me believe all was well? Why insist that I remain at Culdrose? Why indeed had she pressed me to tell her something that she must have known?

This violent reaction consequently made me consider that not all the problem was of my making. Clearly Emma was not indifferent to me. Was she afraid of her own feelings? After all, she'd been assured of my good behaviour. Was she in a situation she didn't know how to handle? Was she lesbian and terrified of admitting it because of the possible damage it might do to her future career or did she, like the patient at Mabledon, discover that she could be attracted by a masculine female? Certainly her reaction was out of all proportion to the threat I posed. It was a question which was not to be resolved for a very long time.

Upon our return to the air station I hurriedly left the two young women, went to the empty chapel, and wept. Only the flickering lamp by the Reserved Sacrament lightened the darkness. There was very little light in my own darkness at that moment. Surely the only answer was to end my life. I could not face such an existence, yet didn't have the courage to end it. I cried aloud to the God I wasn't sure existed and asked why it was so wrong to love.

I was glad of the Chaplain's support. Ken advised me to call Emma's bluff and carry on as normal. It wasn't easy. The rift in our previously warm relationship did not go unnoticed amongst our fellow-Wrens. I was in a state of shock and hardly able to eat. Even if Emma couldn't always avoid sitting at my table on the mess-deck we didn't speak to each other. I could feel the cold atmosphere and kept thinking about her words – that I repelled her. In her anger – or fear – she'd misused the term – it was she who had repelled me. Semantics apart I knew what she meant. No one had ever said anything like that to me before.

Quite by coincidence I was offered a draft but persuaded my officer not to send me, saying that it offered no advancement. That was certainly true, but nor did I want to dance to Emma's tune. She was furious when she discovered what I'd done, but did not, as Ken had predicted, report me to First Officer. She would have been risking her own reputation too. Mercifully, the awful intensity of the atmosphere lasted only a few weeks and we began to speak to each other again, although sadly, the warmth of our previous relationship was never regained.

Emma did eventually apologise, not for what she's said, but the way she'd said it. Apology or not, I'd forgiven her and in spite of my feeling for her being numbed for a while, I continued to love her for many years. We kept in tentative contact after I'd left the WRNS and I was surprised to be invited to her home for a weekend. I thought it strange that she'd waited until her parents had gone away but nevertheless I enjoyed my visit. She was a good hostess and well versed in her local history, which was interesting. Some months afterwards we met in London – at the Swiss Centre – and again it was a pleasant occasion. She drove me to Charing Cross for my train and as I turned to wave back, flashed her headlamps.

Not long after that meeting she wrote a very hurtful letter to me admitting that she'd invited me when her parents were away so that they wouldn't see her odd friend. Why did she bother to invite me at all? Needless to say it revived the distress experienced at Culdrose two or three years earlier and once more I was baffled by her behaviour.

I wrote to her years later to tell her of my role-change and received an equally unpleasant reply. I had, she said, gone against the God-given 'and attempted to fashion a life that is fraudulent'. (Since she was an avowed agnostic I thought the reference to God was rather strange.) Emma became a very senior officer, so achieved her ambition. I wondered if she also achieved happiness? I truly hoped so.

Although when I came to write the first edition of this book I had not given the matter much thought for many years, the pain of this episode suddenly came back to me. This was a shock and distressing but I carried on writing and once the typescript was delivered to the publisher the sorry affair dropped back into my subconscious. Why had this been the part of my life to give me greater sadness in its recall than any other? Was it because it was never properly resolved?

About five years after publication of my book, I happened to learn of the death of one of my former officers who had become a good friend of Emma's. With little hesitation I wrote to Emma expressing my sympathy at the loss of her colleague and friend and also enclosed a photograph I had taken of the officer many years ago. I did not expect a reply.

To my amazement I received a friendly letter from Emma, thanking me for the photograph, which she appreciated, not having got a very good one. She also told me of her life's happenings since we had last met. It was more than I could ever have hoped for. After four decades the wound was healed and I was profoundly thankful. For several years we kept in touch and exchanged annual news just before Christmas. Then in her 2006 Christmas newsletter, Emma wrote a PS, inviting me to visit for a weekend.

I was very surprised but pleased that she felt able to do that and we arranged that I would visit in the summer of 2007. It was probably forty years since we had last met, when she had flashed her headlamps and left me at Charing Cross station. This time she would meet me at her local railway station.

Did Emma recall that as we met? Unsurprisingly we had both

physically changed. I assumed that since I had changed gender roles she would have a job recognising me, but she had seen me on television and found me immediately. I had more difficulty recognising her. What had not changed was her kindness and generosity.

I had wondered what it was which had changed her attitude from accusing me of 'going against the God-given' to that of acceptance. During the weekend Emma told me that when she saw me on television, my 'eyes had changed'. I looked 'right', words that paradoxically echoed those of Betty, another ex-Wren friend, although of an earlier generation.

It was certainly not my intention to raise matters from the past during my visit. The fact that she had invited me at all was a sign of goodwill. The fact that I had accepted would surely have assured her that all was forgiven – if she needed that assurance.

From her letters it was clear Emma was sharing her life with another woman and it was obvious when I saw the situation that it was a lesbian relationship. Her partner was a very pleasant and likeable person and clearly meant a great deal to her. My 'hunch' in 1964 had been correct.

Quite suddenly Emma admitted that she had given me a 'very hard time' in the past and was very sorry. She then went on to tell me that at the time she had been very confused about her own sexuality, worried about the effect on her career, had twice nearly married but eventually discovered that she was bisexual and was happier with a lesbian relationship. Much of her life had been spent alone.

'You must have been equally confused,' she remarked.

'No. I always knew what I wanted.'

My heart went out to Emma. Although very successful in her career as a WRNS officer, I realised that her personal life could have been intensely painful at times. The *camaraderie* of the wardroom would not have removed the intense loneliness she must have felt. I understood that she was without a close relationship until after her retirement. That would certainly have then been frowned upon by the service.

I felt very greatly saddened. My feelings for her were not as they had been at the age of twenty-two, which was a mercy for all of us, but I realised that nonetheless, I did care very much for her. For myself I had not needed her apology; all had been forgiven years earlier, but I hoped that it had helped her to make it. If so, then my lengthy journey had been very worthwhile.

In 1964 however, this outcome could not have been foreseen and something had to be done to resolve my increasingly distressing situation. With my agreement Ken spoke to one of the medical officers about my problem. I saw the Senior Medical Officer shortly afterwards, a man who was very sympathetic and known affectionately as 'Doc' by all ranks. He was unable to offer any hope regarding a 'sex-change'. No surgeon would do it; he would regard it as mutilation.' Like the other doctors he was obviously unaware that there had been two female-to-male changes in the 1940s. Unfortunately at that time I didn't know either. What I did know was that the concern to avoid mutilation of the body was resulting in a mutilation of the mind.

My despair was momentarily lifted by the news that, in spite of the distractions, I'd passed the biology exam, but as Miss Coward wrote in her congratulatory letter, 'What are you going to do now?'

There seemed little chance of carrying out my plan of studying in the WRNS and going on to medical school, but there had to be more to life than driving around an airfield. It was unlikely that I'd be offered a commission, even if I wanted one. It was also clear that my efforts at role-play hadn't fooled many, certainly not me. I would carry my gender-role conflict everywhere, like Christian and his burden in *The Pilgrim's Progress*. If only this agonising split between mind and body could be resolved, then perhaps I would be able to apply myself to the business of living.

My next draft came and I took it, returning to HMS *Excellent*, this time as permanent Captain's Driver. In spite of my unhappiness, it was a wrench leaving the good people at Culdrose, especially the Chaplain and his family, but we kept in touch.

Emma seemed reluctant to bid me farewell or even offer good wishes. No one saw me off. An awful pang of loneliness hit me as I watched the hangars and huts recede into the distance as I was driven to Redruth station. Some sailors joined me at Plymouth. One of them was also on draft to *Excellent*. When he discovered that I was going there too he said that I'd have to have a drink with him. As a man I would have said yes, but in my female role I felt it wiser to put him off. For weeks after he kept asking me – probably by now it had become a challenge to him – and I continued to make excuses. Eventually he got my message. I should have refused at the outset. Some assertiveness training at Burghfield would have been more helpful than watching the doctor drop her felt ovaries to the floor!

I'd wriggled out of accepting the sailor's invitation but it was harder to decline an invitation to a friend's wedding a few weeks after my arrival in Portsmouth. It was obviously going to be a very smart affair and I dreaded it. How could I escape? Could I forever make feeble excuses for missing functions without being seen as very aloof? Loyalty to my friend overcame my misgivings.

Mum persuaded me to have my hair set, wear make-up and a hat. (I think the 'Shoes' were still in operation then.) I really did feel like a third-rate drag act and, at the earliest opportunity, tried to wash off the make-up and comb the set out of my hair. The despised hat was left in the car once the service was over. The worst (and unexpected) experience was being announced by the toastmaster. In vain I tried to dissuade him from making my presence known. It was tempting to make a bolt for home, cake or no cake. Of course, I doubt if many people took much notice, so busy were they chatting to their friends and grabbing a passing glass of wine, but at the time I was convinced that they'd be sniggering at the frump who'd entered and wondering what sex I was. It was actually a very pleasant event but for me the day was marred by the conflict between the real me and the role society expected me to play. Some time after my role change I attended the quiet and informal wedding of a teacher friend, Pauline Spencer. She asked me to read the telegrams and afterwards wrote to say how smart I looked and that I made an exemplary Best Man!

The Medical Officer at *Excellent* wanted me to see a psychiatrist at the naval barracks. My heart sank, but I decided that half-an-hour's chat would make a break from driving, which was becoming just as tedious around the dockyard as it had been around an airfield.

The psychiatrist was a kind and sympathetic man but said at the beginning of our interview that a sex-change was impossible. He suggested deep psychoanalysis. This would have meant leaving the service and attending at least twice a week for perhaps two years. He admitted that the treatment would be useless unless I wanted it. Of course I didn't want it and couldn't understand what the point of it all was. They'd not succeed in making me feminine unless they gave me a brain transplant. In this comment, made at the time, I had, although unwittingly, pointed out a link between brain structure and gender identity, a concept which, according to recent research, is very probable and could be a factor in the cause of transsexualism. It would explain why psychotherapy is useless, but at this point not many of my doctors seemed to realise it.

Being the only Wren driver I was on my own for much of the time. As for being 'Captain's Driver', I hardly ever saw the great man and spent most of my time delivering mail and sailors to the dockyard or cleaning the wretched car. Boredom did nothing to improve my mental state. I hadn't recovered from the painful episode with Emma. There were constant reminders. I thought (probably wrongly) that had I not been female in body Emma would have accepted me. I would never be able to live a normal life and bitterly resented it. Tension was building up. I was near breaking point.

I finally broke when a van ran into the back of the staff car I was driving. No one was hurt and the damage was little, but I burst into tears. I was taken off driving. Although my service career was now clearly in the balance I felt no emotion at all and was totally distant from everything. It was as if I'd reached the threshold of my emotions and passed into insensibility as a defence against the pain. Not unexpectedly, the psychiatrist decided to send me to the Military Psychiatric Hospital at Netley, near Southampton, so that I could undergo psychiatric tests. It was a painful reminder of my time at Mabledon, something I'd wanted to forget. At least it got me away from *Excellent* for a day and the tedious non-driving duties I'd been given. I drove myself there – so I'd not lost my nerve whatever people thought.

My unit officer, Second Officer Nancy Thomson, did her best to find me an alternative to driving but I wanted to move forward, not sideways. Of course I could drive (and passed two Hackney

Carriage tests after discharge to prove it) but my present unsuitability was the symptom of a much deeper malaise. I had known for some time that my WRNS career was in terminal decline. Now it was clear that its death was imminent. Miss Thomson listened patiently to me.

'I really want to be a doctor, Ma'am,' I told her during one of our interviews, 'but I could never pass the examinations needed to get to medical school.' Her response was very unexpected. 'You can and you will. I have every confidence in you.'

I couldn't believe what she'd said. No one had ever said that to me so forcibly before. It was like oxygen to someone gasping for air. She had given me the confidence to believe in myself. I could and I would. I left her office mentally several feet taller than when I'd gone in. I would get to medical school. I could and I would.

Even the probability of imminent discharge was seen as positive – it was a chance to study. What job I did in the meantime was irrelevant; I had my goal. Two years earlier the WRNS had said yes to me after many had said no. Now via Nancy Thomson they were giving me the courage to move on. Nor surprisingly my mother was very upset at the prospect of my leaving the service. Nancy Thomson offered to speak to her so Mum drove to Portsmouth with me after a weekend leave. Before my mother left, Miss Thomson spoke to me alone. She had ascertained that Mum was unaware I'd been seeing a psychiatrist. I told her that I wanted to spare Mum any more pain.

'But Wren Rees there is no disgrace in having psychiatric treatment.'

'I know, but my mother thinks that the reasons which drove me to seek treatment before are cured and over. It would make her unhappy to know that I was having treatment again.'

'But why is it so shameful?'

'Because, Ma'am, I am homosexual.' It was impossible to describe myself as anything else at that time. I wished it had been otherwise.

'I understand,' she said quietly.

Second Officer Thomson obviously realised the strain I was under and instructed me to visit her every time I needed a chat. She was probably of more help than the psychiatrists. The service could seem cold and heartless, but there were within it individuals like Nancy Thomson who possessed something not required by Queen's Regulations – love. She probably never realised how much she helped me when I was very vulnerable. Although never achieving my aim, it is certain that without her support I would never have got as far as I have. I remain indebted to her.

I returned to the psychiatrist. He showed me the report from Netley: 'Homosexual'. A discharge had been recommended because it was believed that Wren Rees would not settle in the service. Until my gender role conflict had been sorted out, Wren Rees would not settle anywhere.

A few weeks later, with my shoes even more glossy than usual and wearing my 'Tiddly Suit' (Number One uniform for best), I took the ferry to the Royal Naval Hospital in Gosport in order to appear before the Medical Board. I must have taken longer to clean my shoes than the time I spent before the gold braid of the Board. After inviting me to sit down, the chairman said that in view of the fact that I was never going to settle in the service it had been decided to give me a medical discharge. Had I anything to say?

'No Sir.'

'Thank you Wren Rees.'

My WRNS career was over.

Chapter eleven

The Struggle to Survive

IT was a huge leap from the WRNS back to life in Rusthall. Although my service career had not met my hopes, nonetheless there had been much which was good. I missed the order and, above all, the instant (but sadly, seldom durable) comradeship. It had, like school, offered security. Now no longer part of a uniformed and disciplined group I was to be again vulnerable to verbal abuse and embarrassing mistakes which would doubtless push me into a relatively solitary life. It was not going to be easy. Inevitably there were questions about my medical discharge. I seemed healthy enough. Such questions were parried as far as possible and I endeavoured to get on with the opportunities which were available.

I enrolled for evening classes in chemistry and physics GCE O-level and worked during the day in a rather tedious office job with a neurotic woman boss. It was good to be back in education, even if I did find the subjects hard. The Tech had not offered much in the way of mathematical or scientific training, but, with Second Officer Thomson's words still fresh, I plodded on through the equations and the Periodic Table. After two years I scraped through the physics exam, but failed chemistry. It was a setback, delaying my A-level study for another year, but I was determined to struggle on.

Six months after my WRNS discharge I was fortunate enough to be offered the post of Laboratory Technician at Tonbridge Girls' Grammar School. It didn't promise advancement, but gave me the opportunity to work in a congenial atmosphere. The staff members were friendly and encouraged me in my efforts to better my education. They were more reserved than my WRNS colleagues but the friends I made there stuck by me during the difficult times ahead.

I regarded the pupils as 'kids' although, on the whole, very pleasant ones, and was not unduly troubled by working with the girls. There were, however, a couple of younger members of staff who aroused my interest. In time the attraction wore off and I didn't make the mistake of confessing it. It was however a great strain, so much that Dr Gelber prescribed me Librium (chlordiazepoxide). It made me drowsy, so I stopped taking it after a very short period. I was angry that it had become necessary to take drugs to suppress what were to me natural desires.

My frustration with the situation was greatly worsened by the fact that I began to suffer badly from pre-menstrual tension. Perhaps it was exacerbated by my inherent conflict. My colleague, Mollie, threatened to refuse to work with me unless I saw Dr Gelber. The doctor prescribed diuretics and female hormones which certainly decreased the PMT. If any good came out of this it was to prove to people that doses of female hormone do not make a female-to-male transsexual more feminine. Physical symptoms were relieved but I was still 'in the wrong body'. Neither hormones nor psychotherapy had proved any use in 'curing' me.

For my 1966 holiday I went on a pony-trekking course in the Lake District. I hoped to have some company that way. Undoubtedly I was still missing the comradeship, however transient, of the WRNS. The trekkers were accommodated in double-bunked chalets attached to an hotel. I was no longer bothered about sharing a room; what concerned me was that guests were expected to 'dress for dinner' (as if we'd dine naked otherwise!). This wasn't meant to be too formal but just that trousers were not worn by the ladies. The fact of having to put on my 'best' (which was usually a tweed jacket and skirt) ruined the meals for me.

There was a lively girl amongst the guests, Zoë, whom I found quite attractive, probably because she reminded me of Emma. I was taken aback to learn that they'd both gone to the same school and knew each other. One evening, as we were chatting in the bar, Zoë told me that I had eyes just like someone she knew. She was looking at me very intensely.

'Oh,' I said, 'Who?'

'I don't know if I ought to tell you.'

'Why not?'

Zoë looked slightly uncomfortable, 'Well…it's a man!'

I forced a laugh.

'Why worry about that?'

She obviously found my eyes attractive, but my blue 'male eyes' wouldn't get me very far whilst I was living in the female role.

I found our young Scottish riding instructress, Linda, much more attractive, but as always had to 'stand aside' and be friendly in an apparently disinterested manner – much to my frustration. Linda came to my room on the last night of the course and tried to persuade me to join the group for its party. I made excuses. How could I tell her that what really deterred me was the thought of having to wear my 'best' and risk being asked to dance by a man? As she was speaking to me all I could think of was how attractive she looked in a dress instead of riding kit. I knew that these should have been the best years of my life. Instead I was living only at half speed and missing so many opportunities, not least in relationships, but I had, as Dr Gelber had said, to learn to live with it and do the best I could. At times I found that very hard.

So, in addition to my daily work and evening study, I filled up my life as best I could; one of the most effective 'anaesthetics' was singing, not only with the choir but at singing lessons. I'd found an excellent teacher, Phyllis Sichel, who increased my range to soprano (although she met some resistance to this) and entered me for the local music festival where I did quite well. Several years later she entered me again, this time as bass and I did even better with a Distinction! Phyllis was one of the few people with whom I felt totally at ease and who seemed to accept me as me, however ambiguous I may have seemed. Her very presence was healing.

Perhaps it was because of nostalgia for the comradeship of my service career that I joined the Association of WRNS. They were a very likeable group of women and one of them, Betty, became a good family friend, but I felt out of place and decided that an all-female group was not for me. I remembered this experience when, long after my role change, I was again in an all-female group, this time an adult education class, but felt totally at ease and then realised why. The WRNS Association saw me as female, the class as male; it was the world's perception of me which had altered, not my perception of myself. That, not the physical change, is the essential difference between my former and present roles.

I also became a Samaritan, which was less altruistic than it may seem because it was another part of my 'anaesthetic'. By immersing myself in others' problems I hoped to submerge my own – a motive which is, of course, not peculiar to transsexual individuals. Perhaps I helped some clients. At least I learned that most people are so engrossed in their own concerns that they are not very aware of anyone else as they pass along the street – unless that person is exceedingly weird or obviously distressed. As a result I felt less conspicuous than before. My clients probably didn't notice or care whether or not I wore make-up or dresses; to them I was an ear on legs. With the Samaritans I felt accepted. When attending one of their conferences, I little realised that twenty years later I would be a speaker at several such gatherings.

By now my father had retired. It meant some adjustment for all of us. My mother had been used to running her own ship. Dad had been used to considerable authority and I had been used to having Mum to myself for most of the time. Dad was a kind person and always ready to take me out in his car, but he had a mental block about my own driving. He absolutely refused to let me drive his car, even after I'd got my Advanced Driver's Certificate. It was as if he saw me as a rival. I don't know how my sister would have fared had she taken up driving before Dad died. Mum suspected he may have been jealous because he'd never passed a test, having started driving before they were compulsory. We never understood his intransigence.

The despised tweed suit

81

It was nearing the time for my second attempt at O-level chemistry and thought had to be given to my next step. Clearly it would be very difficult to study for three science A-levels at night school. I needed to go to college full-time. My local education authority gave an undertaking that if I passed the chemistry, and hence gained a place at the local college of further education, some financial assistance would be forthcoming, an offer supplemented by similar promises from a couple of trusts, including the WRNS Benevolent Fund. The exam over, I decided to have a holiday.

My faith had been going through one of its regular upheavals. This time it may have been due to the fact that I'd gleaned enough scientific knowledge to make me doubt what could not be empirically measured. Rowland Taylor, Vicar of St Barnabas Church, who, following the departure of Denys Crouch, had become my mentor, suggested that I spend a week in the guesthouse of a convent he knew, The Holy Name, at Malvern Link in Worcestershire.

It was wonderful, the peace almost tangible. Far from being depressing, the periods of silence (which included meals) were recreative, as too was the beauty of the Malvern Hills, which we could see as we sat in the dining room.

Probably Father Taylor did not expect me to stay in the convent praying, nor did I. The opportunity to walk over the Malvern Hills and visit Worcester, Gloucester and Tewkesbury was too good to miss. Was I misusing the convent's hospitality? I don't think so. During my stay I was moved by the magnificence of the hills and surrounding countryside, impressed by the majesty of the cathedrals, stirred by the music of the convent offices and warmed by the love I met there. One of the other guests was Pam, who was about my age and a very lively person. Her arrival made my visit even more enjoyable and we immediately struck up a friendship. I soon learned that this young woman, who laughed a great deal, was an aspirant, and she intended to join the order.

'Don't think I wouldn't like to have a "good time", get married and have children,' she said, 'I would, but if it's God's will for me to enter the order and I go against this, then I shall never be truly happy.'

This was the start of a lasting friendship. She made me feel secure and accepted. This was so different from some of the WRNS friendships which seemed shallow by comparison. This was real love, unmarred by a sexual element. Pam was to be a very good friend to me and still remains so. She joined the order and forty years later is still a religious.

Although I was sure that Pam – and probably the sisters – accepted me, however 'odd' I may have seemed, even here were reminders of my problem. The first was that we were expected to wear veils when in Chapel. This I hated, so seldom went, in spite of the lovely singing. The second reminder occurred when, at Worcester Cathedral, a well-meaning woman saw me about to go into the tower and called 'You can't go up there by yourself, son!' (Children under twelve were not allowed without an adult.)

It has been said that female-to-male transsexuals, after role-change, look considerably younger than their chronological ages. My own experience shows this to be so before, as well as after, reassignment therapy. This incident was not an isolated one.

I finished my 1968 summer holiday in Truro and while there learned that I'd passed my chemistry exam. The college doors were now open to me. Light was beginning to dawn. It seemed that my goal of medical school was drawing closer.

It was good to get to college and begin serious study. Most of my fellow-students were male, but, unlike art school, I got along well with them, which pleased me. One of them did ask if I were a lesbian but I pretended not to hear. During the vacations I worked as a taxi driver and also at Pembury Hospital laboratory. Both jobs were enjoyable. One day, when I'd gone to the 'Ladies' near the Tonbridge taxi-rank, a woman came down the stairs. She gasped when she saw me washing my hands, 'Oh, I'm in the wrong one!' Without speaking I pointed to a notice which assured her she was not. At the time I was wearing slacks, but women's, stretch and without the now universal fly-front. My blouse and shoes were also women's.

I had a similar encounter some time later which was even more embarrassing and which prompted me to offer my birth certificate to the old lady who was questioning my right to be there. Such incidents, and the distress that I was experiencing following my break-up from Emma, had a disastrous effect on my studies. I desperately wanted to get on with life. Surely by now I could get some professional help?

Florence Gelber had recently emigrated to Canada. Her successor gently reiterated that a 'sex-change' was impossible. He seemed unable to offer any helpful advice. Quite 'off the cuff' he suggested I go to a lesbian club where it might be possible to meet someone to my liking! This I had no intention of doing. How could I make people understand that I didn't want a lesbian affair? I wasn't like them. I left feeling even more of a freak than before – I wasn't even a normal homosexual.

It was to the Samaritans that I then turned. The Director, Dr Dorrit Waterfield, was an old country GP, a wise and caring woman, who was something of a local legend. She was naturally as concerned for her volunteers as for the clients. Dr Dorrit, as she was affectionately known, assured me that I was not homosexual and was certain that in a few years I'd be through this stage and married. In spite of the great respect I had for her, I knew her to be wrong. I wasn't a teenager in the crush stage but an adult in my late twenties. However it wasn't a wasted meeting because we became friends and kept in touch for the rest of her life. Like Marjorie Coward and Father Taylor, she became one of my 'special people'. It was a joy and privilege to have known her.

Father Taylor helped me most. He seemed to understand the hurt I was feeling over Emma. His greatest help was, however, indirect. In his parish magazine he implored the congregation to treat homosexuals with love, not condemnation; they were welcome at church. In 1969 that was a courageous stand to take. He mentioned the work of the Albany Trust, which had been set up to help everyone with any kind of psychosexual problem. I then sent the Trust a donation and asked about their work, but several months passed before I could summon up enough courage to ask directly if they could help me. Probably I was scared of another dose of 'You have to live with it'.

Chapter twelve

Enlightenment

HELP came from an unexpected source – *The Times*. I chanced to see its report of an International Symposium of Gender Identity which told of the condition of transsexualism and the most successful form of treatment which was sexual reassignment therapy, i.e. 'sex-change'.

I could hardly take in what I was reading. At last I knew! I was not an odd kind of lesbian or transvestite, but transsexual. I wasn't unique and could be helped. It was a discovery which was to alter my life. Had it been just chance? Where could I find this treatment? I wrote to the Albany Trust again and obtained the name of their counsellor, Doreen Cordell. My next plan was to contact her. It was the autumn of 1969.

Then suddenly my father died of a coronary thrombosis. He was sixty-two. We were devastated. For a time everything stopped, including my intention to write to Mrs Cordell.

I felt responsible for my mother's welfare. Strangely enough, on the night of Dad's death, I had a premonition of my new role as her supporter. Coincidentally, one of my South African cousins, Merle, happened to be visiting England at the time. She came immediately and was like a sister to me and a daughter to Mum. My real sister was less evident.

Bereavement was a new experience. I felt as if I had suddenly grown up. In a strange way it had a positive aspect. During the upheaval and distress I became aware of the intangible – love. It was real, very real, but not mentioned in my science text-books. Why did so many people show care, especially those who hardly knew us? What did they gain? The words from St John's First Epistle kept coming to mind: 'God is love'.

It was with my mother's blessing that I applied to medical schools for the following year. Realising how hard it would be to be accepted I put a dental school as an option at the bottom of my list.

I didn't want to be a dentist but thought it would be possible to get into medicine 'through the back door' a year later. All the medical schools rejected me but I was invited for interview at the University of Birmingham Dental School. Hastily I borrowed a book about dental surgery which I finished on the train to Birmingham.

I wondered what the interviewing board thought of the tweed-suited frump before them? It was to my very great surprise that, subject to A-level results, they offered me a place. I could hardly believe it. At last the chance of university and a profession; Second Officer Thomson's faith had been justified. Life was getting better.

Something, however, had to be done to relieve the inner stress if I were to be free to study effectively. I wrote to Doreen Cordell telling her that I believed myself to be a transsexual and described fully my experiences and feelings. I awaited her reply with trepidation and hope.

She replied by return of post. Would I, she asked, be willing to see Dr John Randell, a consultant psychiatrist, with whom the Trust worked? He was one of the leading experts in the field and sensitive to the anguish which people in my situation experienced. In spite of my dislike of the psychiatric profession I agreed. Mrs Cordell's reply had been so swift and sympathetic that I was sure she'd not send me to someone who'd tell me to enjoy being a woman! I had nothing to lose – except his fee, which I could pay this time – and perhaps a great deal to gain.

Dr Randell initially saw transsexual patients in his Harley Street rooms. Perhaps the fee was a filtering mechanism; I don't know. I made some excuse for visiting London and set off. My mother had enough to cope with so I didn't want to burden her with anything else at this point. Sitting in the surprisingly sparsely furnished waiting room I tried to collect my thoughts. It was a ritual I'd been through before – hope, wait and be disappointed. Was it possible that this time someone would be able to help me?

My interview was short. Dr Randell was a man of few words. 'You've done most of my work for me,' he said, indicating the lengthy letters which I'd sent to Mrs Cordell, and which, with my permission, she'd forwarded to him.

'I can help you,' declared the doctor confidently. 'Just prove to me that you can live as a man and I will do everything I can to help you.'

Was I dreaming? Someone was saying yes!

'But how can I?' I asked, conscious of my beardless face and female voice.

'More feminine patients than you have done it,' he replied. 'Come and see me in my clinic at Charing Cross Hospital.' I was to learn that Charing Cross Hospital was the home of Dr Randell's Gender Identity Clinic, through which many transsexual patients passed.

As I left his rooms and walked along Harley Street my mind was in a turmoil. Was it really possible that after all these years of searching I'd found someone who was able to help me in the way I wanted? Was it really feasible? How could I pass myself off as male with my voice, menstruation and female form? What about my family's reaction, especially my mother? What about my university place and the attitudes of society generally! If I simply adopted male attire wouldn't I look just more butch than before? The doctor could perhaps relieve one major problem but many smaller – and larger ones – would arise in its wake.

In one way my move to Birmingham might be an appropriate opportunity to change roles but would the university accept my changed status? Could I change my wardrobe and documentation in the few weeks left before term began? Would I tell my friends and family or live a double life: male in Birmingham and ambiguous but officially female at home?

In spite of my longing to assume the male role I felt uneasy about rushing into it. Mrs Cordell and Dr Randell both agreed with my caution, the former advising that, if possible, it would be better to gain the security of professional status first. There was much preparation for such a step, she said, and it would give my family and friends time to readjust. Inevitably there would be stresses but at least now there was hope which would make them more bearable.

I decided to 'hasten slowly' and resigned myself to a few more years in the female role, but this time with a promise of eventual release.

Chapter thirteen

First Steps

I MET James in my first term at university. Like me he was doing the first year of the Bachelor of Dental Surgery course and was older than the other students.

He was probably the first male friend I'd made during my adulthood. James treated me as a person, a friend, not an object, nor, thank goodness, a woman. He had a depth about him which seemed lacking in many of our younger colleagues. Later James, his wife Sue, and their children, became my surrogate family and have been loyal and supportive friends throughout all my various vicissitudes. Without them my life would have been infinitely more painful that it has been. They have given me much joy.

Yet in spite of new friends and opportunities, my first term was not happy. My illusions were being shattered. Many lecturers were poor teachers and many students thoughtless and badly-behaved. University was not heaven on earth. The first MB/BDS course was tedious, going over a lot of old ground in a very dry way. My digs, in Acocks Green, were excellent, but a long way from the campus so it was difficult to invite people back to my room. I hated living in a large city and yearned for the peace of the woods near my home in Rusthall.

Each time I passed the railway station it was tempting to board the next train home, I was lonely, worried about Mum (now living alone), concerned about the course which was very taxing and, irrespective of the promise of help to come, haunted by my transsexualism.

It was the young Free Church Chaplain, the Rev'd Daphne Hull, who gave me the support I needed. Probably unknowingly, my young landlady and her husband were also responsible for helping to keep me reasonably calm. John and Wendy treated me as a friend, rather than just a lodger. Nonetheless, tension was part of life, so it was no surprise to be told by the doctor that my stomach upsets were due to stress.

My first vacation home didn't improve matters. Mum knew all was not well. (Mothers have an uncanny faculty for smelling out trouble.) When challenged I told her that the course was hard. I wasn't ready to tell her of my real cause for concern, nor did I think she would be. Had I been pregnant or unhappily married it would have been more acceptable, it was 'normal'. In one way I wanted Mum to know because it felt as if I were living a lie, but on the other hand I wanted to spare her pain – she'd had enough. Father Taylor agreed and said that as treatment was not imminent there was no point in causing her unnecessary heartbreak. But circumstances altered my intentions. A neighbour, Mr Curtis, asked if I'd like to go to the ballet at Covent Garden. Initially his invitation was eagerly accepted, but then doubts arose which I unwisely expressed to my mother. As always, especially in formal settings, I was worried about my frumpish attire.

'Wear a dress then,' said Mum in exasperated tones.

'You know I hate wearing dresses,' I replied.

She made a move to the door.

'I'll ring Mr Curtis and tell him you don't want to go after all.'

'But I do want to go. I just feel awkward.'

'So you don't want to go?'

'Yes…no…oh, God I don't know.'

'You must tell Mr Curtis one way or the other. I'll ring.'

My mother did, on occasions, have the habit of taking over. I felt too confused and depressed to stop her. She returned to the room.

'I don't understand you,' she exclaimed crossly, 'You're not normal. You need your head looking at.'

The tension was too much. I broke down and wept.

'It is being looked at – by a Harley Street specialist!'

Mum was dumbstruck. I explained the situation as best I could. It seemed strange that although friends and neighbours were not in the least surprised when they learned of my condition and proposed treatment, Mum was shocked. I thought somehow she might have known. Hadn't she made comments about my 'changing sex' years earlier? It was clearly too much for her to cope with and she'd pushed it to the back of her mind, hoping it would go away. It hadn't and now it had to be faced.

'I don't understand why they can't give you female hormones to make you more feminine,' she argued.

'But Mum,' I said, 'They wouldn't work and if they did I wouldn't take them; I don't want to be made feminine.'

Doreen Cordell was pleased that the hurdle of telling Mum had been cleared. It had been difficult but it was a great relief to be able to be open with her.

'Of course your mother will find it hard to accept, they all do,' she said, 'but in the end, when they see the results, the families are able to accept the treatment. Indeed many are glad that it has been undergone. It will take time for everyone to readjust but I assure you, they will. I cannot begin to tell you the difference it has made to other patients, not only sexually, but in their careers and social lives. Their whole outlook on life has improved beyond recognition.'

Mum accepted Mrs Cordell's invitation to have a chat with her. She was very impressed, but in spite of that remained unconvinced that the step I intended to take was the right one. I'd overcome one obstacle, that of telling her, but there remained a larger one, of getting her to accept the situation and realise that I wasn't 'being awkward'. It would, I knew, take a long time, but since my role-change wasn't planned until the end of my course it was not an immediate problem. I don't know if my mother then told the rest of the family or friends, but it didn't make a great deal of difference to me because I returned to Birmingham for the Spring Term of 1971.

My hopes of concentrating totally on my studies for the next five years were soon thwarted when I became infatuated with a fellow student, a highly intelligent and vivacious brunette, who as far as I knew, remained unaware of my feelings. Matters were worsened by the embarrassment caused by my ambiguity, such as when the chaplaincy caretaker told a group of students that he'd seem me going into the female toilets and thought I was a bloke. It was a relief to confide in Daphne Hull, whose office was nearby.

Perhaps I'd been hypersensitive. Many students wore 'unisex' clothes and it wasn't uncommon to mistake their sex. The advent of unisex clothes was indeed a blessing. It was not so easy for the male-to-female transsexual. He could not wear a skirt as I could trousers.

It was becoming increasingly clear that to delay help until after my qualification was not going to work. The stress of the present situation would render me incapable of passing any examinations. In addition there was the danger that I'd make a fool of myself over the brunette, careful as I thought I was.

It was a television programme which spurred me into action. Doreen Cordell told me that she was to appear on *Midlands Today*, the local news magazine with one of her clients, Philip, who was a female-to-male transsexual. Daphne Hull and I watched the programme. It was astounding. Philip was totally convincing as a male, no one would have looked at him twice. Having now seen the results of sexual reassignment I had no more hesitation and wrote to Dr Randell to ask if I could begin hormone therapy without delay.

Just before I was due to see him in London, I met a music student, a very attractive and statuesque blonde. She was looking at me in a way which I found unnerving. After some conversation she asked me if I were lesbian and confessed that she was herself. The attraction was obviously mutual, but it shocked me that I should be drawn to a lesbian. I told her of my situation and said that as I became more masculine she would find me less interesting. It was stupid of me to allow myself to become involved with her. In my naivety and vulnerability I believed her declaration of affection to be sincere. It was – until the next person came along! I soon realised that she was an emotionally unstable woman who flitted from one affair to another.

Although our relationship was brief and stormy it gave me my first experience of physical contact, although I refused to be seen less than fully clothed. I found it overwhelming – and even more so when I discovered her fickleness. I can't say it did very much for me, either physically or emotionally. I hated the idea of being in a lesbian relationship but vainly hoped that we'd be able to carry on in a heterosexual way once I'd changed roles.

Although eager to see Dr Randell, I was a little apprehensive. Supposing he refused me treatment for a few more years? On the other hand, supposing he agreed to it? I knew that changing roles would pose many problems. My meeting with him, the most important ever, was amazingly short. My letter lay on his desk. He spoke quietly.

'Answer to your question regarding hormone therapy, yes, it is reversible.'

He didn't tell me that it wasn't reversible after a certain period, but that would not have deterred me. Without hesitation he wrote a prescription for methyl testosterone and handed it to me. I could hardly believe it. 'What effects will these have?' I asked.

'None. Menstruation may stop but it doesn't always. Patients have been known to suffer from an embarrassing discharge after beginning life as a man.'

I wondered why he said that there would be no effects? The effects were soon to become obvious. With hindsight I would not have agreed to such medication without thorough physical and biochemical assessment and subsequent monitoring for side-effects, but such treatment was in its relative infancy and I was only too glad to be offered it.

Dr Randell read some notes then looked at me. 'I cannot do any more for you until you have seen your Dean and found out if the university authorities will accept you as a man. I will, of course, give you my full backing should he wish to contact me.'

The doctor did give me his support as promised, but the strange thing was that he continued referring to me in the female pronoun, even years after I had become Mark. Although willing to give me the treatment he made it clear at an early stage that in his eyes I was a female and a lesbian. It angered me but I didn't realise that help could have been available elsewhere so I tolerated his behaviour. At this stage I saw him as my salvation.

I was unwilling to take the prescription to the Rusthall pharmacy lest they suspected its purpose, so, still apprehensive, I took it into a chemist in Tunbridge Wells. My worry was unfounded because I discovered later that androgens are used for purposes other than 'changing sex' so the pharmacist would not have necessarily reached such a conclusion.

Although I assured my mother that the tablets would, according to Dr Randell, make me less tense, she seemed unhappy and unconvinced. Shortly afterwards however she bought me a gentleman's wristwatch. It was a touching and tangible reminder of her support that she gave unstintingly for the rest of her life.

Once back at university I told Daphne of the latest developments and admitted that the thought of going to see the Director of the Dental School filled me with trepidation. I couldn't overcome the sense of shame which the condition – and society's attitudes – had engendered.

A few days later I sat outside the Director's office literally in a cold sweat. It was a memorable event in one respect, being the last time I ever wore a skirt.

'Well, what can I do for you?' asked Professor Marsland. He was a very positive and friendly man.

'It is, admittedly, the first time that I've come into contact with this,' the professor said thoughtfully, 'so I'm not sure what the official position will be, although as far as the Dental School is concerned, it will be all right. We are concerned with getting students through the course. For these purposes sex is irrelevant. However, I shall have to see the Registrar of the university before I can give you the official "yes". This I shall do as soon as possible.' He looked at me sympathetically.

'You must have suffered a great deal more than I have.'

'I can't believe that, Sir. In your situation I couldn't cope at all.'

'Oh yes you could. People can't understand your handicap, but they can see and understand my wheelchair.'

Within a week or so a letter arrived from Professor Marsland telling me that the university would be anxious to help in any way it could, including with the inevitable administrative formalities. Professor Marsland went even further and arranged for me to be allocated a single room in University House for the next academic year. I was also grateful to see that the administration saw to it that once I'd changed roles, letters were addressed to me in my new name. Someone even went to the trouble of sticking a label over 'Miss Brenda Rees'. Officialdom could be understanding, as I was to continue to discover.

Doreen Cordell had given me the contact with Dr Randell and the benefit of her experience. The doctor had prescribed the hormones. The university had sanctioned my proposed role-change. Now it was up to me.

Chapter fourteen

From Brenda to Mark

MY 'birth' as Mark was due to take place at the beginning of the autumn term in October. It was now March 1971. I was doubtful that it would be possible for me to pass as a man by then but had to trust Dr Randell's assurance that all would be well. I was changing roles but once, whereas he's seen it many times. The results of the hormone therapy were more immediate than I'd expected. Menstruation ceased almost immediately, to my profound relief, and within a few weeks my voice was changing enough for people to ask what was wrong with my throat. Any enquiries I answered by explaining that it was a bad bout of catarrh, which was partially true. The friendly lady in the Students' Union cloakroom continued to enquire about my 'bad throat' for some weeks.

'I'm worried about your throat, dear. It's not getting any better at all. You should see someone about it.'

'Don't worry, Elsie. I'm seeing a doctor!'

My already small breasts decreased in size, then, somewhat cautiously, I abandoned the hated bra that I'd first donned so reluctantly in the WRNS. It gave me a wonderful feeling of mental and physical liberation. Ingeniously, I thought, I made a binder from the now-redundant elastic suspender belt, wearing it to conceal what seemed to me nipples and breasts too large for a male. My sister, Jane, who in her very matter-of-fact way was giving me greatly appreciated support, said that looking bound-up would make me more conspicuous. Many men had larger breasts and nipples than I now had. With glee I dispensed with the binder but continued to wear a vest and thick sweaters until my mastectomy four years later. It was some months before facial hair appeared.

Although Wendy and John said it wasn't necessary, I decided to move out of my digs at the end of the summer term and into University House. I wanted to spare them any gossip, but we kept in touch. Their friendship meant much to me.

Fellow students, noticing changes, began to quiz my friends, but most of my colleagues took the matter very phlegmatically, which was a relief.

I passed my first BDS examinations. To spare my mother stress, I considered staying in Birmingham for the long vacation and getting a summer job. When I went to the Labour Exchange they directed me to the men's section. I wasn't ready for that and decided to bite the bullet and go home even though it would be difficult.

I returned to my former holiday jobs of laboratory work at Pembury Hospital and taxi-driving in Tunbridge Wells, which brought their moments of confusion. Happily the lab staff didn't make any comments, and to my delight, most people who didn't know me treated me as male, even to the extent of issuing me with a male overall. One of my taxi passengers, an old lady, spent the whole journey repeating that she'd been told a lady driver was going to collect her. I feigned deafness.

At a garage, I forgot to collect my petrol receipt. The attendant called out.

'You've forgotten your receipt, mate!'

'I'm sorry, my mind wasn't on my work.'

He laughed. 'Got a piece of crumpet tucked away then?'

I smiled to myself as I drove away. He'd treated me as a man. It was wonderful.

At home I was still 'Brenda' and had yet the daunting task of telling friends and more distant relatives of my change of role. It needed much thought. Would they all accept it, or should I just fade quietly out of their lives? I didn't discuss this very much with Mum, because it was too sensitive an issue, or with Jane because she no longer lived at home, but told me to call in when I felt like it, which I was glad to do. Obviously for some people, like my mother, it was very difficult. I'd left it to Mum to tell the family but realised years later that I should have done it myself and not relied on a sort of osmosis for the news to filter through. One aunt, who had been rather antagonistic, confessed twenty years later that she'd been hurt because she'd not been told directly. It is very easy for those of us involved to assume that everyone knows as much as we do. They don't. In our pain it's also easy to underestimate the emotions which are stirred up in others, especially when there is such a lamentable ignorance of the matter.

For my mother, to whom the situation was so blatantly obvious, it was still extremely perplexing and threatening. Added to her own fears, she had fears for me as I entered a new life. She also saw that she'd lost a daughter, although ultimately she was able to accept me as a much happier son. Because it was a loss, there was mourning and all the associated feelings of grief – anger, bewilderment and even perhaps a sense of guilt. She might have also seen it as losing the possibility of my having children. That would have been the loss of a hope that would never have been fulfilled anyhow.

The situation was made all the worse because I seemed to be blazing a path. There were few guidelines. No one told us how to cope with all this. My sister, Jane, was the first, and for a while, the only, member of the family to support me. She wrote a letter, 'to cheer you up....You are entitled to be happy. I'm sure that everyone will get over it...Lee (her husband) says that he's very happy for you and a little relieved as he's always wanted to call you "mate" anyhow.' She said that she was glad to know at last what the problem was because she'd always known that something was wrong but knew that I wasn't a lesbian.

My sister's unsentimental encouragement was something which helped me immensely. It was a tragedy that in January 1984 she turned violently against me and cut herself off from most of the family, including her own mother.

One or two of the immediate neighbours (and probably others unbeknown to me) knew of my plans and were not in the least surprised. One immediately called me 'Mark' because she said that she and her husband had wondered about my sex for years. I wrote to most of my friends and was in for some surprises. Former WRNS colleagues (including Emma) did not accept the situation as expected. Her friend Meg totally ignored my letter.

I decided to fade from the scene as far as some of my Christian friends were concerned, thinking this would be too much for them to accept, but they doggedly kept in touch with me! To my surprise their reactions were positive. 'I had always been aware that there was a conflict inside you...you had masculine tendencies...', wrote one such friend, Carolyn. 'First and foremost you need to be accepted...' 'What a sense of relief you must have,' wrote Pauline

Spencer, another teacher friend from the Grammar School, 'I knew when I met you just after Easter how much more relaxed you were…I look forward to seeing you again'. Ken, my former chaplain at Culdrose said, 'You must always regard us as your friends…'

Pam, now a Sister at Malvern, said: 'There is always something to thank God for… the progress in the medical field which has made this treatment possible….You will keep in touch, won't you?'

Some letters were touched with gentle humour. My singing teacher, Phyllis, said that it was a major upheaval for her to have changed from soprano to contralto so she had some idea of what I was going through! Another choral society friend hoped I'd be a tenor because they were rather short of them. Her hopes were not met – I became a second bass! An ex-nun friend declared that it was more dramatic than turning a nun into a lady!

Apart from Emma's letter, all those I received were understanding and compassionate. As with my father's death, two years earlier, I became very aware of love. Medical treatment alone would not have been sufficient.

The administrative side of my role-change was the most tedious. Dr Randell had written to various authorities to support my request for a change of documentation and Professor Marsland saw to it that my way was smoothed through such problems as re-registration and issue of an LEA grant in my new name.

My name seemed to be stored in dozens of places: the LEA, the university, insurance companies, bank, NHS, DSS, Department of Employment, doctor, dentist and organisations of which I wished to remain a member. Miss Rees left the Association of Wrens! I greatly appreciated the courteous and tactful way in which Miss Williamson of the Passport Office issued me with a new passport, or the understanding and discreet representative from the local office of the Department of Health and Social Security. Others were equally helpful, to my relief. Years after my role-change I continued to find documents which had somehow been overlooked. Certainly, if I'd had any doubts about the wisdom of my action this would have been the point at which to abandon the plan, but I had none.

My wardrobe had to be changed from 'female ambiguous' to 'male unambiguous'. None of the assistants (usually at Marks & Spencer) took any notice as I handed them such items as male underwear for wrapping. (I regretted that the fly-fronts would be useless).

Some of my female clothes were sold but most were given to my mother, friends, the Oxfam shop and jumble sales. In later years I was to acquire most of my clothes from charity shops and jumble sales, but at that time was either too snooty or stupid to think of buying my male clothes from these sources. It was therefore an expensive exercise.

Marks & Spencer posed no problems but would I have the courage to go into a men's tailors? I decided to buy a man's suit and sports jacket. Cowardice made me go to Burtons in another town.

'Can I help you, Sir?'

There was an eager young assistant at my side. This gave me confidence and later I left the shop with a sports jacket and a suit on order.

It was a little daunting in the fitting room trying to behave as if I'd always lived as a man. What was expected? Worst of all, would my measurements arouse suspicion?

'I always have trouble getting things to fit, being a bit broad in the beam,' I remarked casually to the tailor but feeling anxious. 'It's a family thing, my uncle was just the same,' (or so my mother had told me). The procedure was especially nerve-wracking when the courteous tailor measured my chest and inside leg, but if he suspected anything odd it was not evident to me. I related the incident to my sister.

'Did they ask you which side you dressed?' Jane enquired.

'No, and I don't know what it means.'

'Then you were very lucky and you ought to know for the future!'

Although I didn't have to change my behaviour to fit the male role, knowing the 'clan-jargon' was, as Jane had shown me, another matter. In a matter of weeks I was attempting to do what normally takes years – to become an adult male member of society and know all about man-talk, etiquette and expected behaviour. Dr Randell had emphasised that attention had to be paid to factors which were influenced by social conditioning and said that greater problems were experienced by male-to-female than the other way round. During an early visit he had asked me if I'd used the term 'fibber' because it was more ladylike than 'liar'? I had. Since then both speech and dress have become more casual for both sexes. What is now considered normal for a woman would once have made a navvy blush, but it was a great relief for me to be able to say what I liked without having to pass it through the refining filter necessary for a young lady!

There were numerous pitfalls to be avoided. I had to remember not to let out such comments as, 'When I was in the WRNS...'

It was quite difficult to conceal twenty-eight years of life, but with care and some evasion I succeeded. The WRNS was the only 'female job' I'd done. As time went on and a male past was built up it became less difficult. These problems were totally removed when, fifteen years later, I 'went public'.

There were minor practicalities which would not occur to most people, like mounting my bicycle in a male fashion and pulling off my sweaters in a male way. It was no problem with buttoning up coats because I'd been doing them up the male side since schooldays. Dr Randell, my friends and Jane were a great help in all these matters.

One of the greatest moments of my transition was when I tried on my new suit. The reflection in the mirror was of a smart young man. The frump was no more. It was some time before my mother could bring herself to look at me in such definite male attire, but eventually she became proud to see me looking smart – something she'd been denied when I was in the female role. She especially liked to see me in my dinner jacket and would tell her friends that I was like my father, suited to formal dress, but her change of attitude took a long time. Lacking the courage to make my male debut in Rusthall, I wore ambiguous dress at home but began to wear obviously male attire out of Tunbridge Wells. My first such venture was on a visit to see Dr Randell. With my male clothes in a holdall I crossed the recreation ground next door to our house. Some children there sang out:

'We thought it was a man, now a woman...'

With the hope of things improving, I felt able to cope with what had previously been intolerable. On the train I went to the toilet and donned my jacket and tie. The nun who had been sitting opposite smiled as I resumed my seat. No one else took any notice, I might have been invisible. Was it possible that I looked so ordinary? My elation increased as I went about London and did some shopping. There were no turned heads, no sniggers and no comments. People are anonymous in London but the indifference of the train passengers convinced me that I had merged into the background. On that occasion I found being ignored a very happy experience.

My big worry was using a public loo. What were they like? Did they have cubicles? Gingerly I ventured into the 'Gents' at the Charing Cross Hotel where I was due to meet Mrs Cordell for tea before seeing Dr Randell. It was empty, clean and cubicled. Subsequent experience taught me to use toilets in museums, art galleries and department stores, if possible avoiding public loos. I decided that men weren't as clean as women, most not bothering to wash their hands. 'They think they wee distilled water', Mum had caustically remarked.

Doreen Cordell greeted me warmly, 'You look fine'.

The waiter reinforced her opinion by handing me the bill! Mrs Cordell spoke of the errors many transsexual people, usually male-to-female, make in dressing too extravagantly and behaving in a way which they perceive as feminine but which only draws attention to themselves. I have met one or two female-to-males who try too hard to be 'macho'. Thank goodness that this is now on the wane with society being less bothered about sexual stereotypes than formerly.

After my appointment with Dr Randell I met my teacher friend, Pauline.

'You look super,' she commented, 'How long have you been dressing like this now?'

'This is the first day.'

'That's tremendous. I can't think of you in any other way now.'

Similar comments were to be made by countless people over the next few weeks and months.

I felt very relaxed and happy as we walked along the Embankment, the lights twinkling on the dark river, but when reluctantly changing back into my 'unisex' outfit on the homebound train I knew that my difficulties weren't all over. I was like Cinderella after the ball. Fortunately the train reached Tunbridge Wells without turning into a pumpkin!

I decided to make my new name as similar as possible to my old one so that if people did make mistakes it would not be so obvious to bystanders. It also made it easier when signing my name to retain my former initials. Thus Brenda Margaret became Brendan Mark. The solicitor recommended to me by Dr Randell for drawing up the Change of Name Deed thought this a wise plan and so it seemed for a while. People called me 'Bren' which was totally asexual. In quite a short time I felt that my name should be unmistakably male, so settled for Mark.

The solicitor told me that I'd be able to alter every document except my birth certificate which meant of course that marriage to a woman would be impossible. It didn't worry me unduly at that point, but lack of legal recognition would eventually prompt me to take up a campaign which would change my life. Father Taylor and his assistant curate, David Dunn, witnessed my Change of Name Deed. If I were, as Emma had said, 'going against the God-given', then I had some unlikely supporters!

A few years later I had another Change of Name Deed drawn up. 'Brendan' was discarded and instead I became Mark Nicholas – the latter name because I was born on St Nicholas's Day. Father Taylor thought that with saints' names I couldn't lose! On this occasion I went to a local solicitor who was unaware of my situation, a rather aristocratic man who thought it very strange that I should have reached my mid-thirties before deciding that I didn't like my name! However, he didn't refuse my business.

It was undoubtedly a strain living as both Mark and Brenda. If I had hoped to continue going home after my role-change then sooner or later my debut as male would have to be made in Rusthall and Tunbridge Wells. I anticipated it like an execution. I was under too much pressure to realise that most people are caring and would endeavour to understand. Hadn't I coped with the local kids yelling at me? Surely the neighbours wouldn't be worse?

'You'll have to make the break,' said Father Taylor, 'It's no good living two conflicting roles.'

One of my friend's mothers, a bluntly spoken Frenchwoman who'd taught at the Grammar School where I'd worked, made a similar comment.

'But what about the neighbours, Madame?' I had asked her.

'Bugger the neighbours,' she said. 'You have to live your own life.' She was right. I had to end my ambiguity.

Father Taylor suggested that I go for a week or so to the Anglican Franciscan Friary at Hilfield in Dorset. It would give me a break and the chance to live as a man in an all-male establishment. He thought that once I'd lived in my new role for a while it would give me more confidence to face the people who knew me. It would also act as a preparation for my return to university as 'Mark'.

On 20th September 1971 I set off for the Friary. For the first time ever I left home in proper male attire, praying that I'd not meet anyone I knew. (It had become quite a habit to gaze into a shop window if I saw a familiar face approaching.) It was the 'birth' of Mark and I was determined that whatever happened, 'Mark' I was going to remain.

Chapter fifteen

Freedom and Acceptance

THE train journey to the Friary was uneventful, which was for me an event. No one seemed to take any notice of the small young man travelling alone. It was the most important journey of my life. I wondered what sort of impression I gave to the young sailor with whom I shared a table in the dining car. As we chatted I tried hard not to sound too knowledgeable about Naval matters – my WRNS career was not for discussion. It was to be a long time before I could stop worrying about the impression people had of me. Like an actor I would gradually become more confident in my new role. Unlike the actor I wouldn't be acting and the role was to be permanent. After years of living in the limbo of ambiguity which evoked so many comments and sneers, it was hard to accept that people would see me as a man.

It therefore worried me when the friar who met me at the station carried my case to the car. Did he know or guess and think me too weak or womanly to do it myself? Later I discovered that this was a courtesy extended to all guests.

Not having stayed in a men's community before I was not sure how communal it was going to be. It was a relief to find that everyone had a single room with a washbasin. The showers had only curtains so I avoided those, but the bathrooms and toilets locked. One great source of anxiety was removed. I soon realised that even if I had been 'discovered' this was a place where the reaction would be of caring and respect.

The most difficult part of my stay was getting used to my new name. Having been introduced as 'Mark' I couldn't expect to be called anything else – nor did I want to be. Besides, it was an experience I shared with many others. (My mother related how, when she was newly married in 1938, she inadvertently signed 'Alice Bailey' in the hotel register – to Dad's embarrassment!) Father Taylor had indeed been wise to suggest this 'trial run' in the comparative security of the Friary.

It was the happiest week of my life. For the first time ever I felt free from conflict. I enjoyed sharing in the work and worship of the Community. There was fellowship but also space to be alone if one wished it. I took solitary walks in the surrounding Dorset countryside. Everything seemed incredibly beautiful. Now my burden had been lifted I was enabled to look beyond myself to the world. A great sense of joy, peace and relief enfolded me. A miracle had occurred. When I compared my former life with the life that was now opening up, it could be thought of as nothing less. I thanked God for it. At the age of twenty-eight I had been reborn.

Looking down on Hillfield Friary, Cerne Abbas, Dorset

A year later I met one of the friars again. He'd known of my situation and remarked that I'd become much more masculine during the intervening twelve months. Other friends commented similarly. Changing gender roles isn't, as some people would believe, an immediate occurrence, brought about by 'The Operation'. It is a very gradual process and surgery (if any) is only part of it. The most important part of the role change is the transsexual person's acceptance by society.

It was still very early days when I returned, with some trepidation, to Birmingham, the university and my new home in the oldest and most traditional hall of residence, University House. What helped tremendously was the assurance from the boys with whom I'd studied the previous year that they could no longer think of me in my previous role. To them I was male. James was especially supportive.

Sue arrived in the second year. She was a mature student, too, and one of the loveliest people I'd ever met. James agreed, and later married her, to my great delight. There were other highlights in the term. Shortly after my return, I almost managed to date a girl. She was sitting behind me in the orchestra stalls during a concert at Birmingham Town Hall. During the interval – while my companions were in the bar – she asked me the time. We started to chat and afterwards my friends asked me the secret of my success! The young woman was a nurse and quite tall. Regrettably her enthusiasm waned when she discovered that I was short (5'4½"). She never knew that that would have been the least of her problems! It did, however, give me a few weeks 'romance', discovering where she lived and sending her flowers. In that respect I was more like a gawky adolescent than a man nearing thirty. Although outwardly unsuccessful, the encounter did boost my confidence in myself as a passable male. There were other encouragements. One student, a Welshman, who, like Sue, knew me only as male, saw me talking one day to one of the sisters from the Malvern convent who was also a medical student.

'Y'ere, Mark' he said, 'The other boys say you be wasting your time with 'er!' Sister Christina Mary knew about me and later we shared the joke.

On the whole, things were going very well but there were inevitably awkward, sometimes hair-raising moments. One University House student remarked that she'd seen a girl who looked very much like me in the Medical School the previous year. Another asked if I had a sister on the campus. Such comments were not uncommon. Usually I affected total ignorance of my double but there were times during the succeeding months and years when I was glad of Jane's existence. She probably never realised she'd been to Birmingham University or the Tech!

Occasionally people did get my gender pronoun and sometimes my name confused, which worried me a little but I realised I'd be more sensitive to such mistakes than casual listeners. My most alarming moment occurred one night when I was showering in the ground-floor bathroom. A boy who had been locked out after hours tried to climb back in, through the bathroom window. I froze as his hand came round the frame, but my guardian angel was on duty that night. The windows had been fixed so that they could be opened only for ventilation. Breathing a sigh of relief I told the boy to go to my neighbour's window – he was always letting in late entrants. That was one visitor I was delighted not have seen!

Some time later, when I was living elsewhere, the washbasins were communal, so rather than wash too much of myself, I showered. I had to make sure no one else was around because there was only one door to both showers which locked. Only once or twice did I have to call out that I wouldn't be long – and wasn't! Whilst difficulties with bathrooms had been anticipated, there were some practical problems which had not. At one biochemistry session we had to test our own urine at regular intervals. I was terrified lest the other boys saw that I had to use a cubicle, so I arrived at the laboratory before anyone else to ensure that my times of collection did not coincide with theirs. I probably wouldn't worry so much now, but at that time was exceedingly sensitive to anything which could have disclosed my situation.

Another unexpected practical problem arose some months later when I started the clinical part of my training at the Dental School. The short white jacket with which I was issued was hot to wear in the centrally-heated school and hospital. In their respective locker rooms male and female students divested themselves of their shirts or blouses before donning their jackets. Having not yet undergone a mastectomy I thought it unwise to remove anything. For the same reason I wore a vest under my shirt, so the combined effect of vest, shirt and starched jacket was sometimes uncomfortable.

There were the occasional hiccups with my colleagues. One mature dental student who knew me from my first years, told some of the newcomers of my history. I'm sure he didn't mean to be malicious but thought that it showed a lack of judgement that didn't bode well for his future patients. With a mixture of dismay, anger and apprehension I waited for the questions, comments, strange looks and sneers to come, but none did. A friend said that one girl, on hearing the news refused to believe it. James reported that he'd been questioned but assured me that he'd revealed nothing. This and similar incidents taught me that after a time people tire of speculating, especially if one leads a very boringly respectable life.

One of the things which really bothered me was that my hips and thighs were too large for a normal male. It had worried me when living as a female and did so even more now I was living as a male. A determined effort was made over some years to ameliorate this, both by exercises and dieting. This anxiety became more acute if other areas of life were not going well. It was obvious that everyone took me for male, so my fears were groundless, but nevertheless anxiety overcame reason and I became almost neurotic about it. Sue said that she feared I could slip into anorexia. Fortunately reason returned before I reached that point.

Socially I was like a bird loosed from a cage. No longer was I afraid of social occasions, either formal or informal. People called on me and I went out more than I had ever done. Now I enjoyed buying clothes and dressing smartly. Inside me there was a peacock struggling to get out. Many years later a former fashion editor friend, impressed with my clothes sense and the fact that I managed to look well-dressed on Income Support, wrote an article about me which was published in the *Independent*. I'd come a long way from The Frump in the Tweed Suit.

My new suits gets a formal airing

Having previously avoided dancing I now attended ballroom dancing classes. At first I was terrified of making an oaf of myself but soon realised this fear was not confined to transsexual people. I didn't exactly reach the level of *Come Dancing* but just going to the class was achievement enough.

Jane, Professor of Dance and also our instructor, knew of my situation (I assumed that the Warden of University House had told her, but didn't mind). We talked quite openly about it as we walked to Hall one day,

'Of course, you'll find that older women fall for you,' she told me. I hadn't noticed it then or since, but it was obvious that women did and do like me. To the young women I seemed to be a brotherly/avuncular figure, to the older woman I was to be mothered. Certainly there were never any problems in obtaining second helpings in Hall.

The 1971 University House Christmas Dinner was a great occasion for me. I wore my new suit ('You look very smart' said one of the girls) and, for the first time ever, enjoyed a formal event. The long dresses of the girls, the beautifully laid tables and the flickering candles reflecting in the shining tableware must have meant more to me than to anyone else in that room. I was overwhelmed with delight and thankfulness.

I wrote to Father Taylor and delightedly told him of my new life. He replied, 'My dear Mark...the happiest letter I have had from you and I am very thankful.' He went on to warn me that a homosexual man might fall in love with me. His concern was appreciated but thankfully unnecessary, both then and ever since. Father Taylor assured me that he'd 'pave the way' for me at St Barnabas's, although he felt sure that I'd done much of it myself. Judging by the way I was treated subsequently at church it was obvious that his loving influence had been at work. No one made any fuss or asked awkward questions. It was as it my former role had never been. I was treated as a welcome friend. It never occurred to me that many transsexual people were not treated with such Christian love in their faith communities as I had been in 1971, nor are they today. When, years later, I learned this to be the case, it became my new mission to educate the church.

Writing this, I am reminded of the debt I owe to Father Taylor for his support during what was a period of extreme difficulty, especially as I had no father-figure in my life at the time. Although not from the tradition which calls priests, 'Father', it is a term which falls easily from my tongue when thinking of him. He taught love by his own life.

I decided to go home for a weekend, definitely as Mark, and with no compromise. Rusthall would see me as male and that was that. On the Sunday, returning from church, I passed the Assembly Hall where I knew the Tunbridge Wells Choral Society was rehearsing for the afternoon's concert. I hesitated, then silently praying for courage, slipped into a seat at the back of the stalls where no one would notice me. It was good to see familiar faces on the platform and hear the stirring strains of Elgar's 'Dream of Gerontius'. Suddenly I was aware of a figure by my side. It was the Secretary, Cyril Wood. 'Hullo' he said, shaking my hand, 'How very nice to see you again!' After that courteous gesture I abandoned my plan of slinking away and waited to see the choir members as rehearsal ended. They greeted me warmly. Thus encouraged, I bought a ticket for the performance, knowing full well that it would mean facing many other local people who would recognise me, but in true Tunbridge Wells fashion, people were very courteous. My 'coming-out' had been achieved.

Margaret Mortimore, my former class and music-mistress from the Tech and a member of the Choral Society, wrote to me afterwards. 'How brave you were to come and face everyone like that. It must have been absolutely hellish, but there won't ever be a first time again.' She was right: the worst was over.

As my first term as Mark drew to a close I wrote to Professor Marsland, Director of the Dental School, to thank him for all that he and his staff had done for me. His prompt reply was typical of him.

'I am sure that all concerned have been only too pleased to help in any way they could...If we have made it easier for you to continue at university and to become accepted by your fellow-students in your new role, we are delighted.'

I was delighted too. So ended my first male chapter.

Chapter sixteen

Facing the Neighbours

WITH the coming of the 1971 Christmas vacation I knew that the most difficult part of my acceptance would be in Rusthall and amongst friends and family. It was imperative that I remain as Mark and not, through the pressure of fear, slip back into an ambiguous state. Inevitably the person most affected was my mother. She was the one who had to cope, not only with her own bewilderment and anxiety, but also with facing people on a daily basis. She'd coped with crises before, albeit it for a different reason. When my sister had become pregnant my parents had been very shocked but rather than hide it away my mother had announced it to all the groups to which she belonged, such as the church choir and Mothers' Union, 'It's better,' she said, 'that you hear it from me rather than through gossip.'

I knew she would eventually come through it and she did. As Jane had predicted, Mum told people outright that she could see how much happier I was as a man than I'd ever been as a girl. At the time, however, it was hard for us. I think we were both glad of Jane's support.

Local people were kind and understanding. In retrospect I believe that it would possibly have been easier for me and other people had a definite announcement been made. Few were told but everyone knew. It was not until I publicly 'came out' in 1986 that people then felt able to talk to me about it. They had not been sure how to treat or address me. To many it was something of a mystery – had my 'sex-change' just happened? Hearsay was not really helpful, but I was sailing uncharted seas. With hindsight I would have approached the problem much more openly.

Most Rusthall people carried on as if nothing had happened and treated me as courteously as ever. I am sure that the fact that my parents, especially my mother, were so well-liked, must have been in my favour. Having known me for over twenty years as 'Brenda' it was understandable that some people found it difficult to remember to call me by both a new name and a new gender pronoun. I did not expect them to break the habit overnight. After all, it took me some time to get used to it myself.

If I had realised beforehand how many people recognised the male person under my ambiguous appearance it would have been easier to have confronted them with my intended change instead of pretending nothing was happening, but it had not been something we discussed with all our neighbours. Inevitably there was gossip, but it was a nine-day wonder. The only real problems I had at home – and still do – were from a few ignorant teenagers to whom I was not a person but an object to scorn.

On the whole, the people who seemed most able to accept my new role were those I saw frequently. Others, once they met with me again, soon realised that I was the same person but much happier and better adjusted than before. Some people said they felt more comfortable with 'Mark' than they had ever done with Brenda. The former secretary of the local Association of Wrens, to which I had briefly belonged, made an interesting comment. Betty said that she had noticed that in my female role my eyes had had a distant stare, as though I were gazing as something far away but after my role change they had had expression in them. She added, 'I felt immediately that the real person was behind those eyes now.' Her observation had been echoed by Emma.

The people who found it most difficult were often those who seldom saw me, although they were few. To them it was a new problem but for me it had been lifelong, a fact which most of those who saw me frequently seemed to have been aware. Perhaps on paper it could seem very strange and perhaps threatening. One ex-WRNS friend said she could not cope with it then admitted that her father had turned out to be homosexual and consequently her parents' marriage had broken up. I feel almost certain that had we met she might have taken a different view and also realised that my condition was not to be confused with homosexuality.

One problem was that, 'sex-change' as the unenlightened media still insisted on calling it, was then a relatively unknown phenomenon. Whilst being hurt and angered by past unkindness, I had to allow people to get over their perplexity and embarrassment.

The media did, however, serve a purpose. Hadn't *The Times* given me the information I'd so badly needed? Now the *Daily Telegraph* added to our knowledge. A neighbour gave us a copy of its Colour Supplement (10 December 1971) which contained an article by a medical journalist, Wendy Cooper, entitled 'Gender is a Mutable Point'. It was both well-informed and sensitive and not only gave me information and reassurance but helped those around to understand. It was the first piece of positive journalism I'd read on the subject. I wrote to Mrs Cooper, who said that the article had brought a tremendous response; many had been grateful that the subject had been aired in a responsible manner.

Wendy Cooper later interviewed me in Birmingham for a piece which was published the following year. True to her word, I remained totally anonymous and the article was very sympathetic. I decided then that she was a journalist of integrity and I have never doubted her. It was Wendy who encouraged me in my own writing efforts.

Not all journalists were so 'transsexual-friendly'. Mrs Cordell asked me if I would speak to Sally Vincent, who was writing for one of the broadsheets. She seemed very pleasant, but her subsequent articles and television appearances revealed that she had little or no understanding of the transsexual condition. In 1994 the *Guardian* ran a long article written by Sally Vincent which showed that in twenty years her thinking on the topic had not progressed. She was heavily criticised, not only by transsexual people but also by others including doctors, lawyers and fellow journalists.

Mrs Cordell also put me in touch with Philip, the young man I'd seen on television. He was the first female-to-male transsexual person I'd knowingly met. I enjoyed the company of Philip and his female partner, who had had a baby by another man. Philip treated the baby as his own and to the outsider they would have appeared as a happy young married couple with a baby, but the law would not allow him to marry his partner, because in its eyes he was still a woman.

Unlike me, Philip had not had the support of his family; nor do many transsexual people for a variety of reasons. Maybe the relatives see it as something shameful, or perhaps it threatens their own sense of self. I realised how fortunate I was. Another contact from Mrs Cordell was 'Hugh'. Unlike Philip he was aggressive and bitter, one of the saddest female-to-male individuals I have ever met. It made me realise that, although for the majority a role change releases them into a new and fuller life, some have inherent problems which it cannot cure. It is the psychiatrist's task to sort out those who would benefit from the treatment from those who have other problems. Transsexualism may be one of their problems but on the other hand it may just be masking something else.

I suppose it was a compliment that over the next couple of years Mrs Cordell asked me many times to meet her transsexual, journalist, social worker and doctor acquaintances. I was pleased to be able to do something for her.

The New Year, 1972, saw me returning to university with more personal confidence, but I found the course hard and only just managed to struggle through my second BDS examination and consequently had to have a *viva*. Sweating over my books I wondered if, in years to come, I'd remember the Krebs cycle or the branches of the trigeminal nerve. The answer was no, but I managed to satisfy the examiners so was able to go home to Rusthall secure in the knowledge that I would be returning in October for the start of the clinical course. In spite of my near-miss with the exams I felt that to have got through the year had been no mean achievement. It had also been the happiest year of my adult life. Now I would have a well-earned holiday.

I had a good summer, with a spell in the Franciscan Friary in Northumberland, a week in Durham and then a few days at the Malvern Convent. I looked forward to seeing Pam again but what I hadn't expected was an opportunity to help someone who was possibly transsexual.

Erica had been a guest at the Convent but so disturbed that she'd attempted suicide. Knowing my situation, the guest Mistress, Sister Vivienne, asked my advice. I suggested she contact Mrs Cordell. Shortly afterwards Erica visited me. It was traumatic because my own unhappy memories were still fresh and I re-lived my pain as she told me of hers. Erica subsequently became Eric but so eager was he to change roles quickly that he took double the prescribed amount of hormone and had to have part of his liver removed because it had become cancerous. Until I knew of his overdose, I felt guilty because it was due to my contact that he'd had the treatment. Had he died without telling me this I don't know how I would have coped. Thank goodness he recovered. The experience also made me realise that perhaps I was at risk too. Did we really know what the long-term effects of drug therapy were going to be? Was it a risk worth taking? I decided it was. Clearly Charing Cross Hospital was concerned because I was called for a liver scan, which was clear, but nonetheless I was taken off methyl testosterone for good.

I was worried by Eric's illness and also by his behaviour. When he visited me later I couldn't help noticing his obviously padded pants and deliberately strong handshake. Later he underwent a phalloplasty (the construction of a penis). He had some problems with it (most do) and from what I could gather it wasn't functional. Eric was obviously impatient to be 'fully male' and was working very hard to fulfil his perceived stereotype. We have to be realistic. His longings for what was impossible cost him a great deal. He returned to his native Sweden and married (which he was legally able to do) but it was a relatively short-lived affair. Any envy I may have harboured over his phalloplasty and marriage soon vanished.

Back at university, I began to feel like a proper dental student, having been issued with a short white jacket and a cabinet full of dental instruments. We were now based at the Dental School in the centre of Birmingham.

Life was even better than the previous year. I was more confident in my role and becoming closer to my aim of a profession. There was also another reason to make me happy and it was totally unexpected. Her name was Gwen.

Chapter seventeen

Gwen

WE'D met on my recent holiday to Durham and discovered that we were neighbours. Gwen was a nurse at the Birmingham General Hospital, which was adjacent to the Dental School. Having enjoyed each other's company on holiday it was natural that we should continue with our friendship. I had realised very soon after meeting her that I found her attractive. It was obvious that she liked me but I was worried, torn between wanting to become involved and believing that I should not because of my condition.

Once again I turned to Father Taylor. He replied, 'You cannot go through life being thoroughly detached unless you give up being human.'

He was right; I knew that. Before making my feelings known to Gwen I dropped broad hints that all was not normal genitally. When I told her the full story she was neither surprised nor shocked and said that she'd suspected me to have a hypospadias. (This is a congenital malformation of the male urethra, whereby the opening is on the underside of the penis. Sometimes severe cases are wrongly assigned as female at birth.) It had, I decided, been a good idea to fall in love with a nurse. She assured me that it was no problem for her because she was frigid.

We began to see a great deal of each other. How wonderful it was, after years of isolation, to go about with a special woman friend. My happiness reached its peak at Christmas 1972. I stayed in Birmingham because Mum had gone to her brother's in South Africa. At the midnight Eucharist on Christmas Eve I was almost bursting with delight. Here I was, accepted as a male, serving as an acolyte, singing the carols with a bass voice, training for an honourable profession after years of struggle and with a gentle and attractive girlfriend in the congregation. I could ask for no more and praised God for what I had.

In the New Year Gwen invited me to Matron's Ball. It meant

hiring a dinner suit. I was concerned lest one should not be found to fit because of my hips, but I found one which fitted me without any problem and it was a thrilling experience to walk into the ball, formally dressed, with Gwen on my arm. I thought of all the times I'd yearned to be able to take part in an event such as this. Mr Cinderella had come to the ball. It seemed like a dream. Shortly afterwards I chatted with Sue in the dental hospital lift. Conversation was private but brief, 'You know, Sue, everything is going so well that I feel uneasy. I can't believe it can continue'.

The third year was nearing its end. I had found the work no easier, although my social life had been better than ever before. My clinical tutor had been one of the most difficult men I'd ever met, in a very short time grinding down the very little confidence I'd had. Sue had even remarked that she'd been aghast when she'd heard the way he'd spoken to me on clinic. Sometimes this was in front of patients, one of whom tried to boost me by saying she thought I'd make a good dentist, but the damage was done. The forebodings expressed to Sue were justified when in the summer of 1973 the results of the third BDS examination were published. I'd failed and had absolutely nothing to show for my efforts.

It was a terrible blow. My hopes of an eventual medical career were in ashes – and I'd surely let down Professor Marsland who'd given me so much support. He disagreed, saying that I had worked hard but was unfortunate in lacking the manual dexterity necessary for a dentist. I knew I lacked confidence too. A re-sit was possible, but I felt that my time at Birmingham had come to an end and that I should withdraw from the course.

The decision reached, I experienced a great sense of relief. It had been very stressful. My personal tutor thought that because I'd got on well with the patients, some form of social work might be worth pursuing. I didn't really know what to do but was glad to get away from my sarcastic tutor. He taught me how not to teach, a lesson which was to be of help in the future, but however I rationalised my situation it was still impossible to think of those years of effort as anything but a total waste and of myself as a congenital failure. Later I was able to see that I had gained much there, not least the chance to change roles away from the pressure of home, and I had formed the beginnings of some good friendships, especially with Sue and

James.

At the very time when I needed support my relationship with Gwen had become fraught. Our friendship had, from the start, been beleaguered by her cold and domineering mother, one of the most miserable women I'd ever met. I visited Gwen's home once. It wasn't a home but a house, an emotional refrigerator. No wonder Gwen was such a tense person, lacking in any sense of fun or joy. I marvelled that she had been able to show as much warmth as she did. When she (unwisely, I think) told her mother of my situation, her reply had been. 'Be careful Gwen. These people are very odd, you know!' I wondered how many transsexuals she'd met? Mother would, I'm sure, have found some reason to dislike any suitor for her daughter. Gwen must have found her mother's resentment of the time we spent together very stressful and in the end it was easier for her to dispose of me. When Gwen took me to New Street Station to catch the train home when I finally left Birmingham I sensed a distance between us. As she quickly kissed me I knew that that would be the last time I'd see her. Mother had won.

I needed time to recover and to think. Still reasonably sure of a God around somewhere I decided to join an ecumenical Franciscan pilgrimage which was going to walk the Pembrokeshire Coastal Path. To my dismay I discovered that sleeping accommodation was going to be shared. I nearly didn't go. It was one thing to conceal what wasn't under my trousers but doubly difficult to hide my breasts, however small. In the end all went well, because everyone was circumspect. It had been wonderful to have experienced both great fellowship and breathtakingly beautiful scenery, truly a memorable holiday.

Dr Randell had discussed surgery with me and I'd seen a surgeon, but I didn't think a mastectomy was imminent. Being a major coward I hoped and prayed that such a procedure wouldn't be necessary but when realising the restrictions having breasts placed on me, I knew that without it life would be difficult.

I had been completely thrown by my university failure and it was hard to look in a new direction after so many years of striving for my qualifications. Letting go of those hopes was a bereavement.

My old Samaritan Director, Dr Dorrit Waterfield, came up with a temporary solution. She invited me to help to run her 'half-way house' for alcoholics and ex-psychiatric patients.

After the stresses of the last months it was a joy to live in the doctor's rambling old country house, 'Little Grange', which she shared with her 'guests' and their problems. I didn't mind doing gardening and housework; 'No more study' I told myself.

Dr Waterfield – known to all as 'Doc' – was a woman of immense compassion but she was also very tough, both mentally and physically. By then in her seventies, she'd been fifty years in medical practice, both in the country and the East End of London before the Second World War. She had many tales to tell, which she often did after supper, usually with a twinkle in her eyes. It was an unforgettable experience to have lived with such an amazing woman.

'Doc' agreed with my Dental School tutors that I'd be suitable for social work and backed me as I began to make enquiries. I applied for a place at the University of Southampton for a social work course. It was impossible, unless perjuring myself, to complete their forms without mentioning my condition, so I wrote to them 'In Confidence' – a task I was to repeat many times. My application was turned down. I believed that my history had counted against me and challenged the university. They of course emphatically denied it but I was not totally convinced. This is a dilemma every transsexual applicant faces: hide all and risk dismissal if found out, or tell all and risk rejection. Whatever reasons are given there is always the suspicion that the real cause for rejection is fear of the transsexual. On an application form we are remote: freaks perhaps – not people. After about three months at Little Grange the chores began to pall. I'd had enough of 'No study' and mindless work. I could and should do better. 'Doc' knew that too. With thanks for her kindness, I went home.

It was now near Christmas. What a contrast it was from my happiness of the previous year. I'd been trying to get into social work training in various areas without any success. Had God, if there was one, really got me through all the struggles of getting to university and changing roles, just so that I could do menial work? I drove taxis for a few weeks but in the New Year the work decreased until there was nothing. No trips meant no pay. I became officially unemployed.

I felt that I'd let everyone down, but told myself that it was necessary to be patient, God surely had a plan for me. My mother couldn't see it that way. The tensions caused by my transsexualism had now been replaced by anxieties about my career. Her concern often manifested itself as anger. I was in almost total despair. Mark Dalby, the vicar of the Birmingham church where I'd been very happy, wrote to me, 'Do persevere and if you do your part, God will most surely do his'.

I wasn't sure about that, but then a friend managed to get me work in a local department store where her brother was a director. A year earlier I would have scorned such a job but was now grateful for anything. Paradoxically, the day before I was due to start, the Chief Technician at Pembury Hospital rang to offer me a post in the laboratory. While preferring the hospital I didn't want to let my friend down (or her brother), so declined and went to work the next day in the Hardware Department at Weekes of Tunbridge Wells.

Unsurprisingly I didn't like it and increased my efforts to get something better. (Probably I would have been sacked on the spot if I'd been heard when advising an old lady to go to Woolworths' where the stuff was cheaper!).

The events of one day during my time there focused my fears and frustrations. Had I believed in Fate then it would have been obvious to me that She was out to crush me.

Firstly, I received a copy of the *British Dental Journal,* to which I was no longer entitled. It reminded me of my failure. By the same post came a rejection of my application for the position of Probation Assistant – another reminder. Unlike many of the other jobs applied for, this one had really interested me, but by far the most disturbing event of the day was a chance remark made by one of my colleagues as I arrived in the department for work that morning,

'Oh, it's you I saw by the bicycle shed. I though it was a woman!'

This was a dreadful shock. His words kept going round in my mind. Why had he thought I was a woman? He wouldn't have thought that just because my bike was a woman's? It must have been because of my hated feminine hips.

Although initially anxious, I'd been coping with my concern about my shape. After all, people had been accepting me as male for over two years. This threw me into violent reverse and it was at this point that I became so neurotic about losing weight that friends and family began to worry about me. In spite of the treatment, my body was still much too feminine for my peace of mind. I hated it. In fact there wasn't much to like about myself at all.

Meanwhile, but with little optimism, I continued to look for a better job, but as often as I applied rejections came. Either I was too bright, or not too bright enough, too old, too inexperienced or the work was just not available. A few weeks as a shop assistant had been enough. The post at the hospital was still open so with a great sense of relief I went back to the familiar, and caring, lab at Pembury.

Almost immediately a letter arrived from Charing Cross Hospital. A bed would be available for me the following month for a bilateral mastectomy.

Chapter eighteen

The Next Step

I WAS terrified. It wasn't the actual surgery or the prospect of pain which frightened me but the possibility of dying under the anaesthetic. My slender faith had never been strong enough to remove the fear of death, yet this fear had positive results. It produced in me a heightened awareness of the wonder and greatness of human love and the beauty of the world around. I left Mum at Tunbridge Wells station, buoyed up by her love and the good wishes of many friends and neighbours. As the London-bound train sped through the Kentish scenery, resplendent in its May dress, I was held by its loveliness. It was as if I were seeing it for the very first time – the countless greens of the new leaves, the blossom and the rolling downs. All was fresh and intense, illuminated by a bright but gentle sunlight which made every detail clear. Every moment of that journey was cherished.

My anxiety was considerably lessened by the cheery ward clerk at the hospital who told me that cases like mine were always allocated single rooms. Visitors soon began to arrive, one of the first being my teacher friend, Pauline. I was overwhelmed by what seemed to me undeserved concern. I decided that as far as possible I'd enjoy my stay.

The staff seemed kind and my fellow patients friendly. I met several when helping with the tea next morning. In one of the other single rooms was a slight young man with a scarred chest. We had a chat and he confirmed what I'd suspected, that he was also female-to-male transsexual. The scars were from a mastectomy but he was just recovering from a hysterectomy. Ian was a friendly person and spent much of the morning with me, trying to allay my fears about the imminent operation. He said that he was able to go swimming. The scars were certainly faint. I'd always believed that life would improve after such surgery but was less certain about a hysterectomy. That, however, was not mentioned by the doctor and

I had no wish to rush into it, my view being that if I couldn't see my uterus, why undergo the risk of surgery? As far as I was concerned, with my breasts being the most visible reminder of my past, they were the most important things to remove.

Ian had had an unhappy home life and because of missed schooling was virtually illiterate. Not for the first, or last time, I thought how lucky I had been.

The patient role was an entirely new experience for me. I was now the one with the name tag around my wrist, not the white coat on my back. Although never achieving my ambition to become a doctor, as a dental student and lab technician the patient had always been someone else. Now it was me. It was my turn to show trust. My hospital stay was to prove of emotional and spiritual as well as physical benefit.

As I signed the operation consent form my feelings were of apprehension and incredulity. After years of struggle I was about to undergo what had been thought impossible. I was afraid but knew that my fear and any discomfort would soon be forgotten when I enjoyed the benefits of a flat chest.

On the day of the operation I felt strangely calm. Was it because of the love which I knew was being directed at me? This serenity didn't last long. My experience with the pre-operative procedures was unhappy so by the time the kindly anaesthetist arrived I wanted to go home and struggled with her. Eventually, exhausted with anxiety, I succumbed and woke up in the recovery room with a bound chest and drainage tubes protruding from the crêpe bandages.

In a short time I was wheeled back to the ward and was conscious enough to ask the attractive blonde nurse accompanying me if she were Scandinavian. She was, but to my dismay, belonged to the theatre, not my ward. Later that day the surgeon visited me and expressed satisfaction with my general condition. Unlike women who had similar surgery I was healthy. There were to be no problems.

Although feeling a bit light-headed I was able to ring my mother, who was relieved to know that all had gone well. It must have been a very strange experience for her, firstly seeing her daughter become more masculine then undergoing surgery which some would deem a mutilation. It was the removal of a very visible sign of womanhood. In addition to her natural concern for my well-being she must have had very mixed feelings that day.

Gwen had always been scathing about agency nurses. She must have had in mind the one who attended me, who, after showing an appalling carelessness in basic procedures, as a final insult brought me a urinal bottle instead of a bedpan. She was an exception. The regular nurses, both male and female, were kind, friendly and efficient. Ian said that he felt embarrassed when the nurses washed him but it didn't bother me at all, in fact I enjoyed it. He, like many people, believed that in hospital he'd lost his dignity, but what do we mean by dignity? Perhaps we lose our pretences. I never found having a kind and gentle nurse of either sex doing personal things for me humiliating. Dignity means 'worth'. They treated me as if I were of worth. I thanked God for people with such vocations and gratefully accepted their loving care, and of course 'fell in love' with several of them as well!

Mum visited the day after surgery, laden with bits and pieces, including some lilies-of-the-valley from our garden and a small vase in which to put them. Their fragrance delighted me as I awoke the next morning. In spite of the journey she visited me many times during my ten-day stay. My mother and I had undoubtedly become much closer once the initial upheaval and shock of my role change had worn off. I sensed that my relationships with others had also deepened. Was it because my inner conflict had been resolved? Freed to be myself, I was now able to be more honest. The acting and hiding were over.

Several friends, including Father Taylor, also made the journey from Tunbridge Wells to see me. Some people called two or three times. I'd not seen some friends for a long time so enjoyed the opportunity to 'hold court' like royalty. The nurses teased me about the large number of cards which arrived. I really did feel 'enfolded in love'.

However, I was greatly saddened and perplexed by the fact that my sister neither visited nor wrote. Mum, obviously equally upset, said that Jane didn't approve of my treatment.

'But Mum,' I exclaimed, 'She was the first person to back me!'

Was Jane jealous because I was getting so much attention and remembering that while my parents had given her all their support when she became pregnant, she was not admired but regarded as 'a naughty girl'? Would she have continued to support me if the rest of the family had turned me away?

Of the many cards I received there was only one which proved disappointing. It was a very formal one from Gwen. She was still very much on my mind although it had been over a year since we last met. When I telephoned to thank her the conversation was stilted, although I did make her laugh once. It was to be our last communication.

Some time later I wrote to congratulate her on the fact that she'd won a gold medal for nursing, but she did not reply. Afterwards I heard from the people at the church we both attended that Gwen had met a man she was going to marry and had left St Peter's. I wrote to congratulate her – which was sincerely meant – but for my pains received a very unpleasant telephone call from her fiancé, a belligerent Welshman. He asked me what sex I was and said that Gwen didn't want to hear from me again. Furious, I said that it was a pity Gwen hadn't the courage to tell me herself instead of getting someone else to do her dirty work. For some reason I was perceived as a threat, but the threat was in her mind not mine. I was certainly no longer in love with her, but genuinely wished her well. It was sad that she could not realise that. With such a man I doubted her future happiness, but she had made her choice. I hope her Mother approved.

At the Eucharist on the day of my discharge the chaplain spoke of God's love being shown through others and told of a patient who had said that had she not been in hospital she would not have known the depth of people's love. That was exactly how I felt, not just about my hospital stay, but about the whole process of changing roles. There had been much pain, but out of this had come the joy of experiencing love. Would I have been so aware of this had my life been 'normal'?

Yet, on reflection, perhaps I was too grateful, somehow feeling exceedingly obliged to anyone who treated me as normal, as a person. It took some years to realise that it was wrong to feel amazement and fawning gratitude because someone was being accepting and caring to me, a person who happened to be transsexual. Did it not demean myself and others to imply that it was out of the ordinary to show love to a fellow human? Why should I be less worthy of love than the next person? I am certain that my friends would not have wanted me to feel 'umbly grateful'. I had to learn not to debase myself.

I was surprised (and relieved) by the speed of my recovery and the relative lack of discomfort. The worst bother were the vacuum bottles which drained my chest. They sat neatly in my dressing gown pockets and I labelled them BILL and BEN. The only real pain experienced was when the drainage tubes were removed. Although very sharp, the pain was short. With the dressings removed I was able to see my 'new' chest for the first time.

My breasts were gone and the only scars were about three or four inches long which were almost under my arms. I was very pleased. In the years before this surgery I had wondered how I might react at this moment. Would I be shouting for joy that I'd lost a despised part of my body? In the event it wasn't like that at all.

Immediately after the surgery I'd been bound up, then, by the time the dressings were shed I had become accustomed to having a flat chest. In a way it were as if my breasts had never existed. They had been a bad dream and I'd woken up. Yet even though there was no sense of euphoria, I did feel that something alien had gone from me and I was becoming more normal. The only strangeness was when I suddenly realised that a bit of me had been removed. I wanted it gone but it still felt odd to think that it was somewhere else. But was it 'me' any more than my hair cuttings? I wondered if this were a common feeling for people who had had surgery.

I was sorry to leave the Charing Cross Hospital. It had been a wonderful opportunity to see many friends, make new ones, to reflect and learn. The fact of my mastectomy seemed almost incidental especially as I was still swathed in bandages and not yet fully able to appreciate its benefits.

My few days' convalescence was spent at the Retreat House in St Albans which was staffed by the Sisters of the Holy Name from Malvern. My good friend, Sister Pamela, a former nurse, was there, so I was in good hands. Mum insisted on paying for a taxi to bring her to London then take me on to St Albans. I appreciated it, not just for the convenience but for what it symbolised – her acceptance. I wondered too if she were attempting to atone for her earlier lack of understanding, for which I never blamed her anyhow. Perhaps it helped her to do this for me.

My first week as Mark had been spent in a religious house, the Friary. Now, after another step in my role change I was again with the religious. Over the years a few people have accused me of going against God in what I did, but not the religious. They showed only acceptance, understanding and love. As Pamela remarked, if the treatment made me more of a whole person, how could it be wrong? It could only bring me nearer to God.

Exactly three weeks after my operation I was back at work in the laboratory. I was stiff and sore (perhaps my GP's partner had been just a little too enthusiastic to sign me off) but it was not long before all was forgotten. With it now behind me I had to turn my thoughts to a future career.

Chapter nineteen

Hospital again

PEMBURY Hospital Laboratory was a sympathetic and congenial environment. I could have stayed and studied for the State Registration in Medical Laboratory Technology but my experience had shown that science was not my strong point. I didn't want any more abortive study. Besides, I wanted to deal with people, not impersonal samples in bottles.

But where was I to go?

Daily I prayed for guidance until, deciding that it was unlikely God would write the answer on my wall, I sought help through a human agency. I went to the Vocational Guidance Association in London and vowed that whatever they suggested, I would do, believing it to be God's will.

Teaching or social work was recommended. This had to be a joke. My efforts at getting into the latter hadn't been successful. As for teaching, it filled me with horror. Hadn't kids made my life hell enough already? However I had to keep my vow and told myself that if it were God's will, it would all work out.

I decided not to attempt an immediate entry into training college even if a place were available, but to stay at Pembury and study for an A-level in English Literature at night school. Although the course had begun I joined a class and seven months later passed with Grade A! This was my field, not the sciences. Coincidentally, my sister had also been studying English, but had been on a two-year course. Jane had rather pompously told me that one needed two years. She failed. Whilst Mum was delighted at my success she did her best to hide it from Jane for fear of her anger.

It didn't take me long to decide on a college. Perhaps it was the memories of my spilt orange squash in the cathedral porch or a recent visit with some Franciscans, but I felt that Canterbury was to be my place. It was also far enough from Rusthall for me to be unknown but close enough to get home in a reasonably short time. I made an application to Christ Church College Canterbury, which at the time was changing from a teacher training college to a college of higher education, which was to prove beneficial to me. I should have expected it – they asked for my birth certificate.

At that time I wasn't astute enough to realise that a passport would have been equally acceptable. Besides, I'd discovered an omission in my earlier changes of documentation. I'd not bothered about my GCE certificates so they were still in my old name. Although later I had them changed there wasn't time to get it done, so I wrote yet another 'In confidence' letter to sort it all out. I strongly resented the fact that it was necessary. The GCE certificates were my responsibility, the refusal to permit a change of birth certificate, with all the subsequent embarrassment, was the Government's. My determination to fight this grew, although it was to be some time before I went to the courts.

The response of the Registrar, Tom Hetherington, was thoughtful and kind. My initial impression that the college, an Anglican foundation, was a caring institution, was to prove correct.

Early in 1975 I was interviewed at Christ Church and offered a place on the new BEd course that was to begin the following autumn. My main subject was to be English literature. One of my interviewers, Dr Lorna Kendall, was Head of Divinity, and implied that she would have liked to have seen me on that course. I was interested, but couldn't do both. Little did either of us realise that it would later become a reality.

The greatest obstacle to my taking up the place at Christ Church was financial. Understandably, having already funded my dental course, the local education authority was prepared to support me for the second and third years only. My total savings were £400. In order to cover my living expenses and fees for year one a minimum of £1,400 would be required. I almost despaired, but was encouraged by one of the sisters at Malvern.

'Look here, if God wants you to do this course, as you believe and I believe, the money will come. Stop saying "If I go to college" and say "When I go".'

I tried to follow her advice but found it hard not to lose hope over the next few months. When I'd almost given up, the Vicar of Rusthall, Canon Mantle, obtained a grant for me from a local charity. Suddenly things gathered momentum and funds came in from various sources. Never did I have £1,400 handed to me, but by the end of my first year at college, all expenses were met, and my £400 was still intact. That was also something of a miracle.

With the possibility of college ahead I plodded on at Pembury and also began to write more purposefully than hitherto, due largely to the encouragement of Wendy Cooper with whom I'd stayed in contact. I sent a piece about my experience of changing roles to BBC Radio 4 *Woman's Hour*. To my surprise I was invited to Broadcasting House to meet Doreen Forsyth, the producer. She told me that with personal matters they usually interviewed people because it was less embarrassing than reading a script in front of a microphone and production team. I was invited back at a later date to record an interview with her. I was delighted. The topic didn't seem quite so important as the fact that I'd been asked. Doreen Forsyth was a warm and sensitive interviewer. I couldn't have had better for my first, but certainly not last, broadcast.

Two months later, in September 1974, I was able to listen to myself on the radio. My colleagues at Pembury were not deterred by the fact that it was transmitted during working hours. Someone had brought in a transistor radio and we all listened in the relative privacy of the cytology department. It was strange to hear my own voice, but by no means an unpleasant experience.

The unused script I sent on to *Woman*, which spurred them on to send Christine Sparks, their Assistant Features Editor, to interview me. They didn't use my Wendy Cooper-approved manuscript but I was reasonably content with the piece they eventually published in March 1975. Although happy enough with the text, I was less pleased with the headings, 'One woman who dared to take this great step, tells… "why I changed my sex."'

I'd said nothing of the sort and was furious to be described as a woman, but subsequent experience with the media taught me that it wasn't always the journalists who did the damage, but the sub-editors who wrote the headlines.

My holiday that year was four days' camping with Sue (James didn't mind!). It was a joy to be with someone who was so open and such fun. Although I loved her dearly there were no sexual undertones and it was a very honest relationship. She was like a sister and often helped me to sort out things with regard to relationships, whether reassuring me that I would be acceptable to a woman or picking up the pieces when I'd discovered that I wasn't! She too had met Gwen and her mother and likewise sensed the emotional coldness there.

Later that year I went with Kathleen and Bill, two friends from the Franciscan Pilgrimage, to Scotland. On the Isle of Mull the only accommodation available was one single and one double room. Bill and I had to share a double bed, but since I'd remembered to take pyjamas and Bill was very circumspect, it was no great problem – though it would have been had I not had the mastectomy earlier in the year. At one stop there was no door on the gents' loo, so having made sure the coast was clear, I used the ladies'.

Such incidents made me long for surgery which would, I thought, remove such problems. The next procedure would be a hysterectomy. I wasn't pushing for one, but the matter was raised nonetheless when I saw Dr Randell a few weeks later. I told him that there were difficulties in obtaining the hormone tablets.

'Well, it shouldn't worry you too much since you've had a hysterectomy.'

'But I haven't.'

Two weeks later I was at St Mary Abbott's Hospital in Kensington for an appointment with Mr Bower, the gynaecologist.

I hoped never to have that experience repeated. It wasn't the physical discomfort of the internal examination which bothered me, but the reminder of my remaining female anatomy, an anatomy which I abhorred. Mr Bower and the attending sister were very kind and understanding but nothing could have removed my feeling of hatred for my body.

I began to have misgivings when Mr Bower announced that he'd operate as soon as possible. Was it really necessary? After all, I couldn't see what was inside. If it were possible, the construction of a phallus was far more important to me. My own GP, Dr Mary Fletcher, told me not to dither and said that a phalloplasty would not be possible until a hysterectomy had been done. Dr Dorritt gave similar advice. 'If an organ isn't being used, it's safer out of the way.' I told her of my fear of anaesthetics, adding that I was the biggest coward in Kent. 'Ask them for some valium to calm you down, old chap. It's nothing to be ashamed of; no one enjoys operations.'

I was admitted to St Stephen's Hospital, Chelsea on the 20th August 1975, still wondering if it were all necessary. The charge nurse, Mr Cannell, explained that because the female gonads and uterus were being blasted with androgens (male hormone) it was wise to have them removed. I was still unconvinced.

Irrespective of the medical aspects, I wondered if perhaps it were right, that I, outwardly healthy, was justified in taking up a bed in the hard-pressed National Health Service? Pauline Spencer, again one of my most faithful visitors, quelled my doubts. She said that prior to my treatment I had been but a shadow; now I was a real person. That was justification enough. She was right. What had been existence was now life. I was still myself, no longer struggling with a role for which I was manifestly ill-suited.

Once again I was amazed and humbled by the number of cards and visitors I received. Gill was one of my visitors. We had met during the Franciscan Pilgrimage in Pembrokeshire. She brought along some snaps of that holiday, including some of myself, taken without my knowledge. These boosted my confidence immensely. Even after five years in the male role I still worried lest I looked odd, but her photographs showed not an ambiguous being but a definite male. Ruefully I asked myself if the law would ever grant me the dignity of a legal status which was congruent with my social role.

The experience with the anaesthetic was even worse than expected and my recovery slower than anticipated. I was glad of the pain killers and sleeping tablets. One night I tried to do without them and, too late, regretted it. In my growing discomfort and weariness I asked myself if it had all been worth it, but it was too late for such questions. I prayed the Orthodox Jesus Prayer, 'Jesus, Son of the Living God, have mercy on me, a sinner', and eventually fell asleep.

My wound was becoming increasingly swollen and tender. The Registrar diagnosed a haematoma (an abnormal accumulation of blood) and said he would drain it the next morning. I didn't know what that would involve, didn't have the courage to ask and towards evening felt more and more afraid, increasingly uncomfortable and very alone.

It was strange that at this time the person I most wanted to see was Gwen, not as a girlfriend, but as the nurse beside my bed. Although she clearly found close relationships difficult, on a professional level she was compassionate and efficient. I would have trusted her with my life, but Gwen wasn't there and I was fearful. An analgesic eased the pain but not the fear. Once again I repeated the Jesus Prayer. When I awoke the discomfort had lessened but, more importantly, I felt calm.

It proved impossible for the haematoma to be removed completely. My wound continued to seep blood. The expected twelve to fourteen days in hospital passed and I began to wonder if I'd be fit to start college. Tests showed that the haematoma had made me very anaemic and an immediate blood transfusion was ordered.

Suddenly I felt very frightened and ill. Apparently I was more unwell than I'd realised and began to reproach myself. Wasn't it really a self-induced illness? In spite of Pauline's and others' reassurances I questioned the morality of my treatment. The cost had been too high, both financially and emotionally. If Mum had been worried when I'd had my last 'op' she'd certainly got reason to be concerned now. Obviously I'd been wrong in believing that it was God's will to have this surgery.

That afternoon the Chaplain's Assistant, Violet, and her priest, arrived as pre-arranged for a Service of Anointing (Unction). For me it was more than a means of seeking healing; it was a personal re-dedication. Shaky as my faith was, I'd been very aware of God's love during the previous few weeks.

The day after the blood transfusion I was discharged. Mum arrived at the hospital with a hired car and driver to take me home. She also brought a box of chocolates for the nurses, which was typical of her, but no greetings from my sister. That pain would not be healed.

I felt every bump and curve in the road. Perhaps the train would have been less uncomfortable but I appreciated Mum's kindness. I had much for which to be thankful.

Chapter twenty

Canterbury

The Great Cloister at Canterbury Cathedral

SUMMER was now gently slipping into autumn. Cobwebs glistened in the morning light and the air felt cool, although warm enough for me to sit outside during the day.

I was still unwell and needing much more attention than anticipated, but received plenty – from Mum, Dr Fletcher, the district nurse, friends and neighbours, but none from my sister, Jane. Once fit enough I spent a few happy days' convalescence at the Holy Name Convent guest house in Malvern before coming home to prepare for college, which I would be starting a week late.

Mum drove me to Canterbury, an incredibly beautiful journey through Kent, and one which forever gave me pleasure. It was with very mixed feelings that I parted from her. She'd given me so much support and now I was leaving her alone, which I knew she found difficult, but she would be the last person to dissuade me and to see me succeed would give her much joy.

As I walked from the Cathedral after Evensong on that first night I knew I'd made the right decision. It seemed almost a dream to find myself in such a lovely old city. Soon I'd 'adopted' the Cathedral and became more at home there than I did in Rusthall

Church. I felt part of the community.

I'd requested a place in the college hostel because of my still-convalescent state and was very pleased to find that the men on my corridor were friendly and mature. (To my relief Christ Church College had a large percentage of mature students.) I was accepted as one of them and they made me feel welcome. A few students on the lower floors were less mature. Whether it was because I was small, new or looked ambiguous (even though by now I had a reasonable beard) I don't know, but they played several foolish and potentially dangerous practical jokes on me. Geoff, one of the mature students, assured me that they'd treated others equally badly. Apparently previous 'humour' had involved forcing open a locked bathroom door whilst a boy was in the bath and pushing in a live electric floor-polisher! While I didn't fancy electrocution, 'discovery' was almost as terrifying.

My relations with other students were good. Some of the young women seemed to regard me as an older brother figure and I listened to quite a few woes. I was asked to several parties and accepted the invitations with enthusiasm. Few could have realised that this thirty-three year old student was attending parties for the first time in his life. Later on I became bold enough to stand up at a Students' Union meeting and propose a motion, an unthinkable event in my previous role.

Regrettably, not everything went so smoothly. As usual my heart ruled my head. I don't know why I found Mary so attractive. She was pleasant enough but not a ravishing beauty. We had met through a mutual friend and I was instantly drawn to her. The fact that she had recently had a nervous breakdown and found meeting people very difficult left me undeterred. Once she knew of my interest she purposefully, and not always very discreetly, avoided me, which at times was awkward because we both attended the Cathedral. Clearly it was a hopeless cause, but my longing for a close relationship overcame my judgement, so I suffered months of infatuation. Eventually my sanity returned and I was delighted to learn that she had married a very likeable and gentle young man who shared her considerable creative abilities. At least she had not rejected me because of my transsexuality – although that was small comfort. If it weren't my 'middle-sex' body that was being rejected, then even worse, I, the person, was getting the brush-off. I felt that until a normal woman had accepted me then it would be very difficult to love, accept and like myself.

Nevertheless, I was enjoying the academic side of life, especially English literature, but my doubts were growing about my suitability for school teaching. Had I made a mistake about God's will for me? It seemed sensible, however, to stay where I was until the next step was made clear. I knew that Canterbury was a good place to be, with company, intellectual stimulation, and the opportunity to develop my spiritual life. My financial needs were being met and I was fully accepted in the male role, so it was unthinkable to throw all this away.

Just before Christmas I paid one of my regular visits to Dr Randell, although by this time I wasn't sure why I bothered, except to receive a supply of testosterone and be kept on a list for any possible phalloplasty. I had grown weary of his attitude of regarding me as a lesbian and sneering at my religious beliefs, which he saw as a delusion.

'You'll never argue me into Christianity,' he snorted.

'I have no wish to do so,' I replied.

Perhaps in his mind, this 'delusion' was further proof that transsexuality was also a delusion. He never wavered from his assertion that it was solely a psychiatric condition. I never wavered from mine that it was not.

Nevertheless he was sympathetic to the problems engendered by the absence of male genitalia, though very wary of the available surgery. I believe his misgivings were genuine. It was a very difficult and risky procedure and the results seldom satisfactory, either functionally or aesthetically. He wasn't willing for me to be a 'guinea pig' and said that sometimes the phallic constructions hadn't 'taken' and either dropped off or had to be amputated.

I found the idea of someone dropping their phallus at the bus stop grimly amusing. Eager as I was to have a penis I had no wish to submit myself to perhaps ten operations, great pain, scarring and risk of infection in order to acquire something which was useless, ugly and without sensation. For the time being I would wait and see how procedures developed and just grit my teeth over the difficulties which I had to face. Even with these practical problems, such as the inability to urinate standing, I never had one moment's regret about my role-change.

Although at home with Mum for most of the Christmas vacation, I spent Christmas itself in Canterbury with the Anglican Franciscan friars. It was one of my happiest ever. I felt at ease with the brothers and the thought of joining the Order passed through my mind, but I dismissed it. Yes, such a life would solve my problems of career, financial worries, aloneness and the failure to form a close relationship with a woman. I'd also be a 'somebody' wearing a uniform and 'belonging', as with the services. No doubt there'd be opportunity for further study too, but they were wrong reasons, a 'cop-out' because I failed in secular life, not a positive calling. Expediency was not the same as vocation.

Having decided against a religious habit, I then spent some money Mum had given me for Christmas on an ex-hire dinner suit. When trying on the trousers I found one pair that were very tight around my waist, but extremely baggy around the seat, which filled me with relief – somewhere there was a man with bigger hips than mine. I wore the suit for a New Year party in Rusthall and have worn it frequently ever since for singing with the Tunbridge Wells Choral Society and other choirs. Ten years earlier I would not have gone to our friends' party, let alone dressed up for it. My former life seemed so very remote and unreal now, like a nightmare from which I'd awoken.

With some growing doubts about teaching, my return to Christ Church was made with mixed feelings. Even the novelty of living in college was diminishing, although it had advantages, one being its proximity to the Cathedral. I attended the Eucharist and Evensong there daily and, when feeling fraught, often went in at other times and found a quiet corner where I would just be still and let the peace and beauty of the magnificent building and its vibrant stained glass seep into me.

The presence of Mary and her 'avoidance behaviour' did not stop me from visiting the place which had become so important to me. The readily-available fellowship and worship were aspects of Canterbury life which I was later to miss greatly. Whatever else was going on in my life, I knew that Canterbury was right.

Chapter twenty-one

Debbie

THE grey, damp weather reflected my state of mind, as, laden with suitcase, I plodded wearily from the railway station through the empty Canterbury streets towards college for the start of the 1976 summer term. By now it was clear to me that I had neither the desire nor the ability to teach children, but what else was I to do?

In addition, there was still the 'non-relationship' with Mary as we each continued to pretend the other did not exist and played hiding games around the Precincts. My hopes at the beginning of the course had crumbled.

I was in something of a mental vacuum, but what I had not realised was my emotional vulnerability. My unacknowledged longing for love made me liable to fall for any woman who showed the slightest affection – or didn't, as with Mary. Debbie walked into this void and I grasped at the chance of a relationship, pushing aside the obvious warning signs.

She was four years my senior, attractive, highly intelligent, talented and available, and yet she was working in a job far beneath her intellectual capacity. I didn't want to find out why she was unattached or why a professional person was doing such a menial job. Friends who knew her cautioned me about Debbie's moods, but I chose to dismiss their warnings – after all, hadn't I suffered from PMT?

I was very shocked to discover that Debbie had been told of my situation by her friend Kate. She had obtained the information from an indiscreet woman she'd met from Tunbridge Wells. Kate freely distributed news of my medical history around the Cathedral, which was later to cause me considerable distress. The fact that she was obviously enraged by my relationship with Debbie caused me to wonder later if their own relationship had been more than mere friendship. It was a thought which gave me no comfort.

Soon I discovered that Debbie's infamous moods were more

than female 'off-days'. They were disturbing. Without warning or apparent reason her face would change and she would become as a stranger, totally cold and non-responsive. Days would pass before she would speak to me again, during which time she was either engaged in frenetic activity (which was sometimes obsessive tidying-up) or had taken to her bed. Afterwards there was never any explanation; it was as if it had never happened. In the end I could no longer ignore all of this, but it was so wonderful to have found someone who hadn't rejected me and who accepted me in a physical relationship that I clung on, hoping that somehow things would get better.

Debbie seldom met my friends a second time because she was certain that they'd talked about her. She received compliments with a strange grimace and I recognised something that had been bothering me – there was a peculiar distant look in her eyes that made me feel uneasy. Sometimes physical contact seemed the only way in which we could communicate.

When in a 'good mood' Debbie was very warm and loving, often embarrassingly so. She was a gentle and understanding partner and by her acceptance helped me to come to terms with my own body. What I'd read years earlier in Dr Gelber's *Medical Post* had become demonstrably true: a woman could have a satisfactory sexual relationship with a female-to-male transsexual partner. For me it was less satisfactory, but that was predictable, given my lack of equipment.

Although then a member of the church (we both were) I felt no guilt because of my relationship – after all I was barred by the law from marriage, a restriction in this instance which was to prove a mercy. I believed that I loved her and she me, although after she'd left me I felt defiled. At least I learned that there was more to a relationship than sex. It wasn't my inability to penetrate which ended our liaison but her illness.

My belief that Debbie was mentally ill was reinforced by both Dr Randell and Dr Dorrit Waterfield. The former thought that she was suffering from a form of schizophrenia which needed treatment, but assured me she could be helped. Dr Waterfield suspected manic depression. Both advised me to disentangle myself immediately.

How could I? She was becoming increasingly depressed and

seemed to need me, but the seriousness of her illness was made very clear during a weekend spent at home with me. She exhibited bizarre behaviour that was very distressing, both for Mum and me. I knew then that our relationship was over. Her tormented eyes haunted me for a long time, but I had to break free. Eventually the decision was taken out of my hands. Convinced that I'd set people against her she left Canterbury and a few months later returned to her native Australia, denying that she had any problems.

It was dreadful to see this illness destroy a person who was crying out to be loved but who could not maintain a relationship. I was heartbroken because of my inability to help her. I had to let her go but prayed that she'd find healing and peace. It hadn't been all negative. She had shown me that it was possible to be accepted by a normal woman in a physical relationship although it was not knowledge that was going to be of much use to me in the future.

Debbie had also helped me to overcome my nervousness about being seen partially unclad and got me to the swimming pool for lessons, where no one took any notice of me, but for these salutary experiences the price had been high.

Chapter twenty-two

Coping with Sexuality

WAS celibacy the answer? After all, I'd not had much success with my sexual relationships so far.

Just after my role-change my friend, Sister Pamela, had remarked that by choosing to live as a man I had, in effect, opted for celibacy. It was unfair to expect a woman to enter into a permanent relationship knowing that her own sexual fulfilment would be denied. (What about *my* fulfilment, I asked myself?)

It was interesting that female friends who were married took an opposing view. Without exception they said that they would have still married their husbands had they been transsexual (if the law had permitted it, that is) because they loved them as people and there was more to a relationship than sex. Sue felt it was important to get to know the person first; it is the person one loves not the body. The message was that love overcomes physical flaws.

As for the denial of sexual fulfilment, the Canadian research, and latterly my experience of talking with female-to-male transsexual friends and their partners, clearly shows that far from being denied, women find transsexual men good lovers.

Sister Pamela might have been thinking of the problem of not being able to father children, but that is no longer an insurmountable obstacle. Children have been born to partners of female-to-males following artificial insemination by a donor. The particular family I know is one of the happiest and most loving it has been my pleasure to meet.

My reply to Sister Pamela was that I had not chosen celibacy. It was only in my former role that I had been truly celibate because it would have been psychologically, and probably therefore physically, impossible to have had sexual liaison with either a man or woman. After my role-change it became possible, even taking into account my physical limitations.

As for choosing to change roles, what is choice? There's a

difference between the kind of choice which involved deciding whether to wear a red or green tie and one such as taking the opportunity to jump into the firemen's blanket because the flames are licking under the door, or staying put to be roasted alive. A role-change is the latter type of choice.

Sister Pam conceded to my view of myself as a forced celibate, a state which could change with circumstances. If someone loved me and I her, assuming that she was not already in a sexual relationship, would it be right of me to deny her myself? What good would come of it?

My Canterbury GP thought I should not exclude the possibility of a liaison with a woman. He believed that people with problems of this nature often form better relationships than 'normal' people (he called them 'grey') because they are accepted in spite of their problems and loved for who they are.

A priest adviser said it was wrong to impose celibacy upon myself as it was a negative decision. He was certain that many of his colleagues would conduct a religious ceremony in place of the standard marriage and added that God would recognise what the law would not. I did know of such services taking place privately and the people involved regarded themselves as truly married in the sight of God. From my observations it seems that such partnerships are more long lasting than those of 'ordinary' people.

Sex, my friends told me, was over-rated and love could overcome such difficulties. I am ambivalent about a physical relationship, but my misgivings are not for moral reasons. They are perhaps peculiar to me; I do not know if others share them.

Firstly, I am afraid of rejection. This has been my main experience so far. Since I do not believe that women judge men by their genitals and am aware that they can have satisfactory sexual relations with female-to-males, then my transsexual state is not necessarily a reason for rejection. My conclusion is that my lack of success must be due to my lack of acceptability as a person. One flaw has been my appalling lack of judgement – I should have heeded warnings about Debbie's moods. My feelings of being rejected for who, not what I am, are reinforced by the fact that amongst female-to-males I am unusual in not having a partner.

Secondly, I did not find the sexual experience with Debbie as exciting as one might expect. For me it had been frustrating and uncomfortable and had given very little relief. On the other hand there has been research into the feelings of the partners of transsexuals and they seem to be positive. One woman who had been sexually active for years with several genetically male partners said that her transsexual lover was the first man (she used that word) to induce an orgasm in her. To my knowledge there have not been questions asked of the female-to-male transsexuals themselves, so I do not know if my discomfort and frustration is limited to me or common amongst us.

For these reasons I believe that life would be better were I totally asexual, but I am not. It lurks in the background and when I've reached a stage of smug detachment, it leaps in for the attack. It might be provoked by a particular woman, or a sex scene on the television. I recall being aroused in my teens by *Lady Chatterley's Lover* when it was first published. There's a conflict between my feeling of wanting to be vicariously involved and the knowledge that it will leave me frustrated. Usually I turn the television to another channel.

Certain women (unwittingly!) left me in a state of arousal for weeks or more. (This was the case before I underwent any hormone treatment so it cannot be due only to that.) This is far more difficult to cope with than a book or film. It is therefore sensible to aim for detachment, but that's difficult if the sources of arousal are unexpected. At the same time I yearned to have a satisfactory and loving physical relationship. Neither total detachment nor a relationship seemed possible.

For years I hoped that a good woman would come into my life whose love would enable me to overcome my fears and frustrations, although was fully aware that I would have very little to offer her. With increasing age I realise now that the chances of this happening are exceedingly unlikely. Perhaps age too will render me less interested in such matters, although in my late fifties I was horrified to find myself in love with a woman at least fifteen years my junior. She 'cured' me with total indifference.

Now, having been unintentionally single for life I realise that for me the benefits of being alone outweigh the disadvantages. Of course it's not always enjoyable but then nor are partnerships. Life with someone one no longer loves must be a greater hell than physical aloneness. I believe that it is better to affirm the positive, the fact that I do have many good female friends, rather than yearn for the unobtainable wife.

Chapter twenty-three

A Degree of Uncertainty

DOREEN Cordell was dead.

I'd heard the rumour but didn't want to believe it. Dr Randell confirmed the news during my end-of-term visit. I knew she'd been ill with a brain tumour and had been shocked when, on the telephone, this articulate and highly intelligent woman had been barely able to form her words. Nowadays, when there is a great deal of information, several gender dysphoria clinics, support groups, and trained counsellors available for transsexual people, it is easy to forget just how difficult it was in the earlier times. Then one of the worst aspects of the condition was the feeling of being totally unique and understood by no one. Doreen was a light in the darkness and whilst I owe much to my mother, friends and family, she was the one who, with her fine balance of sensitivity and pragmatism, made my life a better one. Her untimely death robbed us of a true friend.

During the summer vacation I re-wrote my (unpublished) *Woman* piece and offered it to the *Nursing Mirror*. They were interested but wanted an accompanying medical article. Dr Randell was the obvious choice, but I regretted suggesting him. Throughout his article he referred to all transsexual people in their former gender pronoun. He wrote, 'These ladies' (female to male transsexuals) 'have an unfortunate tendency to marry'.

Few were impressed by the doctor's contribution. I was very angry. My journalist friend, Wendy Cooper, was as bothered as I was that no mention had been made of a possible biological cause. She immediately submitted an article to redress the balance. As in the earlier *Daily Telegraph* piece, she mentioned the work of Dr C N Armstrong, a consultant endocrinologist of Newcastle-upon-Tyne and a leading expert in the field of intersexual conditions. He had, in the 1950s, published a 'Spectrum of Sex', which showed that no one is 100% male or female. Transsexual individuals were amongst those who fell midway.

Dr Armstrong believed transsexualism to be a form of intersexuality that was determined before birth and has a possible hormonal cause, which would explain its resistance to psychotherapy. I was to be grateful to Wendy, not only for disseminating this information, but also for mentioning Dr Armstrong. I was to meet him later and find him a very valuable and caring contact.

Over ten years later I was to have another article accepted by a nursing magazine (*Nursing Times*) but on this occasion I vetted who my accompanying 'expert' was to be. Having been known as 'John' in the earlier piece, it was good to be able to have my full name published in the later one – and a flattering photograph!

My friends kept me supplied with relevant news cuttings. One reported that a male-to-female person had been found to have an abnormally low level of male hormone. That alone was not sufficient evidence to destroy Dr Randell's (and Dr Urgup's) theories, but as the years passed more and more evidence pointed to a possible biological basis for this misunderstood condition.

One cutting, from the *Observer* (30 December 1979), reported some seemingly promising research. A Professor Wolf Eicher of Munich and his team had discovered that there was present in all male skin and serum tissue an antigen called H-Y. In male-to-female transsexuals Dr Eicher had found this significantly absent, whilst it was present in female-to-male transsexuals. Normal women do not possess this antigen. (See also the *Lancet*, 24 November 1979, pp. 1137-8).

I wrote to Dr Eicher and could have gone to Munich for such a test but was not able to afford the trip. After that this line of research seemed to drop out of sight. My medical acquaintances said there were problems with laboratory tests. That particular ship had run aground, to my great disappointment, but on reflection I wonder if it would have been as helpful as I'd initially thought? Supposing I, or anyone else, had not had the expected results, would we then be regarded as not truly transsexual and therefore be denied treatment and possible legal recognition? I think my initial delight at this apparent breakthrough stemmed from my earlier concern about the condition being perceived as 'imagination' and therefore not real. It is hard to throw off the feeling that we must justify ourselves before we can be taken seriously, especially by the law.

Dr Louis Gooren of Amsterdam, the world's first Professor of Transsexuality, believed that transsexualism was less likely to be genetic and more likely to be developmental with its origin possibly in the brain.

Over the last few years there has been an increasing amount of evidence to suggest that there is a degree of sexual differentiation of the brain. This has been observed in animals, and researchers were reaching the same conclusion in respect of humans. From this it is reasonable to postulate that the transsexual condition might be due to some developmental cause, the brain sex not being congruent with that of the body. Dr Anne Moir, a geneticist, author of *Brainsex* (London: Mandarin, 1991) made mention of such a possibility, which was encouraging, but the real public fanfare for this theory came in 1993 at the Council of Europe's Twenty-Third Colloquy on European Law, entitled 'Transsexualism, Medicine and Law' and held in Amsterdam.

Amongst the learned papers was one delivered by Professor Gooren. He said that sexual differentiation of the brain takes place between the ages of three to four years. Once that has occurred, it cannot be undone. (Thus no female hormones would have done me any good.) He referred to post-mortem findings on transsexual brains, which showed a difference from those of non-transsexuals. Professor Gooren did not dismiss totally the possibility of environmental causes in early childhood, but unlike Dr Randell, he was not dogmatic. What he did assert most firmly was that transsexuals do not choose their condition – something which all transsexuals know. Previously few people had believed us. Some, especially religious fundamentalists, still do not. If, as they assert, there are early psychological factors which contribute towards the differentiation of the brain then I await with interest to learn of those that cause the development of transsexualism. What influences are common to transsexual people? Apart from the condition itself transsexual people seem as diverse as the rest of society. The burden of proof must now surely lie with the 'nurturists', not the biologists.

Dr Armstrong, by then in his nineties, was delighted that his belief that transsexualism was not a psychiatric condition, had at last been vindicated, but all this was a long way off. I was still trying to cope with the results of the Canterbury gossip, which was seriously affecting my peace of mind.

Tom Hetherington, the Registrar of Christ Church College had assured me that my papers were kept secure in his office. 'No one will ever learn anything from us', he said. I knew that, but people were learning a great deal from Kate, Debbie's erstwhile friend. It was worrying me so much that I enquired about getting a transfer to another college. Mr Hetherington was sympathetic but felt the only way to cope with gossips was to ignore them and carry on as usual. Of course he was right, but in the meantime Kate was making life unpleasant.

I discovered that several of my new friends had been informed of my past. One, Jane, wrote to assure me that she was not shocked by Kate's revelations, '…but by the vindictive way in which the information had been imparted'. Two male friends had also been informed but said nothing until I raised the matter. Tony said that he'd been embarrassed because although the information had been thrust upon him it was as if he'd broken a confidence. They all knew that if I'd wanted to tell them I would have done so. It certainly didn't break any friendships, to my relief. In one way I wished I'd known sooner since up to then I had been very wary of going to the loo with either Tim or Tony for fear of them becoming suspicious because I always used a cubicle.

Many years later I experienced a similar event. A new curate had arrived in our parish and someone took it upon him/herself to tell her of my transsexual status. But why? What angered me was that on both such occasions the person responsible for divulging my personal medical history was a member of the church.

According to Kate all Canterbury was talking about me. I felt sure that the worthy citizens of that city had better things to do but nonetheless the situation did undermine my confidence, especially as I was also increasingly unhappy with the teaching course. It was tempting to hide from 'all Canterbury' but I resolved to do the opposite and was thrilled to be accepted as a server at the Cathedral. To appear so deliberately in the public eye was my way of saying to everyone, especially Kate, who attended the services, 'Here I am, neither ashamed nor afraid. Just look and see that I'm quite ordinary'.

A little time later, after much poring over history books, I was also accepted as an official cathedral guide. Sometimes it was hard to believe that I was actually standing up in front of a crowd of strangers and addressing them. Whilst unhappy with teaching children, this was a form of teaching which I thoroughly enjoyed.

Kate didn't drive me out. Instead she left the city herself some months later. My feeling towards her was not of hatred, but of pity. It had been a very unpleasant episode, but had it been ten years later such a thing would not have happened because by then I had 'gone public'. There would thus have been no confidences to break.

Although I'd been advised to finish the teaching course it was still causing me concern. I'd stated my interest in helping adults to read so had been put onto the Infants' course 'in order to learn how to teach reading.' It was the wrong step. For my teaching practice I was allocated to a very good infants' school where the staff were supportive but my conviction that teaching was wrong for me remained. It proved more stressful than dental practice.

What could I do? It was impossible to give up after so many people had shown confidence in me. Would I be able to cope with being a non-achiever yet again? On the other hand, was it honest to take up a grant knowing that once graduated I would avoid teaching? I felt trapped.

I was unashamedly envious of the six students who had recently started at Christ Church on a new BA course in English Literature and Religious Studies. For me it was an unfulfilled dream, yet I could never justify undertaking a non-vocational course, one which would be for interest, a 'want' rather than an 'ought' Nonetheless, I sought Mr Hetherington's advice. He kindly contacted the University of London and ascertained that it would be possible for me to transfer, but only as a first year student the following academic year. It was disappointing. I'd wanted an immediate transfer and most certainly didn't want to be a mature 'fresher' for a third time.

The following day my tutors came into the school and told me that I did not have the right personality for teaching children. I'd failed my teaching practice. It spared me the anguish of having to make a decision. Although the future was yet again a question mark, I felt at peace.

It was a relief to go home for a rest. Mum was concerned but supportive. While occupying myself with job-hunting I continued to go to Canterbury to attend the English Literature classes with our excellent tutor, Sister Jadwiga OP. Those I would miss. When term ended I was due to visit Dr Gelber, now in Canada. After that perhaps I'd be able to sort out something. It was silly to rush into anything 'on the rebound'.

The telephone rang while I was at home one day. It was a student friend at Christ Church to tell me that the Principal, Mr Berry, wanted to see me. Perplexed, I left straightaway on my little motorbike, returned to Canterbury and reported to Mr. Berry.

'Why have you been saying goodbye to people?' he asked me.

'I've failed my teaching practice; that must mean the end of my time here.'

'Don't you want to do the BA course?'

Mr Berry told me he'd been in touch with the university authorities with the result that I could immediately transfer and graduate two years hence – the same time as I would have done had the BEd been completed.

My mind was in a whirl. Of course I wanted to do it but felt that given my age and the time already spent studying I shouldn't do so. As fast as I raised problems Mr Berry demolished them. I left his office euphoric but still beset with 'oughts'. One of the tutors, obviously party to what had been going on, chastised me for my doubts,

'If the Principal has gone to the trouble to get you onto this course, the least you can do is to complete it.' Said Miss Moss, 'Besides, he wouldn't have bothered if he'd not thought you capable.'

I realised that the staff had been concerned, a fact I'd been unaware of until then. Yes, I would do the course. Birmingham University had enabled me to live as a man and now Christ Church College was giving me the opportunity to become an arts graduate.

Both changes had brought a feeling of 'rightness', of calm and satisfaction and both had engendered growth, socially and academically. Had they also brought spiritual growth? That is less certain. My frustration with the teaching course had led me to think that God had made a mistake – or maybe I'd misread the message. Now I believed that this had had to be the route to the BA. Where I went after that was in God's hands. My duty was to work hard and do my best.

There remained one huge obstacle to the course – finance. It meant a visit, metaphorical cap in hand, to the Discretionary Awards Committee of Kent Education Committee. I wondered what they saw? A perpetual student who couldn't face life outside the college environment? One of life's failures? A ne'er-do-well? A victim of circumstances?

The chairman asked me if, were I in their position, would I award myself a grant? I had to be honest,

'No, Sir,' I replied.

'Well, God,' I said silently, composing my thoughts outside the committee room. 'If you want me to do this course, you'd better find me the money!'

I got the award – but they said it would be the last one! Finally, in 1979, I got my degree. I was Mark Rees, BA Hons (London). Hadn't people said years ago that I'd never be able to 'change sex' or get a degree? They were wrong. Some miracles take time though.

College became the place I wanted to be, and the course was one which I enjoyed. It was good. I felt that I belonged. My new fellow students made me very welcome and the staff worked hard to fit me into the timetable so that I could gain the necessary units for my degree. Dr Kendall had got her way – I was reading Religious Studies at last.

My delight at Mr Berry's offer was further enhanced by my now imminent visit to Dr Gelber in Canada, which was to take place during the 1977 summer vacation. Florence proved to be as generous and gracious a hostess as I would have expected having experienced her concern and care as a doctor. After my return to the UK I saw her only about two or three times again, when she visited her sister who lived in Tunbridge Wells, but we kept in touch by letter. It was a cruel irony that having spent her life giving so much to so many people, she later suffered from a appalling degenerative disease which eventually robbed her of her faculties and ended her life. She was undoubtedly one of the special people in my life and I count myself very fortunate to have known her.

Florence, as she asked me to call her, hadn't met me since I'd assumed the male role. She was amazed at the transformation of her former patient and said that she couldn't think of me as the same person. Nor was I any longer that unhappy young woman who had anxiously entered her surgery seventeen years earlier. Florence said that it needed effort to think of me as a female; even when she saw me in bathing trunks she could only see me as male, in spite of being a doctor in full knowledge of the situation. (She'd certainly seen more of me than most people!) I expressed my concern to her about the scars on my chest, but she assured me that some men suffer from a condition known as gynaecomastia, which causes them to develop breasts, which necessitates a mastectomy.

The British Columbia scenery was magnificent, the services excellent and the people most hospitable. It was a memorable visit. For a while I felt joyfully free, free of my past, until I happened to meet some people who were from Canterbury. They didn't know me but it made me realise that one can never feel totally free if hiding a past. The world is a small place. The only way of escaping from the past, as I was to find out, was to acknowledge it.

With perhaps excessive optimism, I'd taken some of my written articles with me and submitted them to a local magazine, *Westworld*. On the day of my flight home they rang me to say that they wanted to publish my piece about the Cornish Furry Dance. Ironically, the material for this had been gleaned during my time in Helston with the WRNS. At least some reward had been reaped from that otherwise difficult period.

I was thrilled. It was to be my first published article under my real name and was not about being transsexual, which was good. I didn't want people to think that was my only topic. It was to be the beginning of a very modest writing career and over the next few years I managed to get several pieces accepted by magazines, both local and national. The future was looking bright.

Chapter twenty-four

False Starts

SHE was one of the most beautiful women I had ever met. While I caught my breath she looked up and smiled. 'Hullo' she said. Her dark eyes smiled too. What a contrast from Debbie's tormented look. Perhaps that's why I fell instantly in love with Fiona. The odd thing was that it wasn't physical. As we talked I felt that our communication was at a much deeper level than I'd known with either Gwen or Debbie. Fiona was cultured, good-humoured, highly intelligent, and a deeply committed Christian (although not of the fundamentalist type), but most importantly, she was a young woman of immense compassion, 'a very lovable person' as someone described her.

However, I had fallen in love with someone who did not want any involvement, indeed someone who behaved at times as if she were terrified of involvement. There were traumas over the next few years whilst I tried hard not to force my attentions on her, and she appeared to be very defensive, making it clear that I was just an acquaintance. But when she learned of my situation she showed great sensitivity, saying (quite rightly) that it must have cost a lot to share so much of myself. She was, for reasons I do not know, less able to share herself. It took me fifteen years to realise and accept that I'd never be any more than a casual friend, but it has been nonetheless a much happier relationship than any of the others. Gwen and Debbie vanished from my life with a certain amount of acrimony. My relationship with Fiona, casual as it may be, painful as it has been, continues. I know that if free, she's willing to meet me when I visit London. Perhaps I fell for her on the rebound after Debbie, but I'm glad to have done so. My life has been richer for having known her. As someone said to me, 'Better a friend than an ex-lover'.

I'd met Fiona just after returning from Canada in September 1977. On this occasion I was looking forward to going back to Christ Church College a few weeks later to begin with my literary and theological studies for the BA.

Life was opening up still further. I was involved with college and Cathedral activities. The following spring saw me in a college production of *The Mikado,* which made a great change from the oratorio singing I'd done in Tunbridge Wells. It was fun, but it would come to an end in a year or so and thought had to be given to a future career.

At the age of thirty-plus it was time I had one. I felt sure that God had guided me onto the BA course, that there was some reason behind it which would unfold as time went on. The last thing I was going to do was panic; that would show a lack of faith.

There was something I'd thought of long ago, even before changing roles, but I'd never articulated it. Now it seemed a possibility, indeed it seemed as if I were being pointed in that direction. It wasn't a career which I sought, but it 'niggled' at me. Other people, including Tom Hetherington, asked if I'd thought about it. To me, and to many who knew me, the priesthood seemed to be my destiny.

I wasn't so sure about parish work – the vicars I knew seemed to spend much of their time in paperwork and meetings – but I felt very drawn to chaplaincy work. The notion of becoming a chaplain, maybe taking a higher degree and being a lecturer and pastor to the students was a very attractive one, but first I had to be ordained.

Realising that my situation might have made it difficult, in July 1978 I wrote to the then Archbishop of Canterbury, Dr Donald Coggan, to seek clarification. His reply was couched in sympathetic tones but the message was a blow. The Church of England did not at that time ordain women and because, in the eyes of the law, I was a woman, ordination would be impossible.

I was very angry and grew more so as the consequences of my situation in law became more obvious. It wasn't my physical state which caused the problems (although I would have preferred to have been a normal male) but society's reaction to me. It seemed that I was to be denied both a normal family life and a career despite my role change.

Women could become deaconesses but I didn't think they'd take too kindly to one with a beard! When I considered lay work, my former Birmingham vicar, Mark Dalby, who was then on the staff of the Selection Board, said that a bishop would think it very odd for a man to apply. The chaplain of a London hospital where I applied for the post of Chaplain's Assistant asked me why an intelligent man like me was applying for such a post. I could do better than look after the altar linen! He was very sympathetic when I explained my situation. Later, women were accepted as deacons and I considered applying, but, after a chat with a respected priest friend, decided that I would not be doing myself any good as the Church would only accept me as a woman, not as a man.

The legal situation made me very angry, but the attitude of the Church made me sad. From the impersonal law I expected nothing, from the Church I expected more but did not get it – except from individual members. Officially I did not exist except as a woman. Over the years I tried to get some undertaking from the Church to look into the plight of the transsexual person both from a pastoral and a legal angle. In 1993 I wrote to every diocese of the Church of England, forty-one in all, and received only five replies. It might be said that the Church wasn't ready for it, but when would it be? I was reminded of a hymn parody...

'Like a mighty tortoise
Moves the Church of God...
Brothers, we are treading
Where we've always trod...'

Over the next few years I tried in vain to get some church-related work and at the same time had to stand by and see former fellow students achieve what I'd hoped to do, small comfort as I signed on at the Job Centre. When I'd graduated I bought my own academic gown as an act of faith; I might need it as a chaplain. Twelve years later, I sold it – 'worn once'. There was a bitter irony in the fact that by the time women had been admitted to the priesthood – and I fully supported their fight – I had become a disenchanted agnostic.

My last couple of years at college, however, were unmarred by the knowledge of the future. Still blissfully certain that God had a plan for me, if I believed that if I did my best everything would work out. Up to then they were the happiest two years of my life.

Christ Church's Summer Ball of 1979 marked the end of my college career. I was delighted to have with me my sister, Jane, who was in very good humour. I could see in her my mother at her best.

Fiona came too, although I hadn't expected her to accept my invitation.

Early the next morning, in spite of having had little sleep, I slipped out and went to the Cathedral for what was probably my last eight o'clock Eucharist there. It was a beautiful summer's morning and the Cathedral chapel was cool and peaceful. I felt a great sadness at leaving the place which I had loved so much. Yes, there had been pain, but that is part of being human. Overwhelmingly these had been the richest years of my life.

Before leaving Canterbury I rang Sue's mother and learned that Sue and James had just got back from their two years' of voluntary service in Swaziland. It was a joy to hear Sue's cheery voice. I felt very happy; my friends were back safely and Fiona had come to the Ball. Jane was friendly and my degree course was completed.

Although happy with my academic course I had been continuing to seek opportunities for surgery. Dr Randell had said that he knew of no viable phalloplasty but if I found anyone able to do it he'd be interested in hearing about it. Although it was clearly a very difficult procedure I kept hoping that something might be possible. If successful, it would be both practically and psychologically beneficial. As one nurse friend bluntly put it,

'A lump is better than a hole!'

I drew several blanks but then wrote to Dr Armstrong in Newcastle-upon-Tyne to ask if he knew of any such surgery. He gave me the name of a plastic surgeon at the Royal Victoria Infirmary, Mr Edwards. The sympathetic and friendly reply which I received from Mr Edwards was very encouraging and so, in December 1978 I went to Newcastle to see him.

He had a much more helpful attitude than Dr Randell. To Mr Edwards I was a man with a handicap, not a deluded woman homosexual. After examining me he said that my situation was very similar to that of a bad hypospadias. Mr Edwards proposed, if I were willing to be a guinea pig, to use a new technique, which would have utilised the *gracilis* muscle in the thigh to construct a penis. I liked and trusted him so was willing. Before any further steps were taken he wanted to have the opinion of the endocrinologist and I was invited to return to Newcastle for tests at a later date.

Shortly after my final degree examinations the following summer

I was admitted to the RVI for biochemical tests and physical examinations. I met some of the members of the Gender Dysphoria Panel and realised that I'd struck gold. This panel was composed of psychiatrists, physicians and surgeons, a psychiatric social worker and latterly, a lawyer. Treatment of transsexualism was multi-disciplinary. I regretted that it hadn't been possible to have found this group ten years earlier. They all treated me as if I were a person of reasonable intelligence. It was also reassuring to undergo tests in order to assess the right dosage of hormone for me, something which, in my opinion, should have been done at the outset of my treatment.

The Professor of Endocrinology, Stuart Hall, examined me. In addition to the expected examination he also pinched the skin at the back of my hands and said, 'Male'. He then looked at my brow and said again, 'Male'. I was puzzled by this and later asked a medical friend why the professor had looked at this and what he had found. 'He was looking at the supra-orbital ridge,' James told me, 'They differ between male and female.' I'd taken with me photographs of myself as a child which Professor Hall was very interested to see. He classified many of them as male. Almost apologetically, they said that they wanted me to see a psychiatrist before surgery would be considered.

The other member of the panel I met was Dr Armstrong, who although well over retirement age, served as Consulting Endocrinologist to the panel. He was a splendid gentleman, immensely knowledgeable and compassionate. We kept in touch until his death at the age of 101. Dr Armstrong was still alive in 1996 when the first edition of this book was published but by then his sight was too poor to read it so I recorded it for him on tape, which he greatly appreciated. Onerous a task as this was, it was the least I could do for a man who had given me personally and the transsexual community at large such valuable professional support. He also lived long enough to learn of the brain research being done in the Netherlands which strongly indicated that transsexualism could have a biological basis. Dr Armstrong's thesis had been somewhat scorned for decades by some who stuck doggedly to their psychological explanations so the Dutch scientists' findings gave him delight. He had certainly been a man before his time.

The consultant psychiatrist on the panel, Dr Kurt Schapira, came beaming into my room. Here was a psychiatrist I was happy to meet. We had a very friendly discussion and I felt that he had treated me as a person of intelligence rather than a patient who was probably psychologically unbalanced. Dr Schapira admitted that he wondered what psychiatrists were doing in this particular field because if transsexualism were a psychiatric disorder then we would have to be regarded as deluded. From the transsexual people he had met that was clearly not the case.

Of course I understand that it is necessary for people who present as transsexual to undergo a thorough psychological assessment before undergoing the irreversible medical and surgical treatment that they desire but for their own good and that of the professionals involved in their treatment. That however is a very different matter from regarding the transsexual condition *per se* as a form of psychosis. In my own experience of meeting many transsexual people over a long period of time I know that most of them are more than just sane, they are also very well-balanced, highly intelligent and sensible.

In order to give the panel as much information as possible I had taken with me an exceedingly rough draft of this book. Dr Schapira eagerly accepted my offer to lend it to him and took it away to read. He re-appeared the next day and announced that he had sat up until 1 am the previous night because he found it so interesting. The doctor's enthusiasm persuaded me to think seriously of publication. If it had enlightened him, it should others. With regard to this condition, enlightenment was something that was much needed. Perhaps I would be able to play my part.

Another welcome visitor was Sister Vivienne from the Holy Name Convent, Malvern, who was now on the chaplaincy of the University of Newcastle. She was an ex-physiotherapist and not at all embarrassed by 'medical matters'. Her view was that the proposed surgery was morally justified and she added that the medical team was probably pleased to have such a co-operative and articulate patient.

I was deemed suitable for 'corrective surgery' (their words) i.e. a phalloplasty, and waited to hear when that would take place. Fiona asked if it were necessary to 'go through all that pain' but I thought that ultimately it would be worth the suffering in order to achieve something which might help me like myself a bit more and ease practical problems.

Months passed but I heard nothing which was unsettling because having left college I didn't want to go straight into a permanent job with lengthy surgery awaiting me. I drove a taxi and did some odd jobs, but nothing very inspiring. Eventually Mr Edwards wrote. He had had second thoughts about the phalloplasty mainly because he was to retire shortly so could not offer much after-care. I declined his offer of a cosmetic appendage, deciding that if I were that bothered by a lack of strategically placed bulge it would be better to stuff my underpants with old socks rather than go through the risk and pain of surgery to obtain a similar effect.

As with many other things which are unobtainable, I attempted to rationalise myself out of the desire for a phalloplasty, but not before seeing a different surgeon at another hospital. I was immediately suspicious because he airily drew diagrams but made no mention of the possible problems. My then GP, Mary Fletcher, thought me wise to wait until something satisfactory was developed.

If, I thought, my whole identity depends on the presence of a few inches of probably numb and non-functional flesh, then my problems are psychological, not physical. If the world accepted me as male then I should accept myself – and the world included people who were very well aware of my situation. As Professor Milton Diamond said in his book *Sex-Watching* (Prion, 1992), 'Our most powerful sex-organ is between our ears, not between our legs.'

Putting aside the psychological benefits, what of the practical implications? Those who have had urethral constructions have experienced many problems. I do not consider having to use a catheter four years after surgery, or a jug permanently, a 'successful' outcome. Constrictions sometimes develop and, because of the urethra, the area is prone to infections.

As for sex, the benefits seem questionable. Erectile tissue cannot be transplanted, so a prosthesis has to be inserted. I have heard (admittedly anecdotally) of a couple of deaths due to the female-to-males' bladders being pierced by the prostheses during intercourse. From the point of view of the woman, there are no cases I know of where women have insisted that their female-to-male partners undergo this surgery. In fact relationships have broken up after a phalloplasty. My woman friends tell me that few women are impressed by the size of a phallus. If they do not want children and experience orgasms when making love with their female-to-male partners, I cannot see how a phalloplasty would benefit such relationships. Were the surgery (both for sex and micturition) safe, and the constructed phallus sensitive, aesthetically pleasing and functional, then it would be a different matter, but with the present situation in this field I believe that it is wiser to make the best of what one has got. For me, the price is too high. Many people have ended up worse off than before – some even to the point of suicide. I do not want to be one of them. In retrospect I was glad that Mr Edwards had changed his mind.

So I did not return to Newcastle for a phalloplasty but in 1985 had 'chest revision surgery' instead, having in the meantime visited the Gender Dysphoria Panel about once a year. For some time my chest had been causing me some concern because where the breast tissue had been removed adhesions developed which had resulted in unsightly concavities. I returned to the Charing Cross Hospital to see the surgeon. He suggested I rub the affected parts with cold cream. It was useless. The plastic surgeon member of the Gender Dysphoria Panel at Newcastle agreed to do what he could to remedy the situation.

As before I went through a terrible period of anxiety, especially since my experiences of anaesthesia had been bad before both previous operations. I very nearly opted out but felt that I had to overcome my fear. In the end I was sent home because my blood pressure had rocketed. My home in Kent was considerable distance from Newcastle so it was an apparently wasted journey but I had to trust the doctor's judgement.

Florence Gelber, now a practising medical hypnotherapist, happened to be visiting England at the time and taught me self-hypnosis, a tool which was to be a great help to me in many situations. I was enabled to control my fear and went back to the hospital in Newcastle and underwent the surgery. It would have been impossible to have bettered the care I received, especially from the anaesthetist, Dr Harvey. While there I was visited by some friar friends, Jude and Colin-Wilfred, from Alnmouth Friary, and when my surgery was over went there for a few days' convalescence. Again the religious welcomed me in my hour of need.

I continued to visit Newcastle until the NHS funding changed and, in spite of being on Income Support, I was unable to get help towards my considerable train fares. Newcastle and that part of the North-East had won a place in my heart, but I was going to have further, very unexpected, opportunities to visit my much-loved 'Geordie-land'. Before then, there were to be some dramatic changes.

Chapter twenty-five

The Dole Queue

THE two years leading up to my graduation had been the happiest of my life but what followed was a time of great frustration and disappointment. The country was in an economic recession and no employer was very keen to employ someone who was over thirty with no relevant experience or professional qualifications. Nor was an employer offering less intellectually demanding work going to engage someone who was probably better educated than he was and likely to leave as soon as something more attractive offered itself.

There was also the dilemma I faced over application forms. Should I 'forget' about my WRNS service and hysterectomy in the 'Health' Section? It became my policy to tell potential employers only what they needed to know. I was, and had been, in general good health so why complicate matters and perhaps risk being immediately rejected? It was some time before I discovered that an employer would have been within his legal rights to dismiss me for failing to reveal what the Government regarded as my true sex. I'd been turned down for one job I really wanted – an assistant warden and tutor at a Hall of Residence because I'd been regarded as male and a woman was required (although it was not stated in the advertisement). Would I have got the job if I'd declared my 'true sex' I wonder? Ironically it was not long after the Church had told me that I could not apply for ordination because I was female!

During the three years after graduation I had several jobs I would not have even considered a decade earlier, when I didn't even have a degree. To quote my former tutor, Dr Kendall, 'they were not commensurate with your ability' – nor with my education, which had cost a great deal.

One job I took was as a porter at Pembury Hospital. I didn't think anyone in that part of the hospital knew of my role-change, but my security was shattered when one of the nurses remarked on my shape (about which I was still – and remain – very sensitive) saying I'd look better carrying a handbag. She actually asked if I'd had a sex-change! I tried to stay calm.

'Whatever makes you ask such a strange question?'

She looked me up and down.

'Hmm. Perhaps not. You've got too many male characteristics.'

Perhaps she thought no more of the matter but my self-confidence, already greatly eroded by my inability to get a decent career, was badly dented. My friends tried to reassure me but it was easier to dent me than bang out the damage.

I did not stay long in that job although had enjoyed the contact with patients, albeit fleeting. A couple of years later I was again working for the NHS, this time as a badly paid part-time stores assistant, counting toilet rolls and sweeping floors. My colleagues (all male) seemed friendly enough but mentally I felt totally isolated. We lived in different worlds. One day I found a crude drawing on my table in the staff room, showing a vagina and penis and the words. 'Which is you, Mark?' This was the final straw. It had been depressing and frustrating to find myself apparently unable to find anything 'commensurate with my abilities' without having to tolerate something like this. I decided it was better to do voluntary work than this job, which was diminishing me. With my doctor's support I gave in my notice. A year had been enough.

In spite of the fact that afterwards I signed on for the dole for a very long time I never regretted my decision to leave. One advantage of it was that it gave me material to write an article, 'Unemployment and the Dark Night…' which was published in the *Church Times* in October 1981 about the spiritual and emotional cost of under-employment and unemployment.

Life was made even worse by the fact that a local woman had told her children of my gender role change in revenge for me having chastised her boy for deliberately breaking glass in the recreation ground next door to my house. That was 1981 and ever since then I have been continually harassed by the local children. At first I found it very difficult and almost reverted to my pre-Mabledon state, but, especially after I'd 'gone public' and received much support, I found that I could cope. 'And anyway,' I thought, 'why should those ignorant buggers drive me from my house?'

When I realised that they did not harass me unless in groups and usually to my back, I knew that they were cowards. If challenged they remained mute. It still annoys me, and it's very boring, but they are the ones with problems, not me. One day I deliberately walked slowly past the would-be tormentors so they'd have to shout for longer and probably get sore throats. One of them, obviously irritated because no reaction was forthcoming, yelled, 'You deaf?' I was even amused by one boy, who perhaps having seen me on television could think of nothing more abusive than, 'Film Star!' One day, when I was in the local baker's, one very troublesome (probably troubled) youngster flung open the shop door and yelled at me. He left before the ladies working there could get hold of him. At least, being known, I was certain of support and, with few exceptions, most local people were angered by the way the children treated me. The boy concerned was later to spend time at Her Majesty's pleasure, which certainly gave me no pleasure. I pitied my juvenile tormentors and hoped that they would eventually make good.

The most unpleasant encounter took place just after the first edition of this book had been published. I was surrounded by a group of jeering children in the recreation ground next to my house. Not content with just verbally abusing me they also threw old bits of food at me and poked me with sticks. (I felt like a wicked sinner being attacked by hell's demons as depicted in representations of the Last Judgement.) From some of the obscene comments made it seemed that they regarded me as a homosexual male who practised anal intercourse. Yet, in the next breath they'd be calling me a woman. (For years such children continually called me Gay Gordon, aware only of sexual connotations, but not the fact that it was the name of an Irish television personality and of a dance.) Reasoning with them was fruitless. When I walked away (I was not going to run) they followed and shouted at me from outside my house. Abuse was not limited to the recreation ground. I was shouted at from a train from which I had just disembarked, in shops and even when I was on the back of a lorry campaigning with the local Liberal Democrat parliamentary candidate before an election. Certainly, especially after 'coming out' I had solicitor's letters sent to some parents and the local police officer visited others but it was very difficult because it was not always possible to identify the culprits. One woman denied that her children would do such a thing, although later incidents proved that they certainly did and worse. She still denies and blames the village for picking on her children. Most, perhaps all, of the children who abused me came from dysfunctional families. Several of them have since been in prison, which is very sad. They did have potential for better things.

In vain I tried to get on to a higher degree course. It was just as well that I didn't because it would have been impossible to afford, but I was desperately missing college and Cathedral life. From time to time I returned to Canterbury to take part in the services but it wasn't the same as being resident; it just emphasised that I was no longer part of the Cathedral community. At that time I didn't feel part of any community. If loss of self-confidence is one casualty of un- and under-employment, a sense of not belonging is another. In another attempt to stave off depression I rejoined the Choral Society as a bass and had as many singing lessons as I could afford with my former teacher, Phyllis Sichel, which helped considerably.

I undertook voluntary work, firstly driving a WRVS van for delivering Meals on Wheels then later became a voluntary tutor for Special Needs and Basic Skills students at the local Adult Education Centre. This was far more rewarding than the soulless paid work I'd suffered. Nonetheless, I dreaded the question 'What do you do?' One friend said that my dole was the salary for being a good member of the community, to which I replied that it was obvious that the community didn't think very much of my efforts! At the same time my file of job rejections grew and I reached the stage of not wanting to apply for fear of being rejected again. There also came a point when such was my loss of self-confidence, acceptance was equally frightening.

My father had never taught me anything about practical work, but nonetheless I managed to do quite a bit for Mum around the house and garden. I was seen as the man of the house now. Unwaged I may have been, but certainly not 'unemployed'.

Although, according to the Vocational Guidance Association, I was a 'fund of original and creative ideas', it was difficult to utilise these to earn money. I managed to sell quite a few of my photographs to local people but in order to get very far capital was needed. If I wanted to sell photographs to jigsaw manufacturers, for example, I would need a better camera but that would have cost a great deal. I did, however, have a photograph accepted by Canterbury Cathedral, which was sold as a card in the Cathedral shop. The income from that was tiny. My writing was spasmodic. There were a few articles accepted, but no real breakthrough – a day of excitement then back to the dole queue.

Having been rejected by the Civil Service in 1983 (for which mercy I was secretly thankful), I decided to stop frenetically hunting and accept that at my age and with my lack of experience and qualifications I would just have to make the best of what I'd got and concentrate my energies on being positive about it. There was much that could be done. Nonetheless I felt let down by God. All my earlier faith and efforts had been unjustified and wasted, but still I clung on, hoping that somehow it would eventually make some sense and I'd find myself earning some money in the right work.

A day which shone like brilliant sunshine throughout those years of 'winter,' was my graduation ceremony in 1980. What a wonderful moment that was when, wearing my academic hood and gown, I bowed to the Chancellor of the University of London, then Her Majesty Queen Elizabeth the Queen Mother, at the Royal Albert Hall. The bearded graduate had come a long way from Wren Rees being encouraged by Second Officer Thomson. In spite of my mother's earlier misgivings about my further study I knew that she was bursting with pride. I knew too that it had further justified my treatment because without it I could never have got so far.

There had been one sour note. I'd invited my sister Jane to come with Mum. She refused. Was she jealous? I didn't want to boast but just wanted her to share my happiness and wished I could have done the same for her. Nonetheless it was a magnificent occasion and a very happy day. The very next morning I was in the dole queue once again.

Eventually Jane cut herself off from me entirely. I never knew why. Her 'reasons', which she relayed via my distressed mother, were illogical. She became so paranoid that she refused to visit Mum while I was at home and even got her daughter to make any telephone calls in case I answered. Then she cut herself off from the rest of the family as well, even ignoring family funerals, until she finally refused to ring or meet Mum at all in case she mentioned my name. I was distressed, not only to be denied a sister, but also to be cut off from my nephews and nieces, who have ignored me ever since then.

I lost count of the times I heard Mum crying herself to sleep at night. This pain was a greater test of my faith than lack of gainful employment. It was all so inexplicable. Surely Jane must have suffered by losing contact with a mother who loved her dearly? However, she convinced herself and others that her family had rejected her and she did not even make contact when Mum was in hospital after a fall.

When she told Mum that 'all this' had happened because she wasn't allowed to wear make-up when she was thirteen, I realised that my forty-plus sister was a very unhappy woman with great problems, but I was powerless, and no one seemed able to help.

So there I was. I'd achieved my ambition of living as a male and gaining a BA but life otherwise seemed very unpromising.

Chapter twenty-six

Rees v UK

With my legal team in court at Strasbourg

'YOU are brave to do this!' people said, 'Fancy facing all those judges.' They were referring to my decision to take the UK Government to the European Court of Human Rights for failing to recognise my male status, a failure which had resulted in loss of privacy and a bar to marriage to a woman. For me it had also meant being denied a possible career in the Church, which had been more damaging than the other two disadvantages.

My personal campaign started in 1972 when I had written to Renée Short MP while still in Birmingham. Over the next ten years or so I was to write many letters to many MPs but the result was always the same: the MP usually wrote to the Home Office or the Registrar General and would then pass on a copy of the reply with a note of sympathy. The reply would say that the sex description on the birth certificate was an historical fact and therefore an alteration would allow us to 'deceive others' as to our 'true sex'.

What the replies never stated was that from 1944 until the *Corbett v Corbett* divorce case in 1970, transsexual people did get their birth certificates amended. I know of one who legally married in her new role.

The Corbett case (High Court 1970 Ormrod J) was cited *ad nauseam* in defence of the Government's stance. It involved male-to-female April Corbett, née Ashley, whose husband wanted a divorce. Mr Justice Ormrod ruled that a change of sex was impossible. For the purposes of marriage April was a man and therefore the marriage was void. Although the Judge stated that his definition of sex applied specifically to marriage it had since been used by the Government whenever sex was legally relevant, so that transsexual people had no legal standing in their adopted roles. In law they remained of their natal sex description.

Angry but undaunted, I plodded on and even got friends to write to their MPs. It seemed a very lone campaign, surely other transsexual people ought to have been doing something too?

My rejection by the Church had spurred me on, but I wondered how on earth it would be possible get anywhere. Shortly before leaving Christ Church College I met the Frenchwoman who had told me to 'Bugger the neighbours' eight years earlier! Madame said that she'd heard of a Belgian female-to-male who had taken a case to the European Court of Human Rights and why didn't I?

So why didn't I? I would. In 1979 I wrote to Liberty (then the NCCL) and was recommended a lawyer, David Burgess, who was willing to do this and in turn he briefed Nick Blake as Counsel. I could not have had a better or more caring team.

Five years and mountains of paper later we flew to Strasbourg for the hearing before the European Commission for Human Rights. I was more anxious about flying than coping with the hearing, although my heart thumped furiously against my ribs as I sat before the Commission listening to Nick present my case and the Government lawyer oppose it. I felt a great sense of unreality. It was difficult to realise that 'The Applicant' to whom they were referring was me.

My application, which was heard on 14th March 1984, was declared Admissible by the Commission. The procedure was that the Commission would then invite the parties to reach a Friendly

Settlement which usually took a few months. The Government, predictably, was not prepared to do this, so on 18th March 1986, two years later, my application was taken by the Commission to the European Court of Human Rights.

Unlike the earlier hearing which had been held in private, this was in open court with seventeen judges. It was somewhat daunting, although Nick of course did all the speaking. 'Whatever happens,' David whispered, 'You'll now go down in the law books and journals. You're making history.'

It had not been my intention to do that, but he was right. I was the first UK transsexual individual to take action against the Government and subsequently saw my name many times in various journals, 'Rees v UK'. 'David and Goliath' I thought.

Unfortunately, on this occasion, Goliath won. On 17th October of that year, judgement was finally handed down. We had lost. It was a shock and a great disappointment. I was greatly saddened that all the efforts of Nick and David were apparently wasted. Nonetheless I was determined to carry on. We would just have to carry on our battles on a different front.

David described the judgement as a Pyrrhic victory and it was clear that the Court did not consider its dismissal of my appeal as the final word on the matter, because the judges recommended that:

'The need for appropriate legal measures should therefore be kept under review having regard particularly to scientific and societal developments.'[1]

In the subsequent inevitable media interviews I declared that although it was an apparent defeat the Government had not heard the last of the matter. My case was the first but others would follow, of that I was certain, a prediction that was to be proved correct. It was not possible for the matter to 'be kept under review' indefinitely. The Court would grow weary of a succession of similar cases. We would not give up and would eventually win. The only uncertain factor was when that would happen.

When the news of the judgement broke I received many messages of sympathy and encouragement from both friends and people I hardly knew. One of the most notable people to contact

[1] Section 47, Judgement, *Rees Case* (2/1985/88/35) European Court of Human Rights 17 October 1986

me at the time was the Liberal Democrat Member of Parliament and lawyer, Alex (Later Lord) Carlile QC, who kindly wrote the preface to the first edition of this book. His words of support were put into action and he was to campaign doggedly on our behalf until the battle was won.

As I had been a lone campaigner, so too for some time was Alex within the Parliamentary sphere. 'Legal Recognition for Trans-sexual People' was not likely to be a vote-winner or an opening to high office. As he stated in his preface, he attempted to interest other politicians 'with mixed success'. I suspect that he had some scornful comments; it was after all a subject that still aroused such reactions. We were very fortunate that he continued to battle on our behalf. Eventually many MPs of all parties were to support the cause but that was not to come about for several years.

It had undoubtedly been difficult to fight a cause almost single-handedly, but the publicity surrounding my Human Rights Court case resulted in other transsexual people coming forward. I saw that my long-held desire to see a campaign group formed became a real possibility.

With Alex's backing I organised a Fringe Meeting at the Liberal Democrat Federal Conference in 1991. It was a total act of faith. I was not certain that it would be possible to get other speakers as well as Alex; whether there would be any interest on the part of the delegates and how I could afford the costs, having been without paid work for a long time. I asked myself whatever was I doing booking a room in a smart Bournemouth hotel?

Thanks to the generosity of some of the transsexual people with whom I had made contact and of a lawyer and a medical specialist who kindly gave of their time, the meeting took place. Alex expertly chaired the meeting for which I was very grateful. It was not a task I would have willingly undertaken. Not for the first or the last time I was immensely grateful for his support.

To my relief I was not the only transsexual person present. One of those who accepted my invitation to attend and speak was Stephen Whittle, a law lecturer. He was to become very active and involved in the subsequent campaign, and was later to receive official recognition of his expertise and very hard work on behalf of those with 'gender issues'.

Alex had ensured that we had some reasonable press coverage. We did not want to address just a few Conference delegates, however sympathetic they might be. Generally the coverage was sympathetic but a subsequent article by a Claudia Fitzherbert in the *Daily Telegraph* left Alex 'incandescent'. It was an appalling piece but we agreed that perhaps it was better to ignore the matter rather than keep it boiling which can sometimes be counterproductive. Certainly it was a reminder that we had more than the challenge to get the law changed; we had also to overcome ignorance. As this piece had shown, a 'good education' was not necessarily a guarantee of an accepting attitude. Claudia Fitzherbert's very unpleasant stance was negated by a sympathetic and informed article in the *Times* by Liz Hodgkinson, who had previously written well-researched books about the subject. We had reason to be grateful to responsible journalists like Liz who fully supported us.

Present at the Fringe Meeting was a councillor from Tunbridge Wells, Beryl Samuel. She was keen to put a motion calling for legal recognition of transsexual people before a future Liberal Democrat conference. As a result the Tunbridge Wells Liberal Democrats submitted several such motions but without success. Nonetheless, I did not regard such apparent failures as entirely negative. Each mention of our cause would bring greater awareness. We would have been naive to expect an overnight change in the law. Likewise, we could not hope for such legislation without a corresponding change in attitudes. My meeting with Beryl was, however, later to lead me in a very unexpected direction.

By 1991 my privacy was no longer an issue and the chances of my ever being in a position to marry were very remote, so why did I feel driven to carry on the battle for legal recognition?

In spite of being open about my situation, it gave me concern to see my screen on the Jobcentre computer, 'Mark Rees Single Female'. It was also very unsettling to know that we had no legal protection. Had I been in employment at that time it would have been quite legal for my employer to dismiss me solely for being transsexual. Or I could have been in trouble for using a 'Gents' toilet'. Given that I had a red beard and was clearly socially accepted as male I would probably also have found myself in trouble if I used the 'Ladies'. After all, I had had problems there before commencing any treatment at all.

In having contact with an increasing number of transsexual people, I began to learn of the problems some experienced because of the lack of legal status congruent with our social roles. A male-to-female transsexual person who was living unobtrusively with a man she had married (unlawfully because she was legally still male) was betrayed and subsequently arrested. The friend of a deceased transsexual person went to collect the latter's death certificate. Thanks to a 'vindictive person' who had telephoned the registrar, the certificate read, 'Mary Smith. Male.' Transsexual people could very easily become victims of such individuals.

My friend Stephen Whittle was also in an untenable legal situation. He had been living with his girlfriend, Sarah, for about twenty years. After undergoing much investigation, the couple was allowed to start a family by artificial insemination. Sarah had four children. Anyone who knew this family would have been very impressed by the loving and stable home which Stephen and Sarah gave to the children, something that many offspring of so-called 'normal' parents are denied. Yet at that time, Stephen, being legally female, could neither marry Sarah nor become their adoptive father. Had Sarah died, the children could have been quite lawfully removed from Stephen's care because he had no parental rights.

These few examples showed how the then current legal situation was causing distress, not only to transsexual individuals but also to other people who were close to them. It could also be disconcerting for the officials (such as registrars, police and Jobcentre staff) whose roles demanded that they follow the law. Legal recognition would also ease life for people other than transsexual inividuals.

The Fringe Meeting had been successful in a very important way; it had brought some of us together which gave me the incentive to move matters on. Again with Alex Carlile's support, I contacted several interested people, both transsexual and sympathetic professionals, and organised a meeting that was held in Alex's office at the House of Commons on Thursday 27th February 1992. Alex's wisdom and parliamentary expertise was of great help. It was clear from the outset that although relatively few in number there were enough enthusiastic and competent people for a campaigning group to start. I felt very happy to see my dream becoming a reality.

A general election was looming and Alex advised us to write to every MP in the new Parliament and ensure that our letter would be one of the first to land on each of their desks. He didn't think that we'd get much of a response and he was right but at least we had some replies. It was a beginning.

Alex's final recommendation to us that afternoon was to repair to 'Grandma Lee's' café opposite the House of Commons. Having firmly decided to set up a group we wondered about a suitable name. Suddenly someone said, 'Press for Change!' It was a spark of inspiration. We all agreed and thus the movement was born and named.

'Press for Change' or 'PFC' as it became commonly called, was to grow and become influential in a way far beyond anything I could have envisaged. 'Grandma Lee's' should have been worthy of a London blue plaque to commemorate the genesis of PFC within its walls but the café and adjoining buildings were later demolished and an additional parliamentary building, Portcullis House, erected in their place. Yet, in time a Parliamentary Forum on Transsexualism, to which PFC was to contribute greatly, would find itself meeting in that very building. There was still, however, quite a way to go.

Chapter twenty-seven

Meeting the Media

A COUPLE of years before my case went before the European Court, I wrote to the producer of *Claire Rayner's Casebook* and asked if they'd consider doing a programme about transsexualism. I felt that it needed some responsible coverage. The producer was very interested and sent a researcher, Maggie Winkworth. She asked me if I'd appear myself. 'Only if I'm totally anonymous,' I said. Maggie explained that it wasn't their policy because it defeated the object of bringing things into the open. It also implied that the condition was something of which to be ashamed. She said that it could help many people, so wouldn't I at least think about appearing? Maggie's words rang true. Of course hiding ourselves would never improve the lot of the transsexual community, either legally or socially.

I discussed it with Mum (after all, I was living in her house) and, to my surprise, she was willing. If people recognised me, would they really treat me any worse than the kids who already harassed me? I agreed and in June (1984) our house was taken over for a day with all the paraphernalia required for making a film. I enjoyed it and so did Mum. She spoke for ages afterwards of the experience and to my surprise and pleasure agreed to be interviewed herself by Claire Rayner. Claire was all that I'd expected her to be and we enjoyed her company. We chatted as if we'd known her for years.

There were still some friends whom I'd never told of my situation, so I was somewhat apprehensive as to their reactions. Although my full name and whereabouts were not revealed, people who knew me would recognise my face. My worry was needless because I was greatly moved by people's reactions. Some were surprised, none were shocked, all were understanding. Maggie had predicted that it would deepen relationships. She was proved right.

Earlier David Burgess, my solicitor, had obtained an undertaking from the Commission for Human Rights that my confidentiality would be respected. It was therefore a shock to receive a telephone call from the local newspaper, the *Kent & Sussex Courier*, in the spring of 1985, asking for details of my case. I was furious and said it was confidential but was told that it had been in the *Guardian* Diary on 12th April. I contacted Alan Rusbridger, the writer of the Diary, who was sympathetic. He said that it had been released from Strasbourg and sent me a copy of the press release. My details were there for all to see. Like it or not, I was exposed. My private life was now public property. It was especially ironic in view of the fact that one of the articles cited in my Appeal was 'Respect for private life' (Art 8). David Burgess was equally angry. He said we could withdraw the case and start the whole process again, but I didn't want to waste another six years.

'I'll risk it. We'll carry on. At least I know what to expect.'

'I think that's the best,' said David. 'Even if we start again there's bound to be some hawk-eyed journalist who will find out.'

Strasbourg's mistake was to change my life.

It was inevitable that there would be media interest; after all I was a pioneer, and, even more interesting for some people, a 'sex-change'. My journalist friend, Wendy Cooper, advised me to speak to the serious press if approached. This would stop the gutter press, who were only interested in 'exclusives'. Wendy joked that I was too boring for the tabloids anyhow!

I 'came out' on 7th March 1986 with a report on the BBC 1 *Nine O'Clock News*. This was eleven days before the court hearing in Strasbourg. John Harrison came to interview me and my mother. He was the first television journalist I'd ever met and undoubtedly one of the best. We met again after the judgement and I was impressed by his professionalism and compassion. It was a great loss to the broadcasting world, as well as his family and friends, when John was killed in a car accident in 1994 during his time as the BBC's Southern Africa correspondent. I felt that I'd lost a friend.

On the same day as my first interview with John, Jenny Cuffe interviewed me for *Woman's Hour*. This was broadcast as I was about to leave for the airport and Strasbourg on 17th March. Jenny was also an interviewer of great integrity and sensitivity. Subsequent experience taught me that not all journalists possessed these qualities.

The Kent & Sussex Courier trumpeted my case with billboards announcing:

My local newsagent refused to display it. I wondered how one could have a 'sex battle', but never found out.

Since my 'coming out' I have, over the succeeding years, had many encounters with journalists and TV interviewers. There were times when I felt almost like a 'one-night stand'. Great interest and sympathy would be affected, they'd get their story – then vanish. I was an object, a story to be exploited at minimum cost. In a way, the media were guilty of abusing us. There were certain TV programmes that clearly regarded us as entertainment. One researcher actually used that term when telephoning me to invite me onto a programme. She did not gain my co-operation. At first I did agree to such invitations, idealistically believing that perhaps it would help people to understand the situation. It might have done to a certain extent but it was often obvious that the minimum amount of research, if any, had been done. I appeared on BBC's *Kilroy* two or three times but refused a subsequent invitation. What infuriated me with these and other similar programmes was the fact that very personal and intrusive questions were asked of the transsexual participants. Those of us who were more experienced deflected them but the media 'newborns' appeared to be mesmerised by the red light on the camera and gave answers which they would probably blush to tell their closest friends. It made some of us feel like voyeurs.

The other 'trick' of the programme makers was to find someone willing to oppose us. Sometimes they had difficulties in finding people to do this so they ended up with one or two 'professional' antagonists whom we'd meet again and again! One notorious opponent was an Exeter GP, Dr Adrian Rogers. During one programme in which I took part he asserted that 'All transsexuals are obsessed by sex.' That was news to us. This statement was quietly and courteously countered by Professor Louis Gooren, whose speciality was transsexual medicine. (Dr Rogers appeared so frequently that we wondered why he was so interested in the topic. Clearly he had little sympathy for transsexual people.) I wondered if the programme makers felt it necessary to find opponents to treatment when discussing other medical conditions?

It seemed that many in the media were obsessed by sex and incapable of interviewing any transsexual person or partner without asking them, 'What do you do for sex?' A friend's partner gave a superb response which I shamelessly repeated when in a similar situation, 'Well, what do you do?' Now that so many of us have 'come out' there seems to be less media interest, but I would urge those new in their gender roles and to the media, to treat invitations to take part with great caution.

It is to be hoped that by now the media is informed and mature enough to realise that transsexual people are to be treated with as much courtesy as anyone else and not to be regarded as an opportunity for a freak show to attract the prurient. To be fair however, I have encountered people from all parts of the media, who took the topic seriously and researched carefully. They were caring and courteous and I was pleased to take part in their thoughtful and responsible programmes which undoubtedly did a great deal to ease the lot of the transsexual community.

Latterly I asked for fees for interviews and was quick to point out that my time, experience, coffee and electricity were of value. I was no longer prepared to be journalist-fodder.

Of all the media I found radio about the best although even that was not without problems. LBC pulled the plug on 'Angela of North London,' a caller who exclaimed angrily that God was cross with me! At the time I dismissed it as the rantings of a fundamentalist, but was later to discover that she was not alone. The religious extremists, although unable to prevent the law being changed, were determined to put every obstacle in our way.

My initial reaction to my unexpected media exposure was one of total dismay but I soon realised that it was very positive. No longer was I looking over my shoulder and wondering 'Who knows?' Nor was I afraid of someone passing on my 'dreadful secret' as Kate had, nor could I ever be blackmailed. I lost no friends but made more. The 'monster' of revelation had turned out to be a friendly kitten.

It was a liberation. I was freed from this fear and also freed to educate others, either directly or by just being seen to live a normal life. I was also made aware of the support of many people, some of whom were unknown to me. Total strangers stopped me in the street, both in my home area and elsewhere to express their support. By hiding I'd been saying to the world 'This is shameful' and 'I cannot believe that you have the capacity to show love'. Of course there were a few who were unpleasant, but only a very few.

My experience showed that there is a great deal of goodwill amongst ordinary people. We transsexual people should tap this resource. By hiding we perpetuate the fallacies about our condition, help no one, and deny ourselves the very thing we want – to be accepted as part of society. There seemed to be a cycle of fear and ignorance that had to be broken. We (understandably) hid ourselves because we were afraid of verbal and sometimes physical abuse, therefore ignorance could not be dispelled, thus we were treated badly so continued to hide ourselves.

The media were partly responsible for this. Quite a large part of the press had in the past displayed dreadful ignorance about the transsexual condition, so one could appreciate why sufferers tried very hard to conceal their past lives. It is perceived abnormality and rarity that make news. If this 'abnormality' is also seen as a sexual aberration, then the 'gutter press' is bound to lap it up eagerly. I had a bizarre idea, that in order to 'help' the newspapers, especially the tabloids, every transsexual person in the UK should ring them and offer their stories. After several thousand calls the editors might beg us to leave them alone. We would no longer be seen as 'scoops'.

Of course nothing as dramatic as that occurred, nor did I expect it to, but subsequent events proved my theory that familiarity would breed, if not contempt, then a lessening of interest from the popular press. Over recent years, with a few exceptions, any media coverage has been more informed and sympathetic, due no doubt to the fact that responsible, intelligent and ordinary-looking people, who happen to be transsexual, have 'come out'. In one way we have been 'hoist by our own petard' because when we wanted media coverage of the delivery of a 10,000 signature petition calling for a change in the law, to 10 Downing Street, there was hardly any mention in the media.

Disappointing as this lack of interest might have been, it served to remind us that we had come a long way from May 1958, when the *Sunday Express* revealed the identity of a female-to-male doctor who was serving on a merchant ship. The doctor had to remain confined to the starboard side of his vessel for the ten days it was docked in Baltimore, USA. On the port side the doctor saw, 'a milling throng of spectators, all intent on glimpsing the male doctor who was really a woman. Most of these people were holding cameras, in the hope getting a picture.'[2] I think they were more curious than callous. They were there because the doctor was a novelty. We are no longer so.

No longer hiding myself, I learned that many people were helped by my media appearances, which was both humbling and gratifying. It was also a great boost to my self-esteem to discover that I could cope with radio and television interviews.

The transsexual community 'adopted' me and I began to receive newsletters from the various self-help groups. They had not been around when I was changing roles and by this time did not need their support, but they seemed to like to have my contributions for their newsletters. Some of my articles might have helped people. In most cases I was willing to answer queries from female-to-males but sometimes found that it was wrongly assumed that because I shared this particular medical condition I wanted to be a bosom pal. I did not. Similar letters also came my way via the media but often I did

[2] Hodgkinson, M *Michael née Laura* Columbus 1989 p138

not answer them because Income Support left little cash for stamps.

After years of isolation I began to meet other transsexual people. That convinced me we were as diverse as any other section of society; in fact we were a microcosm of it. No one can describe a typical transsexual individual. When invited to address an FTM (female-to-male) group I was interested to see that the audience was made up of everyone from Yuppies to Bovver Boys! It was also interesting to observe that the average height was about 5'4", so I felt less conscious of my small stature.

I was delighted to see a number of family members, partners and friends at that meeting. One thing which has struck me about the FTM network is that as a group it is very caring. There is a great deal of mutual support for each other.

The slight uneasiness I'd had about reactions to my exposure in Tunbridge Wells, as opposed to my home village of Rusthall, were dispelled when in May 1986 I was a guest of the incoming Mayor of Tunbridge Wells, Councillor Joyce Hilling, whom I knew personally, at the Civic Banquet. It was a thoughtfulness which I appreciated. In October, when the loss of my appeal was announced, a couple of Tunbridge Wells councillors publicly supported me on Radio Kent. I received many messages of sympathy. It is doubtful that the Government had many cards of congratulations!

Whilst I was angry that my appeal had been rejected, there had come from it much which was positive, not least the awareness of the concern of many people. So many good things had come about because of my consequent public exposure, that it is something I have never regretted.

In spite of the failure of my case a couple of months earlier the year of 1986 ended on quite a happy note. I was invited to be 'Santa' for a children's Christmas party in Tunbridge Wells. The suit was three times my size which left my mother in a state of helpless mirth. It was good to see her laugh. Once known for her good humour the distress over my sister had turned her into a sad person. I also had one of my poems recited at a local public concert in which I took part as a member of a chamber choir. It was well received and in a small way helped to compensate for other disappointments. I was, after all, more than just transsexual.

The following year I had reason to be thankful that I was not a physically normal male. There had been a sexual assault and murder of a young woman in the town. I happened to know her boyfriend slightly and was, as a consequence, visited by the CID. Although without an alibi for the day of the murder, it was clear that I wasn't a major suspect. Nonetheless, their polite questioning left me feeling very uneasy – and I was innocent. They asked me if I'd agree to undergo certain medical tests.

'Don't let me waste your time,' I said. 'As a female-to-male transsexual I am incapable of such an assault.'

For the first time ever I'd been relieved to admit to my transsexual condition. It did have its advantages.

Chapter twenty-eight

Bereavement

THE excitement over my Strasbourg case inevitably died down although there was the occasional TV programme or magazine interview. They were not, however, sufficient to solve my problem of being without regular paid employment. I managed to do some casual paid work such as invigilating for examinations, tutoring a local boy, researching for a doctor friend who was writing a book, and teaching English as a Foreign Language for a couple of weeks during the summer. (After my 'coming out' I did wonder if my EFL employers would want to keep me on, but they did.) I felt I was still regarded as unworthy of anything more. I am certain that my references for both paid and voluntary work would have been impeccable but none were needed.

It was my fifth year of 'signing-on'. I felt humiliated to be so hard-up and without status, and distressed to be rejected both by the 'world' (employers) and my own sister and her family. It was depressing me, so I decided to seek the help of a counsellor. Initially it was intended to be short-term but subsequent events were to make me thankful for her help for very much longer than anticipated.

My sister's third husband was killed in a car accident in March 1987, Ash Wednesday. I grieved for her and hoped that in her distress she would realise just how much we loved her. Perhaps the pain would bring healing of her inexplicable estrangement. Sadly things worsened, and as a result neither Mum nor I attended the funeral.

Late in July 1988 I happened to bump into my sister's two younger daughters in Tunbridge Wells. I'd not seen them for several years and was as surprised to meet them as they were me. My 'Hullo' was ignored. Three days later I received a letter from a solicitor acting for my sister demanding an undertaking that I would not attempt to see the children, especially the youngest one, because

I had an 'adverse effect' on her. The letter made me sound like a pervert in a raincoat. I was furious and shocked. How could my sister do such a thing? Whatever had she told the solicitor? Certainly she wasn't going to intimidate me and I was prepared to go to court to face her.

Mum was devastated. She spent most of the day in tears and uttering her total disbelief that her own daughter could behave in such a way. 'I can't take any more,' she said, 'I must go away.'

She arranged to visit her friend in Clevedon and so, four days later, I accompanied her to Paddington Station and saw her onto the train.

'Don't worry about me,' she said. 'I'll be all right.'

Late that evening the telephone rang. Mum was dead.

That terrible night I knew what desolation meant. Desperate for someone, longing to share my grief with my sister, and knowing that if I rang she'd put the telephone down, I was like a person demented.

I went to a neighbour's and unashamedly wept, not only for the loss of a beloved mother and the loneliness that now faced me, but also for the anguish of my mother. She had been rejected by her daughter, who had refused contact with her for the last eighteen months of her life, and also been denied her grandchildren.

My mother's death certificate stated 'Ischaemic Heart Disease' but I knew, and her friends knew, that she'd died of a broken heart. The pain surrounding her death and the continuing strange behaviour of my sister made it all the more difficult to complete the mourning process and move on.

I was very angry because I believed that Jane had contributed to Mum's death. There was sorrow, too, because my own continuing unemployment had been a terrible failure; my poor mother had had little joy from either of us. I'd wanted so much for her to feel proud of me, hoping that in a small way it might compensate for my sister's inexplicable and unkind behaviour towards her.

I shall never know how I coped. Mum hadn't left any instructions – I wasn't even sure who her solicitor was. After some indecision I decided that Mum should be brought home to rest in the village churchyard where her other daughter, Carol, my twin, lay. At least that way I would have the support of the village community instead of travelling to Clevedon for a funeral in an impersonal crematorium attended by a handful of people. Mum's friend at Clevedon then told me she was glad of my decision because my mother had, the afternoon of her arrival, expressed a wish to be buried in Rusthall.

The vicar, Canon Mantle, insisted that Jane be told of her mother's death. Since she'd not wanted Mum when she was alive I didn't want her present at the funeral, but left it to the vicar to inform her.

Only one member of the family came to me before the funeral. He was my South African cousin who flew from Johannesburg to be with me. I'm sure Lester's generous gesture saved my sanity. It was the first time we had met. The extraordinary thing was he was also female-to-male transsexual, although had changed roles a long time after I had.

Jane accepted him and invited him to her house, although he was transsexual, because she said he'd not gone public. Lester did not know she'd stopped speaking to me before my publicity. On the day of the funeral my dear friend Sue drove from Cardiff and back to be with me, ten hours' driving in all. She, as befits a sister, sat with me in the front pew.

It was a beautiful summer's day and the service in St Paul's Church, Rusthall, was dignified and loving. The gifts of floral tributes filled every available space and over one hundred and fifty people were present – tangible evidence of the affection felt for my mother. Neighbours and friends organised the refreshments afterwards and relieved me of a great worry. To my distress, as I followed Mum's coffin from the house, I was greeted by the jeers of the teenagers from the adjacent recreation ground. Even at the worst moment of my life I was not spared. The only other sour notes were sounded by my grey-and-black-clad sister (Mum hated 'black' funerals) and her children, who refused to sit with, or even look at me. My outstretched hand to my sister as I entered the pew was spurned.

Later in the year I organised a memorial service which was one of the most positive events in that grim period. Having had time to reflect I was able to write the service and take part myself, my tribute to Mum. With my approval, the new vicar, Bob Whyte, whom I had known for several years, spoke of the support my mother had given me during my role change. That I wanted publicly acknowledged. I had been in something of a dilemma because it seemed that my sister should be invited, but felt that if she behaved as she had done at the funeral, or refused to come, she would merely cause further distress. Without her presence the service was a truly joyful occasion and it gave much comfort. Even Amanda Fisher, one of the TV interviewers I had met two years earlier, attended, which I'm sure would have made Mum smile. I think she would have enjoyed the whole event. I dearly wished Jane had been with me, in spirit as well as body. As it was, no member of the family was there.

I did not see Jane again until the summer of 1989, a year after Mum's death. Anniversaries are focal points and concentrate emotions as other days do not, so I was feeling somewhat depressed when I saw my sister in the town centre. I tried to speak to her and asked her what was the matter. She attempted to ignore me but I followed her and repeated my question. We circumnavigated some telephone kiosks, her speed quickening. She had a wild look, like a cornered animal.

'Go away, go away!' she cried, 'I'll fetch the police!'

'Go ahead,' I said. But she didn't, to my regret, because I thought the police might have called a psychiatrist. I was convinced that Jane was, if not mentally ill, at least very emotionally disturbed. Why had she demonised me? Was it me she saw or a projection of something within her which she couldn't handle?

Mum's words came back to me, 'I don't care what she's done, she's still my daughter.'

Now I knew what she meant. In spite of the fear and hatred in her eyes and the way she'd treated my mother and me, she was still my sister and I loved her. That is what made it so painful. I felt so terrible that I called at my doctor's on the way home. By chance he was available and patiently listened to me. 'You've had two bereavements,' he said.

He was right, but how could I cope with my sister's 'death'? My grief over Mum's death would lessen in time. There would always be a scar but a scar was a healing. The loss of my sister was akin to an ulcer. It was always there and the slightest knock would set it bleeding again. In a way it was like a divorce – I had been rejected, although was she really rejecting me or the scapegoat, the demon she had turned me into? I found myself spending more time than ever before thinking about my twin sister, Carol, convincing myself that together we would have sorted out our younger sister, and wondering, of course, what Carol would have been like. That had been a third loss.

My bereavements had certainly put transsexualism into perspective. Like anyone else I suffered from all the feelings associated with a death: grief, loss, guilt, anger and denial. Surely I'd wake up from this nightmare soon? There was also the awareness that no longer would I be first in anyone's life, no longer could I expect to receive unearned love and be secure in the knowledge that I was accepted without having to fulfil conditions, and be accepted as me, whatever my faults.

Bereavement cuts through the whole of life, from the spiritual to the practical. For some time I continued to attend the local church but Mum's death made me realise that I didn't believe in an afterlife. I was haunted by thoughts of my beloved mother as a rotting corpse and of my own mortality.

Human life seemed futile and did not reflect for me, a God who is love. It was one terrible cosmic joke. Creatures with immortal longings were snuffed out at death, all their efforts turned to dust.

I attended church more for fellowship than for spiritual comfort but it left me feeling more isolated than if I'd sat in an empty field. People said 'Hullo,' but nonetheless I'd leave the church alone, feeling that I didn't belong, and return to my empty house. I was fast learning why those who are alone find Sundays and Bank Holidays so difficult. My isolation really hit me when one Easter I was ill, so missed all the services. In spite of my closed curtains, no one called. I recalled my mother's tart remark that no one would notice if one had died 'until one began to smell!'

Soon I stopped going to church. If anyone had noticed, they didn't tell me. Perhaps my faith had been empty? Maybe I'd been seduced by what I'd experienced of purely human love and beauty, of music and the natural world. Maybe it was time I faced the stark reality of our aloneness in an impersonal universe. I felt the futility of it all.

The people who helped me during my acute grief were professionals, Rachel Hillier (one of the doctors at Rusthall) and my counsellor. They provided the net which stopped me dropping into total despair. Most of my friends lived too far away to be physically present but Sue and James welcomed me to their home and I had some happiness with them, even if it were marred by my return to a cold and empty house.

My mother had ill-advisedly taken out an Elderly Home-Owner's plan which left me with a 'Legal Charge' of £20,000 repayable on her death. It meant I had to re-mortgage the house. I remain very angry that my home, once paid for, has had to be mortgaged again. I will be in my seventies when the 'debt' is finally paid. This is three times as much as Mum received. It gave her little material benefit and much anxiety about what would happen to me after her death.

I didn't know how I'd manage to run the house on Income Support and suffered a frugal diet and cold rooms until I could work out just how much I could use the oven and central heating. It was the most desolate winter of my whole life.

Added to all that, my parents had been hoarders and I was faced with the task of sorting and clearing out, which seemed to be never-ending. I felt overwhelmed by the responsibility and saddened that my sister was not with me to help.

With the spring of 1989 came some shoots of hope. Journalist Wendy Cooper persuaded *Wales on Sunday* to commission me to write an article about my life-history. I was very pleased, even if it were about the same old topic. Intermittent media interest continued which, if nothing else, got me out of my shabby and cold house into comfortable hotels, and enabled me to meet interesting people such as Dr Patrick Moore, the astronomer. He was delightful company and very sympathetic to people in my situation. I had the dubious honour too of nearly making the *Wogan* chat show!

In June 1989 I went to Brussels, having been asked to speak at a press conference called to coincide with a meeting of the European Parliament Committee on Petitions. The Committee had passed for debate a motion which, *inter alia*, called for the legal recognition of transsexual people. The following September the full Parliament passed the motion but the UK Government did nothing to implement it here. That was no surprise.

The trip gave me a chance to meet other transsexual people and professionals involved in the field. One of them, a Belgian, became a friend. Present also was a Protestant minister and psychologist, the Rev'd J Douce of the Centre du Christ Liberateur in Paris. His organization was concerned with the welfare of sexual minorities. I was greatly impressed with Pastor Douce. He was a man of true Christian compassion. We corresponded after the meeting and I hoped to meet him again. That wish never came true. Sometime during the summer of 1990 he was murdered.

It was a terrible shock to me and to the transsexual community. Had his love for the outcast been the cause of his brutal death? I believe that he was more than a murder victim; he was a martyr.

It was in 1989 also that I began my public speaking 'career'. Thanks to the recommendation of Br Jude, one of my friar friends, I was 'discovered' by the Samaritans. I was invited to Northumberland to address the North-East Regional Conference of Samaritans. After that I had quite a few conferences to address and later spoke to other groups such as university and medical gatherings.

Although I'd faced TV cameras this was different – I could see my audience. The great advantage was that I could say what I wanted without being limited by having only to answer sometimes trivial questions from callow interviewers.

I met many caring people, and was generously entertained in Samaritans' own homes. One of my major speaking engagements was at the Samaritan National Conference in York 1991. I realised that it was exactly twenty years to the day since I had taken the train to Dorset and begun life as Mark. To my amazement and delight I was also asked to speak at their 1995 and 2000 National Conferences.

Whilst on my 'trips' I was happy, feeling needed, challenged, and valued, and enjoyed the flow of adrenalin and the company, but as one Samaritan said, life is either fast or feast.

These 'feasts' took up but a very small part of my time. For the remaining days, weeks and months, I endured the 'fast' of feeling not needed, in fact of being ignored, of not being valued. My energy was spent in the challenge of surviving, of stretching out the money, of convincing myself that I was of worth in spite of having to shuffle along in the dole-queue to get what many saw as a handout for the idle. One of the worst aspects of the 'fast' was the aloneness – compounded by the knowledge that my sister lived only a couple of miles away.

The entry in my diary for one Sunday read:

Spoke to no one
Saw no one
No one called
No one rang
Do I exist?

Chapter twenty-nine

Something of a Surprise

THE telephone woke me. It was six-thirty on a sunny morning in May 1994,

I recognised Cllr Beryl Samuel's voice, 'Good morning, Councillor Rees!'

'What!'

'I'm sorry to ring you so early, I couldn't wait any longer to tell you. You've been elected!'

'Oh, no...' I groaned. The council elections had been held the previous day. I had neither voted nor attended the count. The local Liberal Democrats had asked me to be a candidate and given me an assurance that it was unlikely that I'd be elected. They were concentrating on other wards and no canvassing would be done in Rusthall. I'd been such a candidate before and to my relief not been elected. Thus assured I reluctantly agreed to their request but privately begged local people not to vote for me. I had no ambition to be a councillor but now the residents of Rusthall had elected me to Tunbridge Wells Borough Council. How could I refuse to serve them? I would not be very popular if I stood down and caused another election to be called. It was an unexpected and very daunting result. Perhaps this was a 'vocation'; had I been called to this ministry? Could I fulfil people's expectations? All I could and would promise was to do my best; I was certainly not going to make promises only to find that they could not be fulfilled.

My most immediate concern was media attention. The press would be much more interested in a transsexual person than in other more hard-working and deserving candidates. Later that day I found a *News of the World* journalist and a photographer waiting outside my house. I was furious and uncooperative. When the journalist said that they'd been waiting for hours to see me I retorted that was their choice. (I hoped that in time the call of nature would remove them from the locality.) My neighbours rallied round to help me; Tina from next door offering a ladder so I could escape over my back fence – in my dinner jacket to sing in a concert that night! Fortunately that measure was not necessary. Some Liberal Democrats also rushed over to my aid, so the journalists gained very little. We learned that a local person had telephoned the newspaper and some thought that the Conservatives were responsible. It might have been a Conservative supporter, but I did not believe that those known to me, including councillors, would have behaved in such an underhand way. My relations with council members of all parties were friendly and courteous.

Nonetheless I was very angry because the resulting article showed a photograph of me that had obviously been taken secretly some weeks earlier. Somewhere there was a person out to damage me. They also supposedly quoted a good neighbour who was very angry because he had refused to speak to them. Yet the piece was so pathetic that I found it amusing, 'Darling of the fed-up Tories'. I imagined myself as a yellow-ribboned 'peke' being fed truffles by a blue-rinsed dowager Tory lady. My question was, why should Angus in Aberdeen or Betty in Bournemouth be the slightest bit interested in the fact that someone, who happened to be transsexual, had been elected to serve the people of Rusthall?

The local press smacked its lips and gobbled up the story so that there was wider Kentish coverage than if it had been confined to the *News of the World* alone. If the person who had attempted to betray me had hoped for my downfall he or she was to be disappointed. Yes, the media attention was tiresome, but it also evoked great support. I had letters and cards from far and wide. My electoral success was announced at the next Choral Society rehearsal and I was overwhelmed to be loudly applauded. Some time later my photograph was in the local newspaper again, but this time just as a councillor, with no mention of my transsexual condition. That was very positive.

The result had been a great affirmation, proving that a transsexual person can 'come out' and, far from being ruined, find that life opens up. It would have been impossible to have stood for election with the ever-present fear of someone 'finding out'. People do accept the situation, then it fades into the background. My constituents were more bothered by dog mess on the pavements than my medical history. After over twenty years, my role-change had lost its novelty. What my election and those of other transsexual people to their local councils did say to the rest of our community is, if you are open and get on with living as normal a life as possible then you can be accepted and integrated into your village or town. It's up to you. Nonetheless, our successes were affirming for all our transsexual colleagues.

While my election had helped considerably in the way I felt about myself, it didn't help in terms of personal relationships. I was a councillor, a functionary more than a person and remained acutely aware of my solitary status, made worse by the knowledge that I did have a sister with children, all of who rejected me.

It was certainly very daunting to find myself as a borough councillor and the Council Chamber was one of the most overwhelming places I'd ever entered. Although I had been addressing (mostly Samaritan) audiences and had had media experience for several years, nothing was as awesome as that chamber. I felt too ill equipped in self-confidence, knowledge and expertise, to engage in debate. My maxim is that if I do not know what I am talking about, then keep quiet. Others usually had plenty to say. I was however, stirred sufficiently by the proposed closure of a county council old people's home in Rusthall to research and prepare a speech, my first, which I delivered at what was to be my penultimate council meeting. To my surprise, even some of my political opponents congratulated me on what the local press called 'a powerful speech,' and they did not even mention that I was transsexual.

What I greatly appreciated about Tunbridge Wells Borough Council was the courtesy that ran through all its proceedings, even if people disagreed with each other. From the first moment I entered the Town Hall in my new role, I was treated with the utmost respect and no unkind reference was ever made to my transsexual status. When I signed the necessary official documents soon after the election, the Chief Executive indicated the newspapers covering my story on his table and said how very sorry he was that I had been subjected to such treatment. He assured me that it was no problem as far as the Council was concerned but if I had any trouble from anyone, staff or councillor, then I should report the matter to him immediately. That was never necessary.

The appellation 'Councillor' did little to deter the local kids however. The dichotomy of my life was vividly illustrated one evening as I left the Town Hall,

'Good Night, Councillor,' said the cheery porter as he held open the door for me. A few minutes later as I cycled home, some kids passed me by and shouted 'Gay Gordon…Brenda…sex-change…'

Life as a ward councillor was, for me, busy, primarily because I lived in my ward, was well known to local people who often stopped me in the street, could see for myself broken pavements and similar, and was pro-active, rather than just reacting to complaints and requests. It is a sad fact however that people appear more ready to complain than praise. They just did not seem to consider that most councillors and town hall staff do their best to improve matters. Nor do they appreciate that councillors do not seek fame and fortune and are not 'out to line their own pockets'. After hearing a woman hint at the doubtful probity of councillors I asked her, 'Are you suggesting that my colleagues are corrupt?' She went very red and walked away.

Before joining the council I had organised tinfoil collections and coffee mornings for various charities and continued to do so. I had also twice rung the local Hospice to tell them about an abandoned property in Rusthall High Street that could perhaps be used as a charity shop, after the unpaid bills had been removed from the doormat. They promised to ring back but never did. Once elected I shamelessly used my title, contacted the owner of the increasingly dusty shop, found some local people to support my project, then rang the Hospice for the third time, 'This is Councillor Rees…' Over ten years later, the shop is still flourishing and supports the 'Rusthall Room' in the Hospice in the Weald.

I was able to continue with my voluntary work at the Adult Education Centre and eventually acquired an official initial qualification in teaching basic skills, although at the time wondered why I bothered since the prospect of gaining any paid work in that field was unlikely. It was, however, to prove useful later in a way which I never anticipated.

Benefits all under one roof

RUSTHALL residents are set to benefit from a new Hospice at Home charity shop in the High Street, which was officially opened by deputy mayor Daisy Fletcher on Wednesday this week.

Cllr Mark Rees, who represents the village, said he was delighted that the shop had opened. "I had seen this empty shop in the High Street for quite a while, so I decided to put the landlord and Hospice at Home in touch with each other to see if something could be done. The plans went from there," he said.

"It has got three real benefits for the people of Rusthall. There are no clothes shops in the village at the moment, so it means people won't necessarily have to go into town to shop, and it also means volunteers can do their charity work locally.

"And, of course, it will also be of benefit to the Hospice at Home charity, which is good news all round," he said.

Pictured are (left to right) Cllr Mark Rees, deputy Mayor, Cllr Daisy Fletcher and Hospice shop manager Stephen Weekes

Photo number 96219/19

Recognition by the media as a councillor
without the appellation 'transsexual'

195

Chapter thirty

Print and Pain

IT was in January 1996, during my term of office, that Cassell published the first edition of this book. The local press made much of this, especially since I was still a serving councillor, but it was sympathetic coverage and several of my council colleagues bought copies and were very positive in their reactions. 'COUNCILLOR'S SEX SWAP TORMENT' was not really a headline that gave me delight but at least it was publicity. If people read my book as a result they should at least see the reality behind the lurid headline. With the Samaritans still issuing me invitations to give talks I was very pleased to have copies of my book with me. Usually every one was sold. My main concern was that my sister would use the book's publication as another reason to condemn me, but that was never to become a problem, due to an event soon to occur.

Cassell arranged for me to do some broadcasts, including one for the BBC World Service, so I paid a second visit to Bush House, my first being at the time of my appeal to the European Court of Human Rights. I considered it an honour to be broadcasting world wide. The other broadcast I particularly found worthwhile was for our local radio station, BBC Radio Kent. I was back at the studio in Chatham and met again the delightful Barbara Sturgeon who greeted me like an old friend. Her interviewing was thoughtful and sensitive and she justly deserved the accolade for broadcasting that she later received. Following the programme I had a letter from a listener in Tonbridge. That was not unusual but although this person, Ann, was clearly trying to appear friendly but non-demanding, my gut feeling was that she was desperate to talk to someone. We did meet and I advised Ann to seek professional advice, which she did, and I listened and reassured as she began the process of changing her gender role. Although by now I had met many transsexual people, Ann/Alan was one of the most anxious people I have ever met, which made the journey all the more arduous. Nonetheless he got there in the end and was an infinitely happier person as a result. Afterwards he wrote to me, '...you have helped me live. I cannot thank you enough for that.' We became good friends and, in 2005, after such ceremonies had been made legal, I was delighted to be a guest at his wedding to his long-term female partner.

On 27th March 1996, two months after publication, I went to Hereford to speak to the local branch of the Samaritans. As usual I found it a very rewarding and enjoyable experience. Yet, inexplicably, I had an overwhelming compulsion to visit the Cathedral for the specific purpose of lighting a candle for my sister before leaving Hereford the next morning. This I did.

I had not had news of Jane for some time, but had previously learned, to my distress, that she was receiving treatment for cancer. I had rung the hospital and the nurse asked if I wanted to speak to my sister. Knowing how Jane had previously behaved I declined and did not ask the nurse to give her my love. This was very painful because I longed to be with her, but felt sure that any messages and especially my presence would be rejected. Subsequently I heard that Jane had been discharged and was apparently all right, but a shudder went through me when later someone casually remarked that she was okay but having some back trouble.

Easter fell the following week after my Hereford visit and, in spite of my misgivings, I bought a card to send to my sister. After further thought I sent it to someone else whom I knew would appreciate it. Jane would just throw it away, probably unopened. Nonetheless, on Good Friday, 5th April, I felt that I must send her one and set out to buy and post it to her. Walking to the shop I felt very depressed, perhaps oppressed, and thought it was probably because I was facing the prospect of another Easter alone. This feeling was so strong that I was tempted to walk past a good neighbour who was cleaning her car and not greet her. She had her back to me and probably would not see me pass by. But what if she did? Monica would think I'd lost my manners.

'Hullo, Monica,' I said.

She turned round. Unusually, she was not smiling,

'Oh Mark, I'm so sorry about your sister,' she exclaimed.

'My sister?' I felt uneasy.

Monica looked surprised and concerned,

'Don't you know? She's died!'

Jane had died two days earlier, exactly a week after I had lit the candle.

No one had told me. In fact, my cousin, Lester's sister, had flown over from South Africa for my sister's funeral and did not contact me. She later apologised and said that the family forbade her to tell me. Yet an announcement in the local newspaper was there for all to see. I was grateful that Monica had told me. Hard as that was it was better than learning it from the obituaries column.

After leaving Monica I walked to Rusthall parish church to meet the people leaving the Good Friday service. My agnosticism did not prevent me from turning to the local Christian community in my time of anguish and they gave me great support.

I never realised that the death of my sister would have caused me so much distress. It devastated me. What I also found disturbing was the surprise of some people that I should be so upset, since Jane had been extremely unkind to my mother and myself. My response was, 'She was still my sister.' Certainly I despised her behaviour but loved her. (It is difficult for some individuals to realise that 'love' and 'like' are not synonymous.) Maybe the intense pain of my loss was because I was also grieving for my twin sister for whom I had never previously mourned. I could have done with her when Mum died and also with the death of our younger sister.

Even *in extremis,* Jane had spurned me. No reconciliation was possible now. That exacerbated my grief. Yet, in another way, I thought myself liberated. I had a ceremonial bonfire and burned all the letters and similar which reminded me of years of pain. It was not such a quick solution as I'd hoped. Was one possible?

Knowing that I'd be unwelcome at my sister's funeral, Bob Whyte, the vicar, and Joyce, the assistant curate, arranged for a requiem to be held in one of the chapels in the parish church. They felt that I needed a ritual and were of course correct. Unlike the very public and joyful thanksgiving service for my mother, this was a very intimate, loving and quiet gathering, with an emphasis on healing and reconciliation. Although steadfast in my agnosticism I found it a very positive experience. It was a beautiful spring morning and I felt truly 'enfolded in love'. I was and remain, profoundly thankful for my friends.

During the course of my life I have been amazed at the number of books which have come into my possession just when I have needed them. Some have been unsolicited gifts from friends, others have just turned up. One that turned up in 'my' hospice shop was a book I'd read years earlier from the local library. It was *Healing the Family Tree* by a consultant psychiatrist, Dr Kenneth McAll.[3] At the time I did not know why I bought it. Dr McAll mentioned that the emotions of the parents can be 'remembered' by a foetus as young as fourteen weeks, and he related case histories that showed how this can adversely affect the individual's mental health well into adulthood. Suddenly light dawned. In her later years my mother was honest enough to admit to me that when she became pregnant with my sister she was desperate not to have another baby. One could not blame her too harshly for this – she was nearly forty and my father was away at sea. The Second World War was near its end but it was still a hard time for everyone. Suddenly my sister's constant, but apparently grossly unjustified, assertion that her family rejected her, made sense. Perhaps too it explained her many liaisons with men. Once born she was most certainly never rejected – indeed perhaps my mother over-compensated – but it was the impersonal unseen early foetus that had been. This realisation has not removed the pain that Jane caused herself and the rest of us, but it has helped to explain it, and confirmed what I had always known, that Jane did not reject me because I was transsexual. It remains a great personal sadness that healing and reconciliation could not have taken place between my mother and Jane on this side of the grave.

In 1998 I lost my council seat – as did nearly all my Liberal Democrat colleagues. I decided that if only 10% of the electorate bothered to vote for me then perhaps my efforts had not been appreciated overmuch and I would welcome a break. At least my seat was lost because I was the 'wrong' party, not because I was transsexual. I had found being a councillor interesting, frustrating, enjoyable, tiring, stimulating and hard work. It was a relief to get away from party politics. That was an aspect I hated. I am not sure that I would want to do it again but was very glad and honoured to have had the experience.

---

[3] McAll, K *Healing the Family Tree* Sheldon 1990 p47

Chapter thirty-one

The Tide Turns

AS one officially unemployed, it was very easy to feel (as my sister once described me) a social parasite and of little worth. Yet, with my charity fund raising, talks to the Samaritans, voluntary tutoring and work as a borough councillor, I felt that my contribution to society was as great as most people who were in paid work. Of course it was embarrassing and demoralising to be reliant on Income Support and I abhorred it, but was doing my best. By then in my late fifties, it seemed very unlikely that I would ever gain paid work. Officialdom, in the form of the Jobcentre, took little account of all that I was doing in the community and the pressure to find remunerative employment was relentless. Again I was experiencing a strange kind of multiple existence: the freak to be abused, the respected councillor, the patient volunteer tutor and the unemployed idler in the dole queue. Of course we all have several roles but mine were so disparate that I was almost in separate pieces rather than composed of different facets of the same person.

The stress was affecting me physically. Stomach upsets were familiar and also I developed alopaecia, which the consultant dermatologist said had no physical cause; it was clearly stress-related. Negative stress (we need a certain amount of 'ordinary' stress) is like a spiral – the stress causes stress-related symptoms, so one then worries about these symptoms and so up goes the stress level still further. My GP sent me for a course of six sessions with the practice counsellor and psychotherapist. She was very pleasant and professional but there was not much she could do. All I was asking for was a paid job which would use my talents and education and where I could find congenial company. My mental energy was running down.

Not long after I lost my council seat the Jobcentre sent me after a vacancy at a shop that sold jeans and working clothes. As instructed I went there and asked for an application form. It was a dreary place with pop music hammering out in the background. That alone would have driven me insane. The glum young man to whom I'd spoken went behind a black curtain on a piece of wire at the back of the shop and returned with a form,

' 'ere are, mate.'

When reading the form I sank into even greater gloom. There wasn't even space for further, let alone higher education qualifications, but then I decided to play the game and answer all the questions honestly, 'Why have you applied for this job?'

'Because I was instructed to do so by the Jobcentre.' I stuffed in every qualification I had gained and under 'Interests' wrote, 'Madrigal singing and Ecclesiastical History.' I was reasonably certain that they'd not want to employ such a 'boring old fart' as they might have privately referred to me. It was therefore an awful shock when I was invited for interview. 'We were interested in your application form.'

It was bad in every way. I'd probably not survive working there for longer than an hour. Memories of previous miserable jobs came back, but what made this worse was that I was no longer young with hopes of moving on to better things. In addition, I would have to give up my voluntary tutoring at the Adult Education Centre where my talents were being used and I was helping people. That was my raison d'etre and the thought of losing it was unbearable.

I walked the two miles to the shop for my interview, hoping that the exercise might lessen my stress. This was surely my nadir. When I reached the shop and was told that the manager had had to go elsewhere, I was both relieved and angry.

'I am sorry that he did not see fit to telephone me.' I said and walked off, praying that was the end of the matter. But would it be? What next? I felt almost suicidal.

Some months earlier, Julie Hudson, the senior tutor in Basic Skills at the Adult Education Centre, had told me to contact Glenys Lake, her counterpart at the local college of further education. I went to see Glenys, liked her very much and immediately felt at home in the environment. Glenys said she would keep me in mind. It became my ambition to work there, but by now had almost given up. Nearly a year later, when I was at the Adult Education Centre working with some students, Julie came into the room,

'I'm glad you're here, Mark. Ring Glenys now. Use the 'phone in my office.'

Immediately after the morning session was over I hastened to the nearby FE college and saw Glenys. She expected me to start work the following Tuesday.

'By the way,' she asked, 'We want people to hold the initial certificate in Basic Skills.'

'I've got it,' I said. My time studying for that had not been wasted after all.

Was I dreaming? I was going to be paid for doing the work I found so worthwhile. Not surprisingly I was in a state of total disbelief. Would I wake up and find myself queuing at the Jobcentre and being sent for some other demoralising and unbearable job?

It was not a dream. From the moment I walked into the West Kent College Study Centre on 5th October 1999 I felt that I belonged there. The combination of work I enjoyed, friendly and helpful colleagues and a very caring boss exceeded my wildest hopes. By now it was just over twenty years since I had gained my degree and left Canterbury, certain that there was a vocation awaiting me. It had been a very long wait for paid employment, 'commensurate with my abilities'. Nonetheless, perhaps some of what I had been doing during those dark years was vocational, albeit unsalaried. I had considered my council work as vocational and what about the talks I'd given to Samaritans and similar, the articles, broadcasts and the publication of my book which had undoubtedly helped people? It had certainly not been my ambition to be a 'professional' transsexual person but perhaps for a while it had been my calling.

My new employment was part-time and that suited me because the salary I received was sufficient for my immediate needs. After all, I was well used to living on a very small income. It also gave me time to do other things, such as writing and giving talks. If it were possible in our economy for everyone to work part-time then I am certain that society would be better balanced and happier than it is at present. Almost overnight my life had changed and I was happier than I'd been for a very long time.

I felt safe at college, safe from the verbal abuse that was directed at me elsewhere.

A few of my colleagues might have been aware of my situation, but it did not worry me. They were professional people and had matters other than my medical history to occupy their minds. Later I became aware that some knew but that was no problem to me, indeed it was to my advantage. Some years after I had begun work there, when about to enter our building, I thought I'd heard the familiar cry of 'Gay Gordon'. I told myself not to be so super-sensitive. The students were always noisy. Later that evening near my home, I heard it again and knew that it had not been my imagination. One of the offender's companions told me that 'M' had seen me at college.

For a moment I was horrified, my safe place was gone. Then I decided that no stupid student was going to ruin what had been so valuable to me – my job and peace of mind. By now Glenys had left, but her successor, Anna, who had previously been one of my staff room colleagues, was informed and was very concerned. With the help of the college computer we identified the culprit, a boy who lived in Rusthall. Had he not shouted at me again that evening he might have remained unidentified. The Head of Faculty said that she was not going to have her staff treated like this and would be able to expel the boy but I asked her not to do so on my account. As an excluded school pupil now being given a chance at college he would not get any better if he were again expelled. All I desired was that he made a personal apology to me. After his admonition from the Head of Faculty, this very embarrassed and unusually tongue-tied boy apologised and we shook hands. It was with sadness that I heard later that he'd again misbehaved and was no longer in college. For me it was a positive experience, insofar that I was certain that in any similar circumstance I would have my colleagues' support.

Many of my transsexual colleagues were very worried that the police check, necessary for those who work with young and vulnerable people, would mean that their places of work would find out about their transition. The support groups, Press for Change in particular, negotiated with the authorities and special provisions were made so that the mandatory checks could be carried out without any work colleagues being made aware of the individual's status. When my CRB check was due I just went to the Personnel Office with my birth certificate and change of name deed and no one turned a hair. Not for the first time I found that being open made life much easier. How could I have coped with the abusive student otherwise?

Some time later I learned from the local police Diversity Officer, that there had been a student, potentially female to male transsexual, at the College who had left because her student colleagues had made her life hell. Recalling my days at the art school I could understand that, but was very sad that rather than speak to the counsellor or chaplain, the girl concerned gave up her course. Either of them would have contacted me and I could have helped her with contacts for specialist advice.

My college job was a very major factor in improving my quality of life in many ways. Yet I was still alone, but in that respect too life had undergone an immense change for the better. I was adopted by a large but skinny black and white stray cat. It had never been my intention to have another animal and it was a matter of pride to me that I would cope alone and not be one of those people who cannot bear to be without their substitute children/partners et al, in other words, their pampered pets. This stray was well known to the neighbours and had probably been through every cat-flap in the road. I decided to feed this nervous and hungry cat but only outside the back door. Patch decided otherwise and persuaded me to let him move in. It was one of the best decisions I'd ever made because he transformed my life for the better and I did likewise for him. For the ten years since the death of my mother I had hated going home, especially after being with friends, to my cold and empty house. It was purely a place of shelter, for which I was of course thankful, but little more. Now there was someone to greet me, even if that 'someone' were non-human. I had responsibility for a living creature and that, I hope, made me less self-centred. Patch turned out to be a very affectionate and good-natured cat: we developed a strong bond and he developed a large girth. It also meant that I had physical contact with another living creature, something that I believe most humans need. (As I write this Patch is purring on my lap, a feline service enjoyed by many writers.) One GP had told me that cats lower one's blood pressure (except when they are being sick on the best carpet) and that was a cat skill that I was to appreciate greatly.

Patch

As for nearly every year since 1986, I spent Christmas 2000 with Sue, James and family in Derbyshire. As I was packing to return home, suddenly a strange and unsettling feeling came over me. I found myself wondering if I would see my friends again. Was something dreadful going to happen? I was soon to find out.

Chapter thirty-two

A Dreadful Fright

'TELL him I'll look after his cat!'

It was Tina, my next door neighbour, calling to the paramedics. She had heard the siren and came out of her house when she saw the ambulance stop at my gates.

Was this a nightmare? If so, I wanted to wake up and find myself getting ready to go to work. Regrettably it was no dream. I had woken up very early that January morning in 2001 and wondered if I'd got 'flu' because I was aching, then realised that this was limited to my upper half. When the local medical centre opened I rang them and to my dismay the doctor said he was sending an ambulance.

Upon my arrival at the Kent & Sussex Hospital, there was the inevitable question,

'Next of kin?'

What could I say? Although I had experienced only slight physical discomfort, this question was psychologically painful, a stark reminder that I was not first in anyone's life. There was little point in mentioning my aunt, who was many miles away, and unbeknown to me at the time, was herself in hospital. Even if I'd known where my sister's children lived they would not have wanted to be known as my relatives and would have refused contact.

'Well,' said the A&E clerk kindly, 'Is there anyone nearby, a neighbour perhaps?'

I hoped Tina wouldn't mind as I gave her name, after all she had a key to my house and telephone numbers of close friends.

It took lab tests for the hospital to be certain that I had actually had a mild heart attack and was then admitted for a week. It was indicative of Glenys' concern for her staff that she was at the hospital early the following morning, eager to assure me that I must not worry about the work and I would get full pay for six weeks. Other members of college staff visited me too and the Study Centre sent a hamper that also included food for Patch. Tina was as good as her word and not only looked after Patch but also kept an eye on the house, contacted friends for me, brought in clean clothes (thank goodness I kept my chest of drawers tidy) and drove me home after discharge.

Perhaps my discharge was the hardest part of that week. During most of my hospital stay I was in a side ward because I was up and dressed and did not need to be under constant observation, so as during my previous hospital stays, I 'held court' for my visitors. It was a delight to see so many friends and neighbours. All that cushioned the blow of what had happened.

Yet, when Tina left my house after bringing me home, I sat on the stairs and wept. Although I knew that she was next door and other neighbours were equally accessible, I felt very alone and very frightened. What had happened? Why had it happened? What was likely to happen? Strange as it may seem for someone of my age, I wished my mother had been with me. Perhaps she was in spirit but I had no sense of anyone's presence. There had admittedly been a warning some time earlier when mild angina was diagnosed. I attributed it to the stress I'd been under and decided that all would be well now that I was happily settled in a job. One of the cardiac nurses told me that they often had patients who'd been under stress for ages but had their hearts attacks once the pressure had been removed.

The hospital had sent me home with drugs and a glycerol trinitrate spray to use if I had an angina attack. As I unpacked and put it on my bedside table, something told me that I'd not need it. Over seven years later I have not needed it but was not to know that at the time. I was in a constant state of fear – made worse by spending so much time alone. Over those few first weeks I was given much support by friends and neighbours which was greatly valued. Many people called, including one of my former fellow councillors. She came bearing home-produced honey and new laid eggs from her chickens. Inevitably visits grew fewer as time passed which is to be expected but must be very difficult for those with chronic illness.

It was a mercy to get back to work. Glenys was typically solicitous and rather concerned that the work had contributed to my heart attack. I assured her that the damage had been done long before I began my employment with the college.

What had caused me anguish was not any physical pain; that I had been spared, but the shock of the event. Everyone was amazed that this had happened to me because I was far from overweight, a non-smoker, a keen walker and cyclist, and a vegetarian. The cardiac nurses said that there was no advice they could give me about lifestyle.

Until this happened to me, I had never realised the profound psychological effect a physical illness could have on one. I experienced inexplicable physical symptoms that made me feel so unwell that one day Glenys sent me home from work and a colleague took me straight to my doctor. After an ECG I was assured that the symptoms were nothing to do with my heart or the drugs that I was taking. Nonetheless they persisted and I was very disappointed to have to cancel a trip to Peterborough to address the Samaritans. With a certain amount of trepidation I was able to get to the King's Lynn and the Ashford (Kent) Samaritans some months later. I was fine once 'on stage' but suffered general anxiety about travelling and being taken ill, whether from my mystery symptoms or from another heart attack.

Months later a trainee GP, Dr Mark Bridle, diagnosed that these symptoms were due to post-traumatic stress and suggested I see a counsellor. It was an immense relief to have the problem recognised. Interestingly, after his diagnosis these symptoms recurred very little. I was immensely grateful to the young doctor. Fortunately I was able to see Vera, the college counsellor, and it was very helpful to talk things through with her. Whatever the state of my heart, my confidence had been shattered and I found myself very anxious about doing things which had previously never bothered me, like getting back on my bicycle and even travelling on a train.

Six months after my heart attack I attended St Thomas' Hospital, London for an angiogram. It was not a painful experience although I was scared stiff. Before I had even been wheeled from the theatre the cardiologist told me that my heart was in a very bad state and I required bypass surgery. The shock of having a heart attack was nothing compared with this and it was little wonder that I became even more anxious than before.

After the cardiologist had made his announcement I felt very cold and began to shake uncontrollably. I was utterly terrified. This was the worst thing he could have told me. How could this have been so? Hadn't I lived an exemplary 'heart-friendly' life?

In the view of the cardiologist, this state of affairs had been brought about by years of testosterone therapy. The prospect of surgery was bad enough but this statement just added to my distressed state. Had I unknowingly caused this disease myself? Should I have undergone the hormone treatment? I knew that it made one more likely to suffer from cardiovascular problems but believed that I could escape it by being sensible in lifestyle and diet. But could I have gone on living in my former role and remained sane? I could not. Nonetheless the cardiologist's words greatly troubled me.

For some years I had been seeing a consultant endocrinologist, Dr Andrew Gorsuch, on an annual basis in order to keep a check on my hormone treatment. He was very sympathetic to the lot of transsexual people and I liked him as a person, especially as we shared a love of choral singing. I contacted him and his response was that without hormone treatment I would have been more, not less, prone to cardiovascular disease. Dr Gorsuch said that eunuchs had a higher rate of heart problems than others. Although my extreme anxiety about possible surgery remained, at least the burden of believing that I had, in effect, caused my own illness, was lifted.

It was my firmly held belief that the years of stress caused by my unemployment was a major contributing factor, and this view was supported by several medical friends. In time I saw an increasing amount of literature that linked extreme stress with illness, including heart disease. One medical friend, Marlene, who was an eminent specialist in the field of stress-related disorders, was unequivocal that this was so but also agreed that conversely, positive thinking could maintain health and assist healing. 'A cheerful heart is a good medicine but a downcast spirit dries up the bones.'[4] I was determined to make myself better. This aim was greatly helped by friends who cut out articles on relevant topics for me. One gave me a piece about the benefit to the heart of being happy. Another told

---

[4] Proverbs Chapter 17 v4

me of someone known personally to her who had been told that he must have a heart and lung transplant. He declined surgery and fifteen years later was still going strong. I realised that healing is not the monopoly of the medical profession.

Yet the prospect of surgery still hung over me. It was one of the worst summers I had ever had. I could hardly think of anything else. My friends were very supportive but no one could go through this with me. Alan, my newly transitioned transsexual friend and former nurse, accompanied me to St Thomas' Hospital in October 2001 to see the cardiac surgeon.

Perhaps I should have been very upset when the surgeon told me that my heart was in such a bad condition that he was unhappy about operating but I was so overcome with relief that surgery was not going to take place that the bad news was overcome. I saw the surgeon again eight months later and he reiterated that it was too risky just to gain perhaps a year of life – if I survived the operation. On this occasion I had a clergywoman friend with me. As we left the surgeon's room she put an arm around my shoulders and said,

'Now start living again!'

She was right. That I was determined to do.

Chapter thirty-three

A Price worth Paying?

WHATEVER the cause of my heart attack, it was a reminder that our gender reassignment treatment does have risks, as indeed does everything else in life.

There was concern at the beginning of my hormone therapy that the methyl testosterone prescribed could cause damage to the liver. It had been remarkably effective in causing relatively rapid development of secondary male characteristics but the risk was deemed too great and so this medication was discontinued. For some time no hormone replacement was prescribed and to my dismay I lost my red chest hairs. I was much relieved not to have also lost my red beard.

Later I was prescribed Restandol, capsules that, perhaps appropriately since they contained male hormone, looked like tiny rugby balls, and had to be taken several times a day. As far as I was concerned, they were inferior to the methyl testosterone because my red chest hairs did not re-grow. I had to be content with fewer hairs and ordinary brown ones.

Many of my female-to-male colleagues were receiving their hormone dosage by intramuscular injections, 250mgm about every three weeks, and found it more effective in developing and maintaining masculine characteristics, and less tiresome than taking tablets daily. I understood that injections were less risky as far as the liver was concerned. Some people had adverse reactions to this, not with the actual testosterone, but with the oily medium in which it was contained. I began with injections of Primoteston then moved on to Sustanon, solely because it was cheaper than the former. Never one keen on medication, especially when it meant sometimes painful injections into the buttocks, I had them as seldom as possible. This was not very helpful because then I found myself becoming a bit lethargic and mildly depressed. People were beginning to remark that I didn't look very robust. A change to monthly administration improved the situation and I felt much better.

Once under the care of Dr Gorsuch, I was made aware of the necessity of keeping testosterone at an optimum level because otherwise one would be in a similar hormonal situation to that of a post-menopausal woman and thus equally prone to osteoporosis. The doctor was initially quite concerned because scans showed my bone density level was verging on the low but that has been much improved with monitored testosterone replacement therapy and prescribed calcium supplements. I realised that the somewhat haphazard hormone therapy of my early years had put me at risk but at least I was more fortunate than some of my female-to-male colleagues who did not have adequate advice and carefully monitored hormone therapy and subsequently developed osteoporosis.

Within the last few years I have begun to experience stiffness and aching for a couple of weeks following the monthly injections. Initially I wondered if it were a side-effect of the drugs prescribed to me after my heart attack, but then noted that it occurred only after the injection. If I missed an injection there were no such symptoms. After discussion with the very helpful local pharmacist, my GP, Mike Lawes, and Dr Gorsuch, I was able to change to a preparation only recently available, Testogel. This has to be applied daily to the skin of the upper arms and shoulders. I was faintly amused by Dr Gorsuch's warning '…to avoid administering testosterone surreptitiously to females with whom you might have contact.' Of course he had to mention it, but knew me well enough to be aware that the chances of my skin touching that of a female were very remote. It was a bit like the warning I'd had from St Thomas' Hospital after my heart attack to 'go easy on the sex!'

Testogel was greatly welcomed by female-to-males, especially those of us who had been suffering tender backsides for many years. One of my colleagues said that he regarded it as his daily anointing, which I thought was a good way to describe it, although few of us were destined for kingship. At the time of writing, this preparation is very expensive which is why I suffered the injection-induced aching for longer than I need have done. I was very loath to cost the NHS more than necessary but life became so uncomfortable that this concern was overcome. Dr Gorsuch told me that as similar preparations come onto the market the price will reduce. It would probably cost a great deal more to treat one for osteoporosis.

Several years earlier I had developed an irritating vulval skin condition. Although it was causing discomfort I delayed seeing my GP because the thought of the inevitable physical examination appalled me. In spite of my assertion that a penis does not make a man I am also painfully aware of my female anatomy. Mike, my GP, was extremely sympathetic and tactful, knowing that my mental discomfort was far greater than the physical.

We wondered if the long-term androgen therapy might have been a causative factor but current specialist medical opinion did not confirm it. Mike was concerned lest it might be pre-cancerous, and referred me to a gynaecologist. It seemed ironic that the part of my body I hated was potentially dangerous and could literally be the death of me.

The gynaecologist, Mr G, was one of the most caring medical men I have ever met. He arranged to see me away from his clinic to spare me embarrassment. So often the transsexual has to cope, not only with his/her condition *per se*, but also with the social problems which it engenders. Mr G had relieved me of that, plus the anxiety about the condition, which he diagnosed as lichen sclerosis. Although permanent, it was non-malignant, which of course was a tremendous relief.

I discover later that other female-to-males had suffered similarly, then read in one of our journals that it was possibly due to the fact that because we'd had 'menopauses' as a result of our treatment, our genitalia were prematurely aged. This seemed to make sense. Dr Gorsuch prescribed some oestrogen cream, which, he assured me, would not feminise me and he was right. Gradually the problem eased and on reflection I realise that it did so after I returned to regular testosterone therapy. The condition was most troublesome when the dosage was low. It has not now been a problem for several years. The situation was ultimately probably a hormonal one.

There is, understandably and rightly, a great deal of emphasis on adequate psychological assessment before transsexual people commence hormonal and surgical treatment. I have been very fortunate in finding an endocrinologist who has been willing to take on transsexual people and monitor their progress. It is to be hoped that this important aspect of care can also be available to all those who undergo gender reassignment.

Some years after my earlier investigations regarding the possibility of a phalloplasty, Mike referred me to a surgeon who was well known and respected in the transsexual community for his skill in the field of gender reassignment. I saw Mr R in August 1996, a few months after publication of the first edition of this book.

My consultation was brief. As soon as he saw the lichen sclerosis Mr. R declared that he would not want to operate because the site would then be hidden and he felt it necessary to keep an eye on it. It was clear that he too feared it could be pre-cancerous. (At that time I had not heard of the aforementioned 'aging' theory.) That it seemed, was that. After my heart attack I realised that even were a surgeon able to use a procedure that would remove the offending tissue, the chances of undergoing phalloplasty surgery were nil.

As before I tried to philosophise my way out of the disappointment. There was of course no doubt that such surgery could be very painful and risky, both in terms of possible complications and aesthetic results. Perhaps it was because now I had to accept that I'd always be 'incomplete', that it occupied my mind more than previously. This was also accentuated because three of my female-to-male friends had opted to undergo such surgery. Additionally, with the otherwise very welcome advent of my college job, I had to use a communal toilet more than before. When at home alone, it did not worry me overmuch, but even now I still worry lest my male colleagues think it very strange that I always use a cubicle.

Another factor is our increasingly sex-obsessed modern climate. Things not previously mentioned are now talked about quite openly. I do not object to serious medical documentaries and articles but constant, often flippant, references to the male genitalia especially in the media, only serve to remind those lacking such equipment of their deficiencies.

The other, non-medical price I have paid for being transsexual, has been the years of, mostly verbal, abuse which I have experienced from local young people. Regrettable as it has been, I was receiving that years before I changed roles so it was not the result of reassignment treatment. At the time of writing that situation has been greatly improved and abuse is far less. Whether it is because the children have become bored with it or because I have reported incidents to the local police community diversity officer, I don't know, but the reduced number of such incidents has been a very welcome relief.

Yet, given all these challenges, never once have I regretted my gender reassignment procedure. No, I am not a perfect male (if there is such a creature) but at least I have been enabled to live rather than exist. The price has been well worth paying.

Chapter thirty-four

Pressing for Change

SOON after our meeting with Alex Carlile in 1992, a small group of Press for Change (PFC) activists gathered at a flat in Hackney and spent the whole weekend signing letters and addressing them to every MP in the new House of Commons. It was quite a daunting task addressing and signing over 500 letters.

The 1992 election was over and the Conservative Government had been returned to power. We wanted to be seen as apolitical but most PFC campaigners admitted that this result was a disappointment. Certainly there were some Tory MPs who were sympathetic to our cause but whatever our individual party allegiances, it was generally felt that there would be a greater chance of getting a change in the law under a Labour administration.

Nonetheless we had a lot of work to do if we wanted to gain support from both Parliament and the British people. Few MPs would want to vote for legislation that had no support from the voters. I had always perceived the campaign as one of water on stone, a slow and gentle attrition of the resistance. We would get there. Some members of our community, understandably perhaps, were quite belligerent, wanting immediate change, but my view was that it was more productive to be patient and always polite. The seemingly awkward civil servants and politicians were, in the main, not 'enemies'. It was just that many of them were bound by rules and woefully ignorant of our situation, as was the general public. With the exception of a very few people who were determined to remain bigots, our only 'enemy' was ignorance, which we would gradually overcome. We were to find that we had many potential friends, both in Parliament and outside. It was a source of great pride to see PFC become an organisation that was respected by those with whom it dealt because of its professionalism and courtesy.

Whilst some people wanted change immediately, the wiser

members of our community realised that good legislation was not made in a rush. Frustrating as it might have seemed there was now opportunity to prepare the ground carefully. PFC spent the period between 1992 and the election of a Labour Government in 1997 very fruitfully. With the advent of the internet small organisations like PFC were able to communicate with many people in a way hitherto impossible. It was soon gaining much support from members of the transsexual community and also giving them a chance to contribute to the campaign in many ways. No longer did they feel isolated in their efforts as I had done twenty years earlier.

Other PFC campaigners took up my idea of fringe meetings at party conferences so we thus made ourselves known to all three major parties and elicited support from other MPs. One of these was Labour Member, Dr Lynne Jones, who, together with Alex Carlile, set up an all-party Parliamentary Forum on Transsexualism in 1994. They were joined later by Conservative MP, Roger Sims, who was recruited to the cause at the 1995 Conservative Conference fringe meeting, by leading PFC campaigners, Stephen Whittle and Christine Burns. Alex was elevated to the House of Lords and Roger Sims retired from the Commons in May 1997 leaving Lynne as the sole chairman of the Forum. The Forum consisted not only of MPs but also medical specialists, lawyers and activists. At the time of writing, both the Forum and the PFC are still functioning. It is clear from the Forum's concerns that the Gender Recognition Act, while a great milestone in the life of the transsexual community, did not solve every problem. There remain many t's to be crossed and i's to be dotted.

Thanks largely to the effort of the Parliamentary Forum and PFC, an Interdepartmental Working Group (IWG) was established in 1999 by then Home Secretary, Jack Straw, to examine the legal status of transsexual people and recommend possible provisions which should be made to alleviate the situation. There were other cumulative factors that possibly contributed to this action; recent cases at the European Court of Human Rights indicated that the Court was losing sympathy with the Government, and the contemporary story in the soap opera *Coronation Street*, regarding the transsexual character, Hayley had evoked considerable public interest and sympathy.

The IWG consisted of representatives of twelve Government departments and deliberated for a year. To its credit it also met members of the transsexual community before completion of its task. Its Report was published in the spring of 2000 and this was to contribute greatly to the development of the subsequent legislation. I reflected on the letters received from the Home Office twenty or more years earlier which told me that a change of registration would not be acceptable because it would enable us to deceive others as to our 'true sex'. By contrast my PFC colleagues, some of whom were legally trained, formed good relationships with the Government officials, to the benefit of all.

One of my other ideas was to gain the patronage of respected people, so that we could have their names on our notepaper. In time we would be able to stand alone, but initially someone like an MP might take seriously a letter from an organisation which had the support of reputable people. I wrote to potential patrons and most of them agreed to give nominal support. One of these was Archbishop Desmond Tutu. That gave me great delight. It has always been my ambition to see Archbishop Tutu in person but that is unlikely. He is certainly a man who is the embodiment of what Christianity should be.

Another way of raising further awareness was a letter to the *Times*. Alex thought it a good idea so I drafted one, which he used as its basis. It was certainly not my intention to sign it – who in the Establishment had heard of Mark Rees? I made considerable efforts to obtain notable signatories: Members of Parliament, eminent medical specialists, senior clergy and academics, but the *Times* declined to publish so many names. They were however willing to do so with just three names, which were of three MPs, Alex (Liberal Democrat) Jerry Hayes (Conservative) and Lynne Jones (Labour). It was published on Friday 8th October 1993. I was sorry that my efforts to gain other signatories were apparently wasted but at least it was another few drips on the stone. For all I know, my letters to the other signatories may have borne fruit elsewhere. One cannot assume that because no benefits are obvious that there are none.

In his Preface to the first edition of this book Alex (now Lord) Carlile QC, stated his intention of getting a Private Member's Bill (PMB) before Parliament. He kept his word and at the earliest opportunity entered the ballot for his PMB to be debated. Usually Members have a very long wait before they are successful but Alex's 'Gender Identity (Registration and Civil Status) Bill' came before the House of Commons on 2nd February 1996. Some of us were in a room in the building near the Commons' chamber and listened to the debate. I was rather surprised – and pleased – to hear Alex mention this book. (*Hansard* – 2 February 1996 col. 1284.)

Yet as is often the way with Private Member's Bills, it was talked out. Alex was experienced enough to know that the chances of it becoming law were not very great but I was sorry that all his effort had seemingly been wasted.

There was, however, a very positive and important result from this apparent failure. For the very first time many transsexual people had been motivated to take action. Prior to the reading of the Bill, they, their families and friends, had raised the matter with their MPs. Largely encouraged by PFC, the community was beginning to come out of hiding and discover that it had a voice. Never before had so many MPs been made aware of the problems we faced. They took up the baton and put pressure on the Government in different ways such as putting forward Early Day Motions and presenting Written Questions.

My prediction, made after my unsuccessful appeal to the ECHR in 1986, that others would follow me to Strasbourg, was beginning to be realised. The trickle of appellants to that court and others, both European and domestic, developed into a steady flow. This was especially so in the 1990s, with PFC encouraging transsexual people to take action whenever possible. The case of *P v S and Cornwall County Council* was heard before the European Court of Justice in 1996. In its judgment the court declared unlawful the dismissal of people from employment on the grounds of their transsexual condition. This declaration was formally incorporated into law in April 1999 as 'The Sex Discrimination (Gender Reassignment) Regulations'. At last employers were no longer able to sack employees purely on the grounds of their transsexual status. Although it was to be a few more years before we were given full legal recognition, this was a very welcome move forward. The refusal of a Health Authority to sanction gender reassignment treatment of transsexual people was successfully challenged in the courts and upheld on Appeal. Others took action over pension rights of partners.

It is sometimes the case that those who initiate projects are not the people who then run them. This was certainly so with PFC. Although the original initiator of the group, I soon realised that others had the administrative and legal skills which I certainly lacked. At the beginning I was also disadvantaged by not having a computer. Technology and expertise overtook my amateur efforts, added to which I was geographically distant from what had become the hub of PFC in Manchester. After twenty-five years of almost lone campaigning I had lost much of my drive and also felt very strongly that there was much more that I wanted to do in life rather than spend much of it in the campaign. Eventually I resigned from PFC.

Nonetheless I answered a plea made by PFC for as many people as possible to take legal action and thus help to build up pressure for legal change. Initially my intention was to apply for leave for a judicial review of the decision made by the Office of Population Censuses and Surveys not to change my birth certificate. We won leave to appeal but the Government solicitor wrote to my then lawyer, Madeleine Rees, stating that they regarded my application as 'unnecessary and wasteful' and would apply for a wasted costs order. After discussion with Maddie, I decided not to risk incurring costs and withdrew. We had already decided to seek a judicial review against the DSS because they would not recognise my male status.

All this dragged on for a couple of years, during which time my local 'rag', *The Courier,* got hold of the story which was reported in what I saw as a negative way: 'The move follows the green light being given to transsexuals to use tax-payers' money.' '...backed by public cash...' and so on. This kind of slant completely ignored the fact that transsexual *people* are tax-payers too. It was indicative of the kind of reporting that objectifies certain groups, such as the unemployed, single mothers, asylum seekers and, in this instance, those who are transsexual. 'Objects' are not people, therefore can been abused. At its worst extreme, depriving individuals of their personhood, has led to some of the worst atrocities ever devised by humankind. Jews, gypsies, the disabled and homosexuals were depersonalised by the Nazis and eliminated. Those 'homosexuals' included transsexual people. Our fellow sufferers also went to the gas chambers.

In 1997 Tony Blair moved into Downing Street and Britain had a Labour government. We were confident that things would improve for us, although not immediately. Regarding my appeals Maddie suggested we wait '…and see what the new Government is going to do…' In the meantime she was involved in other transsexual cases and acted for *P* in the aforementioned successful *P vs S and Cornwall County Council* case. Tragically, this very caring and bright young lawyer died very suddenly in April 2002. We, and many other marginalised groups, had lost a very good friend.

The court battles continued into the new millennium. Eventually the legal victory we had so long sought came about. In July 2002, sixteen years after my Appeal to the European Court of Human Rights, (*Rees v UK 1986*) the Strasbourg judges ruled *unanimously* in the case brought by another transsexual person, Christine Goodwin, that the UK had breached Articles 8 and 12 of the European Convention. These were the same Articles under which my case was heard. After a succession of similar cases brought against the UK Government, the Court of Human Rights had clearly lost patience. Something now had to be done. After a couple of years 'on hold' the Interdepartmental Working party was reconvened and after much discussion and hard work with Press for Change and other concerned groups the draft Gender Recognition Bill was introduced in July 2003.

We were nearly there.

Chapter thirty-five

Unholy Opposition

IMMEDIATELY after the successful and aptly named *Goodwin* case I was once more contacted by the BBC. Clearly they expected me to be euphoric but I was not. After thirty years of campaigning it seemed unreal. Besides, for me, it was too late. It was the refusal of the Church of England to consider me for ordination because I was legally a woman, which had driven me to Strasbourg. The chances of my following that calling at the age of nearly sixty seemed very remote and marriage was equally unlikely. As an ageing transsexual person of very limited means and with poor cardiac prognosis, it was unrealistic to hope that anyone would want to share my life.

My personal disappointments apart, I still felt it necessary to liaise with the Church of England at least, on behalf of transsexual people. Although my earlier efforts to promote some sympathetic interest from the various dioceses had not been very productive, in 1996 I wrote a booklet about transsexualism for members of the Church. Fiona, who now held a very responsible position within the Church, worked through the draft with me in St-Martin-in-the-Fields' cafeteria one afternoon and made some very helpful suggestions. I revised the text accordingly.

PFC had published some booklets on aspects of transsexualism: the medical viewpoint, employment etc, and I hoped that they would do likewise with *The Transsexual Person and the Church* but support was not forthcoming. Nonetheless, having received Fiona's *imprimatur,* I sent the document to several eminent church people, including bishops, and the reactions were favourable, so perhaps my time and effort had not been totally wasted.

In November 2000, after much correspondence with the Church of England's Board for Social Responsibility, I was invited to meet the Secretary, David Skidmore, and Michael Scott-Joynt, Bishop of Winchester. I was pleased to have Susan Marshall, a practising Anglican, former naval officer and qualified barrister, with me for this meeting. The Bishop seemed interested to hear what we had to say and we were pleased to know that at long last the Church was willing to have a dialogue with us. The case of the Rev'd Carol, (née Peter) Stone was in the news at the time, and we thought that perhaps we were able to give the Bishop some relevant information. We were assured that there was to be a working party of bishops, chaired by Bishop Michael, which would be examining the issue and ultimately publishing its conclusions. One bishop said he had been glad of my booklet for this purpose.

At least the C of E had invited us to meet them, which is more than can be said for the Evangelical Alliance, which, early in the spring of 2001, published its report *Transsexuality*, which declared that transsexual people were deluded and their lifestyles incompatible with the will of God. They called for the Government not to grant us legal recognition. Press for Change's invitation to the EA to meet us was declined for a couple of years. They refused to name their so-called experts and had little, if any contact with the leading recognised support groups for transsexual people. Their conclusions had no backing from the leading medical experts in the field. It was a thoroughly discreditable effort and a disgrace to the Christian community. Some of my evangelical friends, who were members of the EA, knew nothing of this publication. One of these friends was so incensed that she wrote to them to dissociate herself from their Report but never received a reply. It did seem disgraceful that the EA's members, some of whom were undoubtedly sympathetic to transsexual people, were not made aware of what had been published in their names.

We wondered why the EA had made transsexualism such a major campaign. It was almost an obsession. Weren't there more important issues for them as Christians, to consider? As well as opposing the Gender Recognition Bill they were also against gender reassignment treatment and asserted that the condition could be cured. Since it was unlikely that many transsexual people would want to have anything to do with them and therefore would not 'taint' their gatherings why their concern? On a wider scale, as one of our activists remarked, even if we received legal recognition, the trains would still run. That has proved to be the case, and from my observations, both rolling stock and punctuality have improved.

In July 2003, on BBC Radio 4's *Sunday*, the EA's spokesman, Don Horrocks, referred to transsexual people as deluded, deceivers and idolatrous. He was challenged on the programme by my former vicar, Dr Mark Dalby, scholar and now retired archdeacon. Mark referred to a female-to-male transsexual member of his former congregation who was fully accepted by everyone as male, indeed he could not think of him as anything else. Horrocks' response was that the individual was probably not transsexual. I knew Mark was referring to me, a fact which he later confirmed. Horrocks' ignorance did nothing to disabuse the notion that many transsexual people had that all Christians were bigoted and therefore to be avoided. I just hoped that Mark's compassionate, well-informed and courteous contribution would have assured transsexual people that there are Christians who do accept us.

Regrettably, some clergy and others took the EA Report as authoritative with the result that some transsexual people were treated with less than Christian understanding and left their churches in distress. At the other end of the ecclesiastical spectrum, in early 2003, the Vatican declared that it would not recognise change of gender roles, which it regarded as sinful. Those Catholics who had undergone such would not be permitted to marry in their new roles, or become priests, monks or nuns.

Ironically (or deliberately?) this announcement was made whilst the Lord Chancellor's Department was working hard with representatives of the transsexual community to frame legislation which would be acceptable to all. It seemed that as far as the transsexual person was concerned, often greater love was received from the secular world than from the body that preached it, i.e. the Church. Yet we did have much support from many church people, both ordained and lay. History tells us that it has usually been the bishops (Lords Spiritual) who have opposed compassionate and socially beneficial legislation in Parliament. One has only to look at their efforts to block the reforming acts of the 1830s to see this trait. It is hard to reconcile such attitudes with those of Jesus of Nazareth.

Whilst the Bill received overwhelming support in the Commons (355–46) its passage through the Lords was less smooth. An unholy alliance of Norman Tebbit, Detta O'Cathain of the Christian

Institute and a few bishops of the Church of England, amongst others, did their best to destroy the Bill. O'Cathain described those of us who had taken our cases to the European courts as 'nasty and devious' which prompted a very angry reaction from Alex Carlile who said that he knew me personally. One of the leading episcopal opponents to the Bill was Michael Scott-Joynt, Bishop of Winchester. This was somewhat ironic and disappointing, given that Susan and I had earlier spent some time with him at Church House, carefully explaining our situation. At least, unlike O'Cathain, he was courteous. (When he heard that I had later had a heart attack he sent me personal good wishes which I appreciated) Bishop Scott-Joynt was joined in opposition by the Bishops of Southwell and Chester, but Peter Selby, Bishop of Worcester, supported the Bill.

Some time prior to the parliamentary debate we began to have our doubts about Winchester's understanding when, after our meeting with him, we discovered that he had put his name to the Evangelical Alliance's report on transsexualism. When the Church of England's Bishops' report, *Some Issues in Human Sexuality,* came out in November 2003 we noted that 'transsexualism' was included together with homosexuality, bisexuality and marriage. Yet again it had been categorised as a form of sexuality. This made us angry. When would they wake up to the fact that, in spite of the unfortunate name, it was a condition of identity, not sexual orientation. It included much of the EA's report, but given Winchester's involvement with this also, it should have been no surprise. Probably few Anglican transsexual people took *Some Issues* too seriously. For most transsexual people it would have been totally irrelevant.

In spite of their efforts, the Evangelical Alliance and other Christian fundamentalists lost their fight to destroy the Bill. The Gender Recognition Act received the Royal Assent in July 2004. Yet, they refused to give up gracefully and persisted with their campaign. As a result, in April 2005 a Statutory Instrument was added to the Act. This concerned disclosure of a person's transsexual status for, *inter alia*, legal, medical and religious purposes.

Probably few of us would have been too upset by this provision, given safeguards, for legal and medical purposes. Yet the SI also gave this right to religious bodies to check whether or not a person was transsexual, so that they could refuse to officiate or permit a marriage of such a person, bar from ministry or any other employment, office or post within a church, including religious orders, and even deny church membership to the individual. Additionally this exclusion also enabled churches to decide 'whether the person was eligible to receive or take part in any religious sacrament, ordinance or rite, or take part in any act of worship or prayer, according to the practices of an organised religion'.[5] A licence for intolerance and bigotry had sullied a compassionate piece of legislation.

How would this work in practice? Would a tall, slightly mannish woman in the congregation or a slight short man be surreptitiously checked out? Or would one of the elders approach them directly? In reality, it is unlikely that any informed transsexual person would wish to go near a religious body that was likely to behave in such a way. It was ironic that Jesus broke through the social and religious exclusions of his day but two thousand years later his so-called followers sought legal sanction to maintain them.

In June 2008 I was invited to address a meeting of 'Changing Attitudes' a predominately Anglican group concerned with the treatment of lesbian, gays, bisexual and transgendered people in the church. I read to them an extract from the Statutory Instrument. They had not been aware of it and were shocked and angry to learn of its contents. One lady, a member of General Synod, was considering raising the matter at Synod. They asked how it could have come about. I had assumed that the extremists had been responsible for this appalling measure but promised to make further enquiries. Christine Burns was able to confirm that it was the combined forces of the Christian Institute (Baroness O'Cathain and her friends) and the Evangelical Alliance. She wrote:

'To answer your question, the government was subjected to very determined lobbying by the Christian Institute and Evangelical Alliance – the latter claiming, of course, to represent 1 million Christians. The civil servants showed me a huge trolley containing 10,000 letters that had been sent to the Prime Minister – each saying

---
[5] Statutory Instrument XXX April 2005

how they feared their faith was under threat if they couldn't know if their Church might be marrying a transsexual or (worse still) promoting one to a lay position within their congregations. (These are the same people, of course, who also painted stereotypes of the "you can always tell" variety). The civil servants and ministers were hearing no alternative viewpoint. Church house was silent on the matter; so was Lambeth. So what do you expect? They were already so scared of wrecking the precarious deal they'd got to get the Civil Partnership Bill through (and remember this was to follow the GRA) so they didn't want to rock the boat and appeasement was the order of the day. And you can quote this entire paragraph word for word if you like.

'This is also why we ended up with the awful fudge requiring people to annul an existing marriage for legal recognition. On the bright side, however, the extremists have been given far less of a concession in the exceptions to the goods, services and protection (which came into force in April). The only exceptions there relate to religious premises where they are being used directly for worship. Thus, for instance, a Church bookshop is as obliged to serve trans people as WH Smith.'

It was really little surprise that some transsexual people detested Christians and in particular the bishops. Regrettably they overlooked the fact that some bishops did vote for the Bill and that we had the support of many Christians. In spite of being a thorough agnostic I was greatly saddened by this. Although angered by the unloving and bigoted comments made by people calling themselves Christian, I felt it necessary to defend the Church of England of which I was a cradle member. At the same time I decided to tell the Church that its behaviour was unacceptable. To my surprise and satisfaction, on the 31st July 2004, the *Church Times* published a letter in which I challenged the bishops concerned to apologise for the hurt they had caused us. I also mentioned in passing that I was thinking of organising a service for transsexual people. A fortnight later, one of the *Church Times'* regular contributors, the Rev'd Dr Giles Fraser, mentioned the Gender Recognition Act in his column. He expressed his lack of surprise that the bishops had sought to derail it, '…another indication of how out of touch the Church is with the culture in which it operates…most people in this country now regard the Church of England as a basket case. They are right.' He went on to declare that the portrayal of the transsexual Hayley in *Coronation Street* '…has done more to help in the pastoral care and understanding of transsexual people than those charged with a commitment to the vulnerable.'

I agreed with that but wasn't convinced that 'most people in the country' were bothered enough to regard the Church at all. Of the total population, relatively few were committed members of any church, and of those, even fewer were bothered about the grave moral decline that some thought would result from the GRA. We were, in fact, opposed by a very small but vociferous minority, who thought they had the right to block legislation passed by very large majority in our democratically elected House of Commons.

The print of my letter was hardly dry before I had an invitation to write a piece for the *Modern Churchpeople's Union* newsletter. This I did and described in detail the shameful treatment that some transsexual people had experienced at the hands of the Church. It was, I suspect, preaching to the converted, but nonetheless some may have found it informative.

To my surprise and pleasure, I received a very supportive letter from a clergyman who had been chaplain at the University of Birmingham during my time there. He congratulated me on my 'measured and clear response to people who seem to prefer a fog of offensive language when addressing sexual matters outside the alleged "norm"…It seems…ironic that in a time when science brings important insights…the Church, or at least strident parts of it, seem to flee to naiveté and fundamentalism…'

A less welcome response to my letter was a copy of a 19th century 'hell-fire' tract written by a Bishop Ryle, sent by an anonymous reader but I learned from the *Church Times* itself that this unknown person sent copies to all writers of letters which included the word 'sex'. I was proud to be one of the chosen.

More positively, the vicar of my local parish, Canon Bob Whyte, referred to my *Church Times* letter in a sermon which he preached at Rochester Cathedral the following Sunday. This was, in my opinion, a courageous gesture. It was a timely reminder, not that I personally needed one, that there were many people in the Church who supported us.

A couple of years later, April 2007, Bob announced in the parish magazine that,

'At its last meeting our PCC (Parochial Church Council) unanimously agreed to make St Paul's a church that welcomes gay, lesbian and transsexual people, believing that we need to make explicit our commitment to inclusivity in an atmosphere of growing intolerance.'

As well as his Rochester sermon in 2004 Bob had written to the Lord Chancellor's Department to support the Bill before it reached the Lords for its second reading, as did other members of the parish. The Department probably welcomed these letters, given that they were almost under siege from the fundamentalists.

Following my *Church Times* letter, Linda, the sister of a male-to-female transsexual woman, wrote to me. She was very angry at the way the Church had treated transsexual people and declared that although she considered herself Christian she was no longer able to go to church but added that the service I was thinking of planning might perhaps be a way back for her.

Her moving letter spurred me on. Although classing myself as agnostic, for some unaccountable reason the idea of a service for transsexual people had been in my mind for several years since I'd learned of a lesbian and gay service that had been held at Southwark Cathedral. I had even been to see the Dean of Southwark, Colin Slee, and his deputy, Canon Andrew Nunn. They were sympathetic but wisely suggested somewhere smaller. The cost alone would have been prohibitive. I knew that transsexual people were less numerous and perhaps less open about their situation than the homosexual community. Although numerically, transsexual people could have filled the nave or more, I realised only a small percentage would want to attend. In spite of little success there I was very glad to have met the two clergymen and certainly did not consider my journey wasted. Now, Linda's letter made me realise that such a service was imperative.

One of the problems with my earlier idea was that there was no apparent 'hook' on which to hang such an event but now the passing of the Gender Recognition Act 2004 gave me an excuse. With the same blind faith that had led me to book a room at the

Liberal Democrat Conference over ten years earlier I decided to organise a service in London.

The decision made, I wondered how on earth to achieve it, but was utterly determined that it would work out. I allowed myself nine months for preparation and, as I was to discover, that was only just long enough. Having always been impressed by the attitude of St Martin-in-the-Fields towards the marginalised I made enquiries there. The vicar, Nicholas Holtam, was very willing to host us, but the cost was still much more than I thought it would be possible to raise. I happened to mention my idea to a woman priest whom I had met some years ago through a mutual friend. Clare replied almost immediately,

'You can always use St Anne's if you want somewhere *small*.'

St Anne's Church, Soho, certainly was small but as time went on I realised that we could not expect a large number. There were three main factors that hindered my making the proposed service public: firstly the opposition of such antagonistic groups as the Evangelical Alliance and Christian Institute, secondly, possible prurient media interest and thirdly, the opposition of certain transsexual people themselves. One transsexual individual, thoroughly embittered by the behaviour of certain parts of the Christian community, threatened to demonstrate outside any service. I felt that was a pointless and unkind gesture that might ruin an event that could be of great help to transsexual people and their loved ones, such as Linda. It also ignored the support we had from the Church, both clergy and lay. All this meant that public announcements were too great a risk. I had to rely entirely on emails, letters and word of mouth, to people I knew might be interested.

The first, very enthusiastic, response came from Ruth Howe, a priest I'd met in 1985 during my stay in the Newcastle Royal Infirmary. She said it was a wonderful idea and would certainly attend the service. Almost immediately some people sent generous donations to fund the event and others offered their services. One lady barrister offered her husband, a professional organist, to play the organ, which he did with much grace and talent.

Although the service was ostensibly to celebrate the passing of the Act, I felt very strongly that it should include a strong element of healing and reconciliation. It was therefore entitled 'Gender

Recognition Act 2004, Reflection and Thanksgiving.'

With the offer of a church, booked for 21st May 2005, an organist, a couple of priests (Ruth and Clare) and several people for the congregation, the die was set. Now I had to organise, compile and write the service. It was a challenge and I was determined to meet it.

Chapter thirty-six

An Unexpected Turn

I HAD had great support after my heart attack, much of it from the members of my local parish church, St Paul's, Rusthall. It was absolutely clear that there was no 'hidden agenda' in their concern and care. They helped because that was their nature, not because they wanted to persuade me to 'give myself to the Lord'. It wasn't that kind of church. My views were known and they respected them. Nonetheless, I was happy to go to some healing services that the church held on a regular basis. Whilst rejecting much Christian doctrine there was one reality of which I was very aware and that was of love. As before, during crises such as bereavement, I had felt very much 'enfolded in love', to use Julian of Norwich's beautiful expression.

Not far from my village there was a well-known Christian Home of Healing, Burrswood, in Groombridge, founded by Dorothy Kerin. It was set in magnificent countryside and I happily accepted invitations to attend healing services there with various friends. There was a wonderful sense of peace there and I appreciated my friends' kindness in taking me. Again there was no proselytising at all.

Shortly after my illness I met a new resident of my village, a woman, whom I liked very much but as I got to know her decided that her religious views were so extreme that they repelled me. Her God was tyrannical as far as I was concerned and initially that drove me from benign agnosticism into angry atheism. Then I realised that her God was a projection, reflecting the psychological problems she had that later became manifest. At least her views had led me to think deeply about things that had been 'on hold' for a long time, then, and this surprised me, I began to wonder if I should again consider offering myself for ordination? I did not especially want to do it, nor did I consider myself fit to do so, but had to respond somehow to the 'nudgings'. Our ever-patient vicar, Bob, wisely suggested that perhaps I might like to undertake an academic theology course before making a decision.

This course was run by the South East Institute of Theological Education (SEITE), which trained ordinands for the ministry and also took lay people who wanted to gain University of Kent academic qualifications. There were sometimes transfers of the latter to ministerial training.

Although I wrote only to make a very tentative enquiry, the Principal, Alan le Grys, invited me for a chat, then, to my surprise, offered me a place on the course. He did say that in my diocese of Rochester I was too old to be considered for ordination. When realising the amount of work that my part-time colleagues had to undertake in order to become ordained, I was very relieved to have been ineligible. As time went on I became more and more convinced that I was too independent to have been of much use to the Church. Instead of preaching traditional doctrine I would have been stirring up the doubters and questioners. Yet I found the course stimulating, greatly enjoyed the company and made some good friends.

Part of the course involved pastoral studies, which I found interesting. We had a lively young woman priest, Justine, as tutor, and her sessions were enjoyable and thought provoking. One evening she told us that we always had to be prepared for the unexpected and as an example related how the organist where she had been vicar suddenly announced that he was changing sex.

My hair stood up, metaphorically, if not literally. Was I never to be free of this? I went home and reflected on it a great deal. Here was a big nudge, of that there was no doubt. Did I really want to be seen as transsexual? Yet, having condemned much of the Church for its ignorance and bigotry, perhaps I should do something about it. Maybe here was a chance to inform potential clergy. After much thought I wrote to Justine, revealed my situation and said I would be willing to answer questions but only if she thought it would be helpful.

Justine thought it would be so and gave me the opportunity to give a presentation to the class that was very well received. (I certainly had no objection to being embraced by a beautiful young woman ordinand afterwards!) With my permission, Justine gave each student a copy of my 'Gender Recognition Act' service sheet. The students expressed their gratitude for giving them insight into something that they could possibly meet during the course of their ministries. I was also able to use my encounter with my female-to-male friend Alan (anonymously) as my 'case-history' presentation in class.

It didn't end there. A year or so later, my former colleagues now ordained, I was studying with a different group. I found that one of the courses involved issues of homosexuality and similar. Nick, my tutor, who knew of my status, asked me if I would mind doing a presentation that involved transsexuality. I agreed but told him that the sole book on the matter in the library (a Grove booklet by O'Donovan) was out-of-date, inaccurate and almost libellous towards transsexual people.

It was a good exercise for me to prepare for the presentation because it honed my arguments against the religious bigots – not that bigots usually listen – but at least it gave my colleagues some food for thought. Again I had a very warm and appreciative response. My piece was a defence of transsexual people being allowed to marry in church. By that time I was able to talk about such marriages from personal experiences. Nick also asked my permission to use the service sheet from 'my service' for future students and very happily I gave consent.

I had been a student with SEITE for some time when I decided to organise the service, but did not mention it to my colleagues then because at that point had not 'come out'. Nor had I reached the stage of formally studying liturgy, but just got on with compiling and writing the service, irrespective of my amateur status. Sometimes I thought it was a bit arrogant of me to attempt this, after all there could well be clergy and bishops present, but who else was going to do it? I squeezed it between my essays and college job and admit that I found it a rewarding and creative task although wondered what an agnostic was doing organising and writing a church service as well as studying academic theology. It puzzled people and, if I am honest, did me too, but something drove me on.

Although it was to be held in an Anglican church with Anglican clergy and probably the majority of the congregation likewise, it was essential for the service to be as inclusive as possible. I knew that there would probably also be Roman Catholics, atheists, Buddhists and probably some agnostics present. As something of a dogma-anarchist myself I kept the liturgy as simple as possible and made love the focus of the whole service. Someone remarked afterwards that I had made history. Certainly as I drafted the liturgy, it was clear that there were few, if any, precedents from which to draw. In order to ensure that my liturgical efforts were of an acceptable standard throughout my preparations I consulted Bob Whyte, Clare Herbert, (Rector of St Anne's Church) and several other people, clergy and lay. They were all very helpful and positive.

I invited Bishop Hugh Montefiore, one of our PFC patrons, to preach. He felt it should be done by a transsexual person but said he would be very happy to give the blessing. Dr Mark Dalby, a friend and PFC patron, was not going to be able to attend the service so neither could he preach but agreed with Bishop Hugh that a transsexual preacher would be the most appropriate. At that point I didn't know any possible transsexual preachers, ordained or lay, but then decided that Bob Whyte, my local vicar, was as suitable as anyone could be. He had known me for a long time and given the transsexual cause much support. I knew that we could rely on him.

By the end of the year there still remained much to do, but I was confident that, given the support that had been forthcoming, all would be well. With the service and the Gender Recognition Act now coming into force, 2005 promised to be eventful.

Chapter thirty-seven

Celebration

PEOPLE assumed that as one of the old campaigners – I'd begun in 1972 – I would be one of the first to take advantage of the Gender Recognition Act 2004, change my registration and acquire a new birth certificate showing my present male status. I did not. As a woman in law I had been entitled to the State Retirement Pension when I reached the age of sixty in December 2002. At first I was unwilling to accept this – after all I was living in a male role – but then a friend bluntly said, 'The Government has buggered you up for years, grab the money!' After reflecting upon the difficulties that had come my way I realised she was right, so accepted the pension. Since I was working only part-time the extra money from the pension was very welcome, although half of it went back in tax. It enabled me to save for extras, like a new carpet.

In order to ease the way for people who had transitioned many years ago the Act provided a simple 'fast-track' procedure for them that would be available until April 2007. One of the unforeseen drawbacks of the new legislation was that if I became officially male before my 65th birthday I would lose my pension immediately. Lynne Jones and Alex Carlile tried to get the Government to change its mind over this but without success. Stephen Whittle said that it would affect only about twenty of us in the whole country. It would hardly bankrupt the Treasury. On the other hand, male-to-female transsexual people who had reached sixty would, after re-registration, be eligible for a state pension. I certainly did not begrudge them that but felt it was somewhat mean to take away my pension once it had been granted. Had I not already been receiving it that would have been a different matter. It also showed what a nonsensical situation it was to grant pensions to men five years after women who usually outlive them.

To other people's surprise this posed me no dilemma. I simply decided not to re-register as male. Then I bought a new carpet. It made me realise how much had changed, perhaps how much I had changed. What difference would it make to my life if I re-registered? I had been living quite successfully as male since 1971. Having been 'out' since 1986 there was no problem with anyone discovering my 'secret', because it was no secret. I was now too old and too agnostic to become a priest so that was no longer relevant. The only reason for requiring such a document would be if I were to marry. By now the grateful possessor of a free bus pass and a railcard I felt that the chances of that happening were exceedingly remote, even if I were still active enough to use my bicycle, walk miles, go to work and engage in academic study. Certainly re-registration would not prevent me, or anyone else in my situation, from being the object of abuse. Yet of course I was very pleased that others were able to re-register with the legal and social advantages that gave them.

Although of little consequence to me this right was one of the most welcome results of the Gender Recognition Act. Transsexual people were now enabled to marry legally in their re-assigned gender roles. It was in 2005 that the first such marriages began to take place.

They were not, however, the first transsexual weddings. Some had earlier married unlawfully, which meant that their marriages were not recognised. Quite rarely, but not unknown, were marriages of two transsexual people to each other. In law they had always been able to marry, but the greatest problem to those involved was that the apparent groom was the bride and the apparent bride the groom, which rendered the event somewhat farcical. It was also possible for homosexual transsexual people to legally marry. A male-to-female lesbian could legally marry her female partner and the converse was true with a female-to-male homosexual and his male partner. This was understandably annoying to non-transsexual gay people because at that time they had no legal recognition of their partnerships.

In the autumn of 1999 two transsexual people I knew, David (female-to-male) and Janeen (male-to-female) went through a legal marriage ceremony in Denmark, a country that recognised the post-assignment status of transsexual people. This meant that their roles accorded with their appearance. David did not have to suffer the indignity of being referred to as the bride nor Janeen as the groom.

They returned to England where they had a service of blessing at their local church with the approval of their vicar and their bishop. The vicar, Canon Hall, regarded his role as 'a privilege to extend the support of the Church...' He added that the ceremony was 'exciting, moving, meaningful and very genuine.' This event was featured on a BBC *Everyman* programme transmitted by the BBC on 24th October 1999. It was very obvious that David and Janeen were highly regarded by their local community. I hoped those transsexual people who condemned the whole Church outright had watched the programme.

In 2003 I was very pleasantly surprised and honoured to be invited to a service of blessing following the legal marriage, also in Denmark, of Susan Marshall, who had been with me when we met the Bishop of Winchester nearly three years earlier. Susan was Bursar and a Fellow of Exeter College, Oxford, and the ceremony was to take place in the college chapel.

When reading the smart invitation, I was delighted to see that dress was formal. At last I would be able to fulfil my long-held desire to wear a morning suit. I thought back to similar formal events which, in my previous role, I had either hated or else shunned. The hellish memory of my pre-transition experience at a friend's wedding, (mentioned in Chapter 10) came back. This really encapsulated how life had changed for the better. I had managed to pick up a grey morning suit, which, amazingly, was small enough to fit me, at the local hospice charity shop. As I had initiated the founding of that establishment I felt the suit was well earned.

Any such an event in the historic college would have memorable, but this was a very special one. Although a delightfully grand affair it was also very warm and friendly. What made it different from similar events was the open presence of many transsexual people.

The service of blessing was both dignified and loving. Clearly the clergy present as participants and guests did not share the views of the Evangelical Alliance. It was a very moving occasion. That was followed by champagne in the Fellows' garden. I was pleased to meet many people I knew, fellow transsexual guests, doctors and lawyers amongst others.

Champagne in the Fellows' garden. I am the smallest fellow!

We then proceeded into the college hall for the reception, which, in its way was as moving as the service. The guests filled the whole hall.

Without letting it dominate the proceedings, the history of Susan's gender role reassignment was spoken of openly. She had apparently tendered her resignation when she decided to take this step but it was refused by the Master and Fellows. Instead they promised to support her, which they did. Given that Susan changed roles during her time there it meant that the students and other staff were also aware of the situation. The student members of the college choir had come back from their vacation to sing for the chapel service and then as we dined. Susan's former colleagues from her time as a male Naval officer made speeches and it was obvious that they too held her in very high regard. The presence of the Master of the College and these former colleagues at the dinner was significant but what was even more so was the fact that Susan's family, including her ex-wife and children, were also present. I was delighted to learn that Susan and her family remain close. Sadly it is not a situation shared by all transsexual people.

There could have been few settings and gatherings more Establishment than this, but I remember the day for the great sense of joy and love, which, as one lawyer guest, Ashley, put it, 'was almost tangible'. Susan, herself a very loving person, deserved no less, but I also found it personally uplifting. It seemed to me that, by affirming Susan, the event affirmed all of us who were also transsexual. Perhaps it was one of the few occasions when I felt liberated and 'normal.' We all need communities to become full people. This wonderful event had enhanced the personhood of those transsexual individuals present, many of whom, if not all, would have experienced what it was like to be regarded as objects and thus abused. Susan had given us so much more than an enjoyable afternoon. We were delighted and happy for her that she had met and married a splendid man who loved her enough not to be deterred by her 'unusual CV' as she put it.

It was good to meet Stephen Whittle, who was also a guest, because I had not seen him for some time. We went for a drink after the reception was over and Stephen told me that he had been diagnosed with multiple sclerosis. I was deeply shocked and saddened by this news. It certainly gave me much to think over. I found myself feeling rather ashamed because in my eyes Stephen had so much that I would have liked to have had. Certainly I did not begrudge him anything at all, but wished that I, like him, could have had a good career, academic success and a lovely partner (later wife) and family. No, I didn't have those things, but irrespective of my supposed heart condition, which caused me no trouble at all, I had my health. I grieved for what Stephen faced and chastised myself for my envy.

Stephen and his partner of over twenty years, Sarah, were legally married on 18th June 2005. Exactly a month later, 18th July, my more recent friend, Alan, married his partner of nearly thirty years. Stephen, although himself a professing atheist/agnostic, was married in church. Alan and his partner, both practising Roman Catholics, married in the local register office because the Vatican forbade such ceremonies. In spite of that, the couple's priest blessed their rings in private. He probably rightly saw it as pastorally important. Alan himself would have been happy enough to have married in an Anglican church and I felt sure that Bob, my vicar, would have readily obliged, but Alan's partner was unwilling to be married in any church other than Roman Catholic. It made me very angry that the Vatican was so apparently rigid and harsh. In a less vociferous way, it was as blinkered as the Evangelical Alliance and Christian Institute. Alan's wedding was such a quiet ceremony that I found myself in charge of both the rings and the bride's bouquet. The registrars, both women, conducted the ceremony with great dignity and, dare one say, love. It was certainly as spiritual as any church wedding I have ever attended. Although on a much smaller scale, it had as much of an impact upon me as had Susan's service two years earlier.

At the luncheon afterwards, Alan publicly thanked me for all the support I'd given him and said that without me, it would not have been possible to have married. That might have been so, I don't know, but had it not been for my broadcast interview on Radio Kent, we might never have met. Certainly my media coverage did bear some good fruit.

The following spring, 2006, I was invited to another transsexual wedding. This was held in a country church. It was one of the most amazing church weddings I'd ever attended and, as with Susan's service, again the love there 'was almost tangible'. The vicar expressed his joy that at long last he was able to conduct the marriage of two people he'd known for a long time and had been party to their struggles. When he pronounced Simon and Jenny man and wife there was a great outburst of applause and I suspect that many members of the congregation, myself included, found it hard not to be moved to tears. This was really the moment when the significance of our achievement hit me: the formal words of the Act had become a reality. Again this was another affirming experience for all of us there who were transsexual.

What was particularly interesting was that it was a church of an evangelical persuasion and some people there were members of the Evangelical Alliance. If they had been aware of that group's views on the matter they had chosen to ignore them. When I asked Simon and Jenny if they had had any problems because of the EA, they told me that there had been none whatsoever because the vicar and congregation knew them as people. That is the crux of the matter.

For Stephen, 2005 was special for his long-awaited wedding and for another very notable event. In May he and another leading campaigner, Christine Burns, went to Buckingham Palace to receive the OBE and MBE respectively for their services to 'Gender Issues'. We were all absolutely delighted for them. These awards were certainly very well deserved. Both were quick to point out that they were but our representatives; others had done a tremendous amount of work too and the honours were for all of us. That was so, but few would have doubted that the contributions of Stephen and Christine were indeed exceptional. This certainly was an affirmation. The heart of the Establishment had officially recognised transsexual people and granted them entry.

Stephen and Christine on their Investiture Day

Although these events were all a great joy to me, my personal special occasion was the service I had organised for 21st May 2005. I was amazed and moved by the support that had been forthcoming from several quarters. There were a large number of friends from Rusthall. Other friends also came, Alan, and notably my school friend Madeline from Nottingham. To my relief, the Rusthall ladies and other friends immediately set to and organised the post-service coffee. I'd not wanted to ask anyone for such help and had had visions of doing it all myself.

There were people from the transsexual community whom I knew and others I had not previously met. Amongst the latter was the Rev'd Sarah Jones. The Bishop of Hereford, Anthony Priddis, had been aware of her transsexual status but had made it clear that he was happy to ordain her. Sarah was a delightful person and the Church is, I am sure, all the richer for her ministry – and for the courage and foresight of Bishop Priddis. I was very pleased to see that Linda, whose letter had persuaded me to go ahead with the service, came with her brother (sister-to-be) in spite of having to travel a very considerable distance. The Rev'd Ruth Howe had been one of the first to arrive, having left Newcastle at about six a.m. Other people also had undertaken very long journeys in order to attend. That made me slightly apprehensive lest the service might not meet their expectations and hopes.

Weeks earlier I had told people that having acquired Bishop Montefiore to give the blessing and the services of an organist, Christopher Bayston, I couldn't abandon my idea, however daunting it seemed. Christopher's talent was an invaluable asset to the service but to my sorrow, Bishop Hugh's daughter rang me a week before the service to say that her father had died. This was a sad note in an otherwise very happy event. What I also found very sad was that some people did not come because they were scared of being identified as transsexual.

Alex Carlile and Lynne Jones were unable to attend but both kindly sent best wishes to the people present. I had asked three serving bishops, including Bishop Priddis, who were sympathetic to transsexual people if they would like to attend, but unsurprisingly because I had been unable to give them much notice, they had other engagements. Nonetheless, Bishop Priddis, Bishop Peter Selby of Worcester and Bishop John Gladwin of Chelmsford, all sent messages of goodwill for the day, which were greatly appreciated. I had invited Margaret Duggan of the *Church Times*, who had supported our cause for years, but regrettably she had been unable to attend because of serious illness. She was however able to write a short piece later which appeared in the *Church Times*.

In the months before the service, as I had busied myself with everything from writing the service to ordering sandwiches from *Patisserie Valerie* in Dean Street, I had wondered if it were going to be worth the effort; after all, support from the transsexual community at large was muted. But throughout the lengthy preparations I thought of Linda and told myself that if only one person were helped, then it would have been worthwhile.

St Anne's, Soho, was ideal for this intimate and quiet service. There were about fifty people present in the congregation. This included at least three transsexual clergy. Also present were the Rector of St Anne's, Clare Herbert, whose invitation to use her church had made the event possible, Ruth Howe, who conducted the agape and gave the blessing at the end of the service, and Bob Whyte, whose powerful sermon gained great approval from those present. Immediately preceding his address in the order of service I had placed a reading from the First Epistle of John, 4:vv7-12. This is the passage about love and Bob took up that theme. Ironically, the service took place very shortly after the Statutory Instrument had been added to the Gender Recognition Act which gave religious bodies the right to seek disclosure of an individual's transsexual status. Bob's genuine anger over this was very evident and he declared that it was time that these Christians started to show love.

Although my adrenalin was running high throughout the service because I was concerned that all should go well, I also felt very aware of people's support. Afterwards I was both relieved and happy because it had been a very positive event. Clare remarked that I'd put together a very good liturgy. But had anyone, especially Linda and her transsexual sibling, R, benefited from it? Judging from the immediate responses it seemed that they had, but it was additionally reassuring to receive written messages during the following days.

One of the first emails I had after the service was from Linda:

'It was a very special occasion and one that I will not forget. I was so glad that R was there and glad to see her happy and at ease in the company of other supportive people It was a real celebration, though tinged with sadness as well…thank you for a very special and important Service and service to the church.'

I was delighted to receive such a positive response and even more so to hear directly from R herself:

'I really enjoyed the service – much more than I thought I would. The feeling of acceptance and inclusion were wonderful…I have to admit that I was nearly in tears a couple of times…Thank you for organising the event – it really was quite a revelation for me to meet such accepting people.'

Other messages and emails spoke of the love and warmth felt at the service and several expressed what an emotional and moving experience it had been for them. Ruth Howe, after her return journey from Newcastle to London to take part, said that she had been delighted to have been able to do so, especially as people had felt included and welcomed. She added that perhaps one day we would have more clergy who are understanding and compassionate.

Alan was very impressed by the clergy present, Bob, Clare and Ruth, who were, '...so understanding and kind that I too had to stop singing twice as tears welled up. How sad that my own church (Catholic) is so blinkered and archaic. So there was a lot of anger inside and the service did show me other ways and healed a lot of pain.'

Susan, who had been with me when we met the Bishop of Winchester five years earlier, wrote:

'My dear Mark,

Well, you did it – and it was a big success, enjoyed by everyone who was there! Needless to say, I thoroughly enjoyed the service too, and the chance to meet Clare, Bob and Ruth. Would that they were more typical of C of E clergy as a whole. So there you are.

You can now relax in the knowledge that all your preparations paid off and that, despite antipathy and even antagonism in some quarters, you brought about something really worthwhile and affirming. Not bad for an agnostic!!'

Susan was right, it wasn't bad at all.

Two thousand and five had been quite a year, with weddings, investitures and the service at St Anne's, but I had one more celebration. In November, after a twenty-five year gap, I was again in cap and gown, this time at Rochester Cathedral, to receive the University of Kent Certificate in Christian Theology – with merit. It was the result of following Bob's suggestion to consider undertaking such a course. (Two years and many more essays later I was to receive the Diploma in Applied Theology, again with merit.)

As I walked back to my seat clutching my pristine certificate I thought, 'I've done my bit for the trans-sexual world. This is the new me now. I want to develop my intellectual side. From henceforth I shall be Mark Rees, transsexual *emeritus*.'

Shortly afterwards I received an invitation to speak to the local police as part of their diversity training. It was good to know that the police were taking seriously the problems suffered by minorities, including those faced by the transsexual community. Although I had seldom had any hesitation in contacting the police if harassed and abused by the local youngsters, others, especially those terrified about revealing their change of gender status, might now feel more able to contact the police via a specifically designated officer. At long last we had the reassurance that we would be treated courteously and our difficulties taken seriously. It might or might not be a coincidence that since reporting some personal abuse I had suffered to Nova, our local diversity officer, the problems that had beset me for decades have almost ceased.

With Nova's invitation to speak to her colleagues my 'retirement' would have to be delayed. During one of the four presentations I gave, one police officer asked me more questions than anyone else, which I hoped, were answered to his satisfaction. Afterwards, with his helmet tucked under his arm, he came to speak to me, 'I've come to apologise. Until now I'd not taken this seriously. Even just before I came in here I was taking the piss out of transsexuals. I'm sorry, I'll never do that again.'

After he'd left, Nova and her colleague, who had organised the session chuckled,

'We wondered if you'd win him over,' they said. 'He's got a heart of gold but is the biggest bigot in the station. Now he'll never let anyone get away with abusing transsexual people. Well done.'

Chapter thirty-eight

A Little Administrative Matter

AS I progressed with this book it occurred to me that in spite of my indifference about re-registering as male perhaps I should do so. Much of the narrative had been concerned with a long struggle for legal recognition so it seemed fitting to include my personal 'closure' in the form of legal male status. A few months after my 65th birthday, which was eight months after the end of the 'fast-track' procedure, I made a formal application, confident that I was no longer going to forfeit my pension as a result. Accompanying the forms to be completed was a list of approved medical specialists from whom reports would be accepted by the Gender Recognition Panel (GRP).

My GP, Mike Lawes, kindly completed the required GP report within a day but the specialist requirement was more of a problem. There were several names I recognised, having met the doctors concerned, both at conferences and sometimes in television studios, but I had not been a patient of any of them. I had known one through the Gender Dysphoria clinic at Newcastle but he had retired. As for my original specialist, Dr Randell, it would have been very difficult to make contact with him without either an exhumation certificate or excellent medium because he had died years earlier. I forwarded my completed forms and explained the reason for delaying my application. My need for the pension was confirmed because even with that and a part-time salary, my income was still too low for me to be required to pay fees to the GRP. I explained the difficulty of obtaining a report from an approved specialist on the list and instead sent a copy of Dr Armstrong's medical report, which had been submitted with my application to the European Commission for Human Rights in 1979.

To my surprise and considerable annoyance, my application was not considered adequate by the GRP. It was stated that I, 'should submit a report from a registered medical practitioner practising in the field of gender dysphoria confirming a diagnosis of gender dysphoria and giving details of how the diagnosis was made.'

How could I possibly do this? I was further annoyed by the GRP's statement that, it would have been 'more appropriate' for me to have made the application during the 'fast-track' period. Although I had previously been indifferent about re-registration, anger now drove me on. I contacted Alex, now Lord, Carlile and Dr Lynne Jones MP, who was still chairing the Parliamentary Forum on Transsexuality. Both promised help if necessary.

It seemed to me that the major problem was the approved list. It listed named specialists rather than Gender Identity Clinics. I would have felt more able to contact the clinic where I had seen Dr Randell, rather than writing to one of the unknown specialists, hoping that I had picked one who would be able and willing to help.

It rather looked as if I, pioneer in our campaign, were going to be unable to re-register, but Christine Burns contacted a sympathetic psychiatrist she knew, Stuart Lorimer, who was one of the GIC team in Fulham, formerly at Charing Cross Hospital. He was very willing to write a report but, quite understandably, wanted to meet me. It was a very agreeable encounter. Stuart asked and I answered all the right questions, although he already knew how I would reply having read my book. I thought it likely that most of the present specialists were probably unborn when I changed roles and Stuart confirmed that he was then one year old. Nonetheless his report was accepted and I was grateful to him.

On 30th May 2008 I heard the post arrive. A large 'DO NOT BEND' envelope dropped onto my doormat – bent by the postman because he did not bother to knock at the door. It was my Gender Recognition Certificate. After a wait of thirty-six years I was now legally male. It was a strange feeling but also a little anti-climactic. The accompanying information informed me that I now had the rights appropriate to a person of my acquired gender, including the right to marry someone of the opposite gender. 'It's a bit late now,' I thought.

Shortly afterwards the General Register Office (GRO) wrote to me with the details to be recorded on my new birth certificate and examples of a pre-1969 and a post-1969 certificate. The choice was mine. Having observed that the earlier certificate gave more details of one's father than mother I decided to opt for the later type. I wanted a document which gave my mother equal status. Also, with a certain amount of amusement, I wrote a note to point out that in paragraph 1 of the accompanying letter that they had sent me the Registrar General was referred to as 'she' but in paragraph 4 as 'he'. It was commendable of the RG to identify so closely with the clients' situation.

A pleasant-sounding lady called Joanna rang me from the GRO. She said it was clever of me to note the error, which they had laughed about in the office. Apparently there had been a recent change, not of gender but of holders of the post. Joanna's main purpose in telephoning was to ask me if I realised that a modern style certificate for someone who was born some time before they came into use might raise some questions. I replied that it was no problem for me, the chances of my needing to produce a birth certificate were remote and also, given my media and other exposure, I was hardly shy about the affair. She was relieved about that but said she had to ask because some people were very worried about anyone knowing of their situation. What a burden they create for themselves and at the same time denying others the chance to be educated. As it happened, a few months after I had been retired by West Kent College my pension providers requested a copy of my birth certificate. I admit that it was quite a relief to send it without the usual bother of an explanatory letter. Recalling the conversation with Joanna, I opted to send the short form copy of my certificate so as not to complicate matters.

My new birth certificate had arrived the day after Joanna's call. This had a more profound and unexpected effect on me than the Gender Recognition Certificate. Suddenly I thought, 'This is wrong!' I was not born a boy (pre-1969) or male (post-1969). Yet I knew that I was never a normal girl. The discussions I had had with David Burgess at the time of my Human Rights appeal came back to me. Our concern was not so much the birth certificate as to legal recognition of one's current gender status. The major problem had been caused by the use of a birth certificate in order to prove identity. That would have been less of a problem if transsexual people had been totally accepted in society. Would the answer have been identity cards for all which showed current status? The present proposals for ID cards have been immensely unpopular. Would another answer have been birth certificates that left gender blank until the child's status was certain? Given that sex is a spectrum, with more people than generally realised falling between the two poles, that would surely have been a more realistic and humane approach. Or is it necessary to put any gender at all?

After a short period of wrestling with my conscience I decided that it was a reflection of my social status. What had been possible had been done medically and surgically but it was a compromise. Compromises might not always be comfortable but they can be more so than the alternatives. I put the new certificate away in the deed box to join its predecessor, one marking the start of my life and my campaign for legal recognition, the other marking its success.

Chapter thirty-nine

Wholeness

MARGARET Duggan, as she had promised, wrote a short and sympathetic account of our St Anne's service in the *Church Times* of 10th June 2005. It was almost a year since my letter had been published in the same paper and I had subsequently received the anonymously sent tract. There was a much more positive and unexpected response to Margaret's piece. I received an email from a Rev'd Graham Noyce, Bishop's Adviser on Spirituality for the episcopal area of Willesden. He invited me to contribute a piece for the area's spirituality newsletter about spirituality and changing gender.

It was, I thought, quite a compliment but felt that as a professed agnostic I was the last person who should undertake such a task. In vain I tried to persuade one of the transsexual clergy to do it, then tried some of my Rusthall church friends, but they were equally unwilling. The consensus amongst these apparently unhelpful folk was that I could and should do it. So I did and to my surprise, Graham was very pleased with the result. It certainly concentrated my mind, especially as the deadline was very close. Ultimately Graham had done me a favour because it is very easy to see the transsexual condition mainly in physical terms, which hasn't always been to our advantage. Now I had to think in broader way.

Although our religious opponents were very vociferous in condemning our 'sin' of undergoing role change it was clear that these extremists, and probably many other people, including some transsexual individuals themselves, had not actually thought through the spiritual significance of the role change. I wonder if it had occurred to these fundamentalists that many of us personally involved would have asked ourselves whether or not it was in accord with our religious beliefs?

Over the years I had come to realise that whether committed to a particular faith or not, in seeking reassignment, transgender people are ultimately seeking wholeness. This is surely a religious, indeed a spiritual quest. Probably no human being will ever find total wholeness but for the gender dysphoric person, gender reassignment will certainly be movement towards it.

Wholeness is about relationships – with our bodies, our loved ones, society, the world and, for some, God. Being an incarnational faith Christianity regards body and self (soul?) as one, so the most basic relationship is surely our self with our body. It is not perhaps something that everyone would think about, but it dominates the life of a gender dysphoric person for whom this relationship is one of total conflict. There is little, if any, wholeness in it. We cannot love our bodies. Some sufferers attempt self-mutilation, such is the loathing of a body that seems completely alien to them.

Even after successful reassignment there can still be lack of integration between the self and body. No surgeon or medication can make one a full member of the new gender role. It is a compromise. Although very thankful for what has been achieved we can detest those remaining vestiges of our former gender, especially if they mean we cannot fully function in our new roles. Some, the more accepting and philosophical amongst us, cope with it better than others do. One female-to-male friend told me that he was able to cope with his 'undesirable bits' by telling himself that because they belonged to him they were male. He accepted his body; it was not something alien and despised. I was sure he was helped by the fact that he had a very loving partner. Generally I think we female-to-males find it hard to feel totally secure in the male role without the right 'bits'. It is difficult to integrate our female parts. My friend was obviously coping better than most and certainly better than me.

The most extreme form of this lack of integration is manifest in the female-to-male who desperately seeks surgery and, ignoring all the risks and warnings, undergoes it in the hope of then feeling 'whole'. If it is a compulsion, rather than a carefully considered choice made over time, then wholeness will continue to elude one. The results can be disastrous, both physically and psychologically. Surgery for the male-to-female is much more successful.

Less extreme are those female-to-males who buy the prostheses that are now available. I can think of better ways of spending my money (such as buying a new carpet!), especially as I've managed since 1971 without one. I comfort myself with the fact that a penis, whether genuine, surgically constructed or a prosthesis, can at times be an encumbrance, and certainly one needs more than that to attract a woman.

However good surgery and modern prostheses might be, we still have to live with this physical incompleteness and ambiguity. It is also necessary to cope with the knowledge that we cannot fully share the physical experience of our reassigned gender or the emotional and mental one of our former role. In these respects we are again incomplete, or looked at in another way, intersexual, inhabiting the centre ground of the spectrum but perhaps with wider views than those on its extreme sides. Of course, probably every human being has feelings of incompleteness for different reasons. Perhaps indeed it is part of being human. For the transsexual individual however it is very obvious.

My past is also that which isolates me from the rest of the community. I was not reared as a boy or as a young man. My experience can neither include normal heterosexual relations with a woman or fatherhood. Before role change my apparent sex was that of a biological female but a woman is a female *person*. That I have never been. I have never known what it is like to be a normal woman. What changed at my role-assignment was the world's perception of me; my essence, my personhood, remained unaltered. My gender role was reassigned, my gender identity confirmed. Had I been a female person, a woman, then I'd still be one and not writing this book. In common with other transsexual people I have also mourned my lost past, an apparently wasted youth and young adulthood. Nowadays people can get help earlier than when I was young but even so can miss out on a normal adolescence and young adulthood with both its pains and joys.

Another area where there may be lack of integration is between our gender roles, past and present. There are transsexual people who deny their past, even to the extent of denying that they have experienced gender transition. Having been forced into openness I cannot deny or invent a past. It has contributed to what I am today and is part of me, however painful it has been. This is not dwelling in the past but accepting that past, present and future are not hermetically-sealed compartments but a whole. It would be absurd to believe that nothing before my 're-birth' in 1971 has affected me now. The whole of my life has contributed to what I am today. In the BBC Radio 4 *Thought For The Day* (12th November 1994) the Rev'd David Winter, asked, 'What are we if we come from nowhere?'

I would also ask, 'What are we if we come from a fiction?'

It is known that hiding secrets is very stressful, so what is already a difficult life is made more so. I am sure this is engendered largely by fear. It may be justified in some circumstances. Knowing the opposition from some fundamentalist Christians to gender reassignment I can understand my friend who is terrified of anyone in his church finding out about his situation. What I find more difficult to understand is why he still belongs to a group that would reject him – or so he thinks. Sometimes one can be very happily surprised. It is risky throwing ourselves on people's mercy but it can also be very enriching and liberating. We are giving people the chance to reject or love us. My experience has been overwhelmingly the latter.

If the tortured relationship between mind and body is at least partially healed by gender reassignment, what then of that between the individual and others? Generally this can mean a blossoming of relationships. If it becomes possible to be truly oneself then it will be easier to form friendships. It is a salutary experience to discover how many people felt there was 'something wrong' before reassignment. The 'something wrong' was the conflict. A comment, which one hears very frequently from transsexual people, is that before reassignment, they felt as if they were 'living a lie'. I recall how, in my early twenties, especially in the WRNS, attempting to act out the role which was expected of me. It was awful and I fooled few, especially those who knew me well.

It is clear that some religious people, especially those at the extremes of Protestantism and Roman Catholicism see role-change as a sin, going against God. I believe that to continue to live in a state of such conflict if treatment is possible is the real sin. In his book, *Free to Believe*,[6] David Jenkins writes, 'God is determined to enable you to be yourself in order that you should become the best you can be'. When we are continually having our gender disputed or

---

[6] Jenkins, D *Free to Believe* BBC Books 1991 p70

are at the receiving end of obscenities because of our pre-transition ambiguous state, it is very easy to become acutely *self*-conscious. The problem consumes the whole of life. Released by medical treatment into a new life, we are enabled to look outwards and direct our attention to the needs of others. In other words, we can now better love our neighbour. We are closer to becoming the best we can be, i.e. becoming closer to wholeness.

It is ironic that whilst in the twenty-first century some religious people seek to deny those who are transsexual basic rights, there were ancient mythologies and civilisations that recognised the male and female in each person, and accepted into their societies those who were probably transsexual. In India today there are men who live as women. They are not only accepted but revered, as are the Fa'afines of Samoa. A clergyman wrote to me of the Maori attitude to an individual who was different, 'To treat that person as special, not suspect. To ask what contribution such a person can make to the common good, not whether they belong or not.'

Whilst these and similar cultures may not have the medical and surgical means to help the transsexual person, they give what is more important – acceptance (which is not synonymous with 'tolerance') into the community. Even with our advanced techniques, a transsexual person's treatment is less than fully effective if this integration into society is not available. Some may see legal recognition as the ultimate acceptance, but I believe that the love of those around is more important than an amended document.

If I am now seen as 'unusual' it is unlikely to be because of my transsexual status. It could be because I don't have a partner, don't own a car, DVD or washing machine, don't watch sports or 'soap operas' on the television, don't walk around with an iPod or mobile phone in constant use but cherish silence. In my 'unusualness' I do find much that gives me joy.

It was immensely rewarding to have tutored students at college, seeing them grow not only in knowledge but also self-esteem. Away from work I am fortunate indeed in living close to the countryside, so relish the changing seasons and walking with my ears tuned and eyes opened to the nature around me. There are few experiences I find more wonderful than going to the woods early on a spring morning, seeing the haze of bluebells under the beech trees and smelling their delicate scent. There is sheer delight in hearing the song of a wren from the hedgerow and standing silently as a deer walks past. There is the joy of being with friends and of experiencing an unexpected act of love. All this makes me feel more whole. I enjoyed all these things in my former role but not to the extent that I do now, freed long ago from the conflict all transsexual people experience.

I have received much love, not only from my beloved late mother, family and friends, but also from caring professionals and people I've hardly known. Neither their love nor medical science has made me 'fully male' but it has made me more fully myself and thus able to contribute to the common good.

My role-change was almost a religious experience. It freed me to live a life that was infinitely more fulfilling than I had ever dreamt possible. It gave me the opportunity to experience love, both given and received, in a much richer and deeper way than before. For that I am truly thankful.

References

Council of Europe F-67075 Strasbourg Cedex	Rees v UK Application 9532/81	Report of Commission 1984 Hearing 18 March 1986 Judgment 2/1985/88/135
	XXIII Colloquy on European Law	'Transsexualism, Medicine and Law' Amsterdam 14-16 April 1993
European Parliament	Resolution	Transsexual Doc A. 16/89 (Adopted 12 September 1989)

Support Groups

ALL the groups listed are affiliated to each other and offer support, access to accredited counselling, advice on where to seek medical care, and information. All have the backing of eminent professionals.

The FTM Network
(This is specifically for female-to-male transsexual people.)
BM Network
London
WC1N 3XX
Advice line 0161 432 1915 (Wed 8 p.m.–10.30 p.m. only)
www.ftm.org.uk

The Gender Trust (Registered Charity)
Community Base
113 Queens Road
Brighton
East Sussex
BN1 3XG
National Helpline 0845 231 0505
(Mon–Fri 10 a.m.–10 p.m., Sat–Sun 1 p.m.–10 p.m.
Office 01273 234024
www.gendertrust.org.uk
info@gendertrust.org.uk

Press for Change
BM Network
London WC1N 3XX
www.pfc.org.uk
This is the campaigning group, set up in 1992 with the backing of Alex
Carlile MP, QC, which fought for legal recognition of gender-role
reassigned transsexuals. It is still active in areas where there remains
discrimination against transsexual people.

GIRES (Gender Identity Research & Education Society)
Melverley
The Warren
Ashstead
Surrey
KT21 2SP
01372 801554
www.gires.org.uk
Unlike the previous organisations this is not a support group but aims
to help transgender people by educating the concerned professionals
and society at large.
admin@gires.org.uk

Inclusive Church
This organisation is able to give individuals names of churches that
welcome lesbian, gay, bisexual and transgender people.
www.inclusivechurch.net